THEOLOGY AFTER VEDĀNTA

SUNY Series, Toward a Comparative Philosophy of Religions
Frank Reynolds and David Tracy, editors

THEOLOGY AFTER VEDĀNTA

An Experiment in Comparative Theology

Francis X. Clooney, S.J.

State University of New York Press

Published by
State University of New York Press, Albany

Printed in the United States of America

For information, address State University of New York Press,
State University Plaza, Albany, N.Y. 12246

Production by Marilyn P. Semerad
Marketing by Bernadette La Manna

Library of Congress Cataloging-in-Publication Data

Clooney, Francis Xavier, 1950–
Theology after Vedānta: an experiment in comparative theology / Francis X. Clooney.
p. cm.—(SUNY series, toward a comparative philosophy of religions)
Includes bibliographical references and index.
ISBN 0-7914-1365-9 (hard).—ISBN 0-7914-1366-7 (pbk.)
1. Advaita. 2. Vedanta. 3. Theology, Doctrinal—Comparative studies. 4. Christianity and other religions—Hinduism. 5. Catholic Church—Relations—Hinduism. 6. Hinduism—Relations—Christianity. I. Title. II. Series.
B132. A3C57 1993
181' .482—dc20 92-14007
CIP

10 9 8 7 6 5 4 3 2 1

In Memory of:

Ignacio Ellacuria, S.J.
Amando Lopez, S.J.
Joaquin Lopez, S.J.
Ignacio Martin-Baro, S.J.
Segundo Montes, S.J.
Juan Ramon Moreno, S.J.
Celina Maricet Ramos
Elba Julia Ramos

Contents

Chapter One:
Comparative Theology and the Practice of Advaita Vedānta

Chapter Two: The Texture of the Advaita Vedānta Text

Chapter Three: The Truth of Advaita Vedānta

Chapter Four: Advaita Vedānta and Its Readers

Chapter Five: Theology after Advaita Vedānta: The Text, The Truth, and The Theologian

Foreword

Frank E. Reynolds

From the inception of the ongoing "Toward a Comparative Philosophy of Religions Project" at the University of Chicago Divinity School (for a basic description see my "Introduction" in Volume I—*Myth and Philosophy*), the organizers and the participants have quite explicitly recognized that the term "philosophy" is being used in a rather broad sense.[1] Thus everyone who has been involved has accepted the presumption that the term philosophy includes *both* "philosophic" enterprises that stand outside the faith commitments associated with particular religious traditions, *and* closely corresponding "theological" enterprises in which such religious commitments play an explicit role.

In the previous volumes that have been published in the Series (*Myth and Philosophy, Mencius and Aquinas: Theories of Virtue and Conceptions of Courage,* and *Discourse and Practice*) the term philosophy has been used in this rather broad sense, and little explicit reference to theology has been made.[2] The only major exception is Francis X. Clooney's essay, "Vedānta, Commentary, and the Theological Component of Cross-Cultural Study," which provided a preliminary formulation of many of the ideas that are more fully developed in the present volume (see *Myth and Philosophy,* pp. 287–316). At the time, Clooney's quite self-conscious insistence on using the term "theology" rather than the term "philosophy" was not called to the attention of readers in any compelling way, either by the editors or by Clooney himself. However, now that a full-length book on *Theology After Vedānta* is being published in the *Toward a Comparative Philosophy of Religions Series*, some further comment seems to be in order.

This is not the place to embark on an extended discussion (either descriptive or normative) of the highly complex relationships between philosophy in the narrower sense of the term, and closely related forms of theology. At least one such discussion *will* be included in an essay that will appear in a collection of essays entitled *Religion and Practical Reason* that will be published in the Series in late 1993. In the present context, a few comments directly related to Clooney's book will have to suffice.

In the present volume, Clooney insists on emphasizing the theological character of his study in order to highlight two very important dimensions of his argument. The first has to do with his interpretation of the Indian Advaita (Non-Dualist) texts that constitute his most important primary sources. The second has to do with his own intellectual identity, and with the closely correlated method of comparative study which he proposes and implements. The issues involved are not minor. They go to the very heart of the highly original and extremely important contributions that Clooney makes to Indological studies on the one hand, and to the theory and practice of comparison on the other.

In most of the best known modern scholarship on Śaṅkara and the Advaita tradition in India, the emphasis has been placed on philosophy in the narrow sense noted above. Given this intellectual background, one of the major achievements of Clooney's book is to show, beyond any doubt, that classical Advaita writings in general, and the work of Śaṅkara in particular, are thoroughly theological. To be more specific, Clooney demonstrates that the Advaita text(s) are deeply and inextricably embedded in a tradition in which the theological authority of pre-existing Vedic scriptures is strongly and consistently affirmed. Clooney goes on to highlight the fact that the Advaitins in general, and Śaṅkara in particular, have formulated their teachings and marshalled their arguments in a genre of theological writing that can best be described as "commentarial" or "exegetical."

Working with this specifically theological character of Advaita discourse clearly in mind, Clooney develops his own interpretation of the Advaita/Śaṅkara tradition that is both original and compelling. Using as background his previous studies of the earlier Mīmāṃsa tradition on which Śaṅkara and the later Advaitins built, he provides the best available discussion of the content of the Advaita doctrine, the character of Advaita soteriology, and the style of Advaita argument.[3]

Important as Clooney's Indological contribution is, the most significant breakthrough that he achieves in *Theology After Vedānta* concerns the theory and practice of comparison. Building on the work of Lee Yearley in *Mencius and Aquinas,* Clooney sets forth and implements his own approach in which he highlights the theological dimension in a way that Yearley did not. Clooney begins with an explicit recognition of his own personal "location" within an ongoing tradition of Roman Catholic theology. He then undertakes an intense reading of the Advaita text(s) that concern him, taking seriously into account not only the intellectual context in which they were written, but also the kind of involved theological reading that they themselves presuppose and commend. After Clooney's own theological orientation and modes of reasoning have been challenged and enriched by this process, he then proceeds to undertake a new reading of what he considers to be the most comparable text(s) within his own Roman Catholic tradition—in this case Thomas Aquinas' *Summa Theologiae* and the commentaries associated with it.

Clooney's distinctively theological approach is characterized by a very high level of hermeneutical sophistication. His perspective is a modest one in the sense that he neither presumes nor attempts to construct any kind of "God's eye view" (or any kind of "view from nowhere") that would enable him to arrive at a synthesis between the two texts or traditions that he is "comparing," or to render any definitive evaluations that would rank either one above the other. What is more, the methods that he *does* use are highly sophisticated adaptations and extensions of the very best contemporary thinking in the area of hermenutics in general, and of reader-oriented literary theory in particular.

For theologians who are committed to a particular religious tradition, *Theology After Vedānta* opens a path toward a new kind of theology of religions that combines two elements. The first is a perspective that is "inclusivist" in the sense that it recognizes the potential truth value and soteriological efficacy of the theologies and traditions of "others." The second element, which serves as an essential complement to the first, is a very hard-nosed method for pursuing potentially transformative comparative studies. It is certainly within the realm of possibility that such an inclusivist, comparatively oriented, potentially transformative theology of religions could revitalize contemporary theological research and reflection not only in Christianity, but (with appropriate adaptations) in other religious traditions as well.

For those who pursue the comparative philosophy of religions in a non-theological mode, Clooney's work is no less important. At an empirical or descriptive level, his interpretation of his Advaita and Christian texts will foster among such philosophers a new kind of sensitivity to the theological significance of the theological data that they study. At a more theoretical or normative level, Clooney's notion of comparing texts and traditions by means of a back-and-forth process of creatively ordered reading deserves serious consideration. The highly innovative and creative strategies that he employs in a theological mode are—in terms of their basic structure—equally relevant for comparativists who identify themselves with secular philosophical traditions.

February 10, 1992

Acknowledgments

Ancient commentators began their treatises by evoking gods and gurus near and far. Less eloquently and solemnly, but no less sincerely, I begin by expressing gratitude to those who helped make this book possible. I am grateful to the Henry Luce Foundation for a Luce Fellowship in Comparative Religious Studies, which enabled me to begin work on this book at the University of Chicago Divinity School during 1989–90, and to the Divinity School for welcoming me as a visiting professor and member of the Institute for the Advanced Study of Religion. Many conversations there, including those from 1986–89 in the colloquia on "Religions in History and Culture," and in a seminar on comparative theology in the winter of 1990, enriched my writing. Discussions with colleagues at Boston College and in the Boston Theological Society have likewise stimulated my thinking at crucial points.

To name but a few of the friends and colleagues who helped me in special ways: Frans Josef van Beeck, S.J., Loyola University, Chicago; David Burrell, C.S.C., University of Notre Dame; Richard DeSmet, S.J., Pune, India; Sister Vrajaprana, the Sarada Convent, Montecito; David Gitomer, Paul Griffiths and Sheldon Pollock, the University of Chicago; Lois Malcolm, currently completing the Ph.D. in Theology at the University of Chicago; Joshua Mitchell, George Washington University, Washington, D.C.; Laurie Patton, Bard College, Annandale-on-Hudson, New York; Louis Roy, O.P., Boston College; John Taber, University of New Mexico at Albuquerque. My fellow Jesuits, at Barat House, Boston College, and at Hopkins Hall, Chicago, have helped me in countless ways, and their brotherhood was a grace at every stage of this project. Finally, I am especially indebted to Frank Reynolds of the Divinity School of the University of Chicago; without his encouragement and support at every point in this project, it would by no means have come to fruition so smoothly and quickly.

On November 16, 1989, I finished sketching a first draft of the ideas that eventually became Chapter 3 of this book, on the advent of truth in the tension between the complexity of one's tradition and the simple realization one accomplishes through total engagement in it. That same afternoon I heard the news of the murder in El Salvador of my six Jesuit brothers and their housekeeper and her daughter. Though worked out in a very different context, their engagement in the truth is perhaps not entirely unrelated to what I have written here. To their memory I dedicate this book.

Chapter **1**

Comparative Theology and the Practice of Advaita Vedānta

I. The Elements of the Experiment

Theology after Vedānta is an experiment in the practice of comparative theology. It proceeds by the cooperation of three distinct activities. First, it is a study of that Indian system of exegetical theology known as the Advaita (Non-Dualist) Vedānta,[1] which flourished most richly after the theologian Śaṅkara, who lived in the early 8th century CE. Advaita is a tradition of sacred and theological texts and commentaries on them, as well as arguments about texts, and the practice of meditation with texts—all of these making possible and necessary post-textual philosophical claims, and culminating in events of realization to which the hitherto indispensable texts are no longer primary. Given the enormous attention, legitimate but exaggerated, that has been paid to Advaita as an epistemological and philosophical system, it has been necessary to engage extensively in a study of that school of thought in its commentarial and theological components.

Second, this book is an exercise in (Christian) comparative theology, as this theology is (re)thought and (re)written after a close reading of Advaita. As such, *Theology after Vedānta* is an experiment in that writing, one which has as its goal the delineation of a better way for theologians to do comparative work: a way that is more practical; more engaged in texts and in the concreteness of multiple theological traditions; more attentive to how learning, writing and true knowledge follow from patient reading; more cognizant of the location of faith statements and realizations not only as prior to theological activity, but also as continually recomposed in light of and according to the requirements of that activity.

Third, and consequently, this book explores the tension between the study of Advaita and the construction of a (Christian) comparative theology, as this is mediated by a reflective reappropriation of reading as a primary practical avenue of knowledge. It is about the array of smaller and larger practices which are parts of that disciplined reading, and about the realizations that become possible and necessary for the theologian who ventures to read carefully in a tradition distinct from her or his own.

This book will therefore attract a variety of readers, including those who may be tempted to read selectively. The interpretation of Advaita which occupies Chapters 2, 3, and 4 breaks new ground in its insistence that we understand Advaita primarily as a theological tradition, and it may be of interest to readers who are not at all concerned with comparative theology. The inquiry into comparison as the practice of intelligent comparative reading, presented chiefly in this chapter and Chapter 5, may be of interest to those curious about the possible uses of reading theory in comparative religious studies, and to those who actually do comparative work; the presentation of a better, textual foundation for comparative theology and of the implied reconstruction of theological practice in general, presented chiefly in Chapter 5, will be of special interest to theologians, including those who specialize in reflection on religions other than their own. But as a whole the book addresses those who are interested in Advaita *and* theology *and* reading *and* comparative work; it is properly understood only when these subsidiary concerns are not separated.

In its broader frame the composition of this book reflects on how I, though not an Advaitin, nevertheless chose to become a reader of Advaita, to engage in that reading with some successes and some failures, and consequently to reflect on that reading and on my enduring though partially overcome exteriority to Advaita; this reflection is highlighted in order to bring to prominence the issues that need to be faced in a rereading and rewriting of my own Christian tradition. Even Chapters 2, 3 and 4, which focus on Advaita and strive for a fair reading of certain Advaita texts, are composed consciously within the margins of my comparative theological interests—even if these are only implicit in those chapters—for the sake of the composition of a better account of how one rereads one's home theological tradition—in my case, the Roman Catholic—after a serious engagement in the reading of another tradition, in this case, the Advaita. In those middle chapters, the issues of the text that is read (Chapter 2), the truth of that text (Chapter 3), and its reader (Chapter 4), are respectively taken up; each issue recurs in the three major sections of Chapter 5, where the earlier chapters' theological and comparative concerns come explicitly to the fore. Even in those middle chapters, therefore, a privileged objective position outside traditions, from which he or she might compare and contrast them objectively, has neither been sought nor attained; this is so, even if at the same time the inevitable subjective factors have been submitted to the discipline of attentive reading. This book intends neither the acquisition nor defense of a privileged objective stance, especially if the acquisition of such would entail the expectation that the Advaita and/or Christian traditions could be located within a broader field of intelligibility, which they would be thought to exemplify. The reader is therefore requested to keep in mind the Indological, theological and literary concerns which appear at least implicitly on every page of this book, and is invited to share with the author the task of keeping distinct though productively cooperative these inseparably and mutually determinative concerns.

Though *Theology after Vedānta* addresses a wide range of issues, these issues are focused through one particular example, a selective reading of certain Advaita texts and a reconsideration of certain Catholic theological texts thereafter. As a practical exercise and limited experiment this book does not begin with general issues, and does not conclude to a general theory of religion or comparison; generalizations will be made only cautiously, even reluctantly. Instead it seeks more modestly to inscribe reflection on such issues within the specific boundaries of one particular case study, in order to illuminate the universal from a studiously and stubbornly particular stance.

In this chapter I introduce the chief features and topics which require balancing in the interplay of the specific and the general, the engagement in an "other," and reappraisal of one's "home" tradition: comparative theology (section II), the theory of practice (III), and Advaita Vedānta (IV). In the light of those components taken together, I conclude by previewing the rest of the book as a commitment to the practice of reading and the important tensions that derive from a permanent commitment to that practice and a recognition of the understanding that is derived from it (V).

II. Comparative Theology

Since every issue taken up in this book will be filtered through the concerns of comparative theology, it is important to describe this project and to distinguish it from the related endeavors of theology, Indology, and the study of religion in its various forms.[2]

1. Calling Comparison "Theological"

The kind of comparison in which I engage bears with it a set of particularly theological problems. Theology, to characterize it in a non-technical fashion, is distinct from the study of religion (with which it overlaps in many of its procedures) because theology is an inquiry carried on by believers who allow their belief to remain an explicit and influential factor in their research, analysis and writing. Believing theologians are (usually) members of believing communities, and have those communities as their primary audiences, whether or not the bulk of their writing is addressed to them. With their communities, they believe in some transcendent (perhaps supernatural) reality, the possibility of and (usually fact of) a normative revelation, and in the need to make practical decisions and life choices which have a bearing on salvation. Theologians do their work with an awareness of and concern for these beliefs, and with a desire to defend and preserve them, even if at one or another moment they may have to question, recontextualize and finally reformulate them in modes of discourse quite different from those already familiar to the community.

These features remain operative throughout theologians' comparative study as well. Comparativists who are theologians are likely to believe that transcendence, revelation, truth and salvation are real concerns, not simply components of the texts which talk about them; that they are concerns likely to affect not only explicit participants in the religious traditions which revere those texts, but also scholars who might read those texts seriously. Two consequences follow.

First, comparative theologians cannot be content simply with cataloguing different traditions' views on these concerns, or with understanding how certain texts make sense to certain communities, or how "their" texts are like or unlike "our" texts, should the allegiances "our" and "their" survive scrutiny. As theologians, they insist on asking further questions about the truth of their own and other communities' knowledge of God. Unwilling to reduce their own tradition's faith claims to mere information which does not require a response, comparative theologians likewise refuse to reduce other traditions' faith to mere, safe information. Knowledge, taken seriously, changes the lives of the knowers; even if research reveals or creates a series of contradictions which make life more difficult for the believing comparativist, to pass over these in silence is only a short-term solution which manages to leave out much of what is most interesting in comparisons, the specific, "thick" details which constitute the substance of communities' religious beliefs and their continuing vitality.

Second, comparative theologians operate within boundaries marked by the tension between a necessary vulnerability to truth as one might find it and be affected by it in the materials studied, and loyalty to truth as one has already found it, lives it, and hopes according to it. Comparative theologians do not wish to reduce the studied traditions to mere, disposable information to be used as they see fit; this reduction would fundamentally distort the other, by depriving it of its imposing structures, its transformative power and its claims to universality—the very features which should most interest the theologian. But there can be no plan by which the theologian can relocate the comparison and the compared religious texts in an arena where the operative principle is a universal, exceptionless respect for all religions as equally true; even were such a relocation possible, it would be likely to devalue from the start one's own community's beliefs about itself—for the sake of comparison, the comparative venture would be shorn of its properly theological character.

2. *Calling Theology "Comparative"*

We need also to admit from the start that this project begins with a particular, peculiar, kind of theological confidence, the view that a faith tradition can claim the world entirely and universally, leaving no part of it unaccounted for, while yet simultaneously and effectively confronting itself uncompromisingly with the particular and stubborn demands that a world rich in particular and irreducible traditions and their beliefs places on the theologian.

In choosing to label *Theology after Vedānta* an experiment in "comparative theology," I therefore use the word "theology" advisedly, endowing it with an attentiveness to what is often unaccounted for or entirely marginalized in a tradition's theology, the fact of its serious theological competitors in other religions. Though I must distinguish the project undertaken here from theology as it is generally understood in the Christian context, I am tempted to call it simply "an experiment in theology," leaving aside the marker "comparative." "Comparative theology" is not meant merely to mark another specialization within theology, nor is it merely heir to the older "theology of religions" and missiology disciplines. It is a project which, though begun modestly and with small examples, intends a rethinking of every theological issue and a rereading of every theological text. But as long as comparative study is not the norm, it would not be of much help to reserve the name "theology" for this way of doing theology.

One may also concede that "comparative" may not be the right word to suggest what actually goes on in the reading of texts and therefore in this book, where the engaged reader is "inscribed" into an ever more complexly composed context, in order to write after and out of it. The distance one might normally associate with comparison is lacking; the images of visual assessment often associated with comparing—looking at things together—are inappropriate. Perhaps another Latin word, "col-lectio"—"reading-together"—might be rehabilitated for this purpose. But for now, "comparative theology" serves to indicate my intention to inscribe within the Christian theological tradition theological texts from outside it, and to (begin to) write Christian theology only out of that newly composed context.

3. *Comparative Theology in Relation to Other Disciplines*

The nature of comparative theology can be clarified by noting its relation to two presupposed but distinct disciplines: "Indology," as one instance from among a wider range of area- or culture- or religion-specific studies often termed "area studies," and the comparative study of religion.

Good comparative study, including good comparative theology, of course depends heavily on the ability of the comparativist to articulate a viable understanding of the "other," in which the encountered "other" is not manufactured to fit the comparativist's prejudices and expectations. The comparative theologian must achieve a certain distance from her or his own starting point, in order to be able to learn from another tradition by understanding it on its own terms, and in a way that can never be entirely predicated on the expectations of one's home tradition, because it reformulates those expectations regarding the home tradition.

This is why credible Indological study is necessary for my project. A credible use of Advaita in a comparative project depends on a prior credible reading of Advaita even if, as conceded above, this reading is not accomplished entirely apart from the comparative agenda. Though in an exemplary and not a comprehensive fashion, the resources of Indology have been crucial to this book. And though it cannot be labeled an Indological monograph, it would also be inaccurate to suggest that only certain parts of it—Chapters 2, 3 and 4—are Indologically informed: the very project of a "theology after Vedānta" occurs due to the reformulation of my theological concerns by engagement in the study of Advaita and its Mīmāṃsā predecessor (about which I will say more below). As my study is Theological, so is it Indological.

The distinction between comparative theology and the range of disciplines collected under the title of "the study of religion" points to the fact that comparative theology, like theology in general, is invested with the dimension of faith. The faith of the inquirer cannot be separated from the faith claims of the inquirer's community; this faith is explicitly at issue in the comparative exercise, as much as is a concern for the truth that may be emerge and claim the scholar more or less profoundly during the project of comparison. While scholars committed to the study of religion are frequently enough believers who are committed to certain traditional formulations of religious truth, such commitment does not need to be explicitly an issue in their writing; often scholars devise ways of distancing their professional work from their personal religious roots.

One may distinguish comparative theology and the study of religion also by their goals. The aim of the study of religion, in the most general terms, is an understanding of religion in its various forms and actualizations, and the accomplishment of this understanding by a methodology which enables one to study and talk about religion(s) comprehensively and productively. Particular studies of particular religious texts, symbols, and practices are often undertaken with the announced goal of using them to understand better the larger phenomenon of religion which they exemplify.

Comparative theology differs in its resistance to generalizations about religion, its commitment to the demands of one or another tradition, and its goal of a reflective retrieval, after comparison, of the comparativist's (acknowledged) own community's beliefs in order to restate them more effectively. In keeping with a concern that is central to both Advaita and (my Roman Catholic) Christian tradition, my emphasis on the local and particular resists the reduction of the two religious traditions compared, or of the comparative reading of them, to examples of how "religion" works or of how religions are to be studied.

Nevertheless, conclusions about religion and comparison can be drawn from this study, and perhaps there will be many. My point is to emphasize from the beginning that any such conclusions need to be carefully elicited from the particularities of this material, and composed in such a way as to invite the reader to engage the material directly and comprehensively, for the sake of a consequent reappropriation of her or his theological presuppositions and commitments.

III. Comparative Theology as Practical Knowledge

Theological comparison is therefore a practice in which one must purposefully and perseveringly engage; more specifically, one of the most important forms of this practice is the activity of reading attentively. Since reading is the practice which both Advaita and Christian theologians have usually undertaken, it is this practice of reading which will occupy us here; and while it cannot be adequately anticipated by a theory about it, its key dimensions—its relation to theory, its temporality, its treatment of particularity, its expectations regarding the transformation of the practitioner—must be understood if it is to be unhindered in its performance.

As reading, comparative theology entails a combination of activity with an incrementally progressive understanding of that activity; as such, it resists labelling as either "mere practice" and "mere theory."[3] Moreover, the understanding is integral to the practice; comparative theology wishes to perform and understand its practice without making the unnecessary and inept claim that it thereby supplements unexamined religious practices with their previously unarticulated theoretical framework, or that it explicitates and succeeds in making available presuppositions known better to the observer than to the participants in a religion. While comparative theology must be distinguished from religious practice, and while it necessarily enters into a critical, intelligent relationship to the materials of the compared traditions, both the familiar and the new, its achievement of this relationship is a continually provisional and practical arrangement in which the comparativist engages in activities—theoretical, practical, interpretive, personal, communal—which are shaped in negotiation with the comparable activities of the communities which are being studied and compared.[4]

As a practical endeavor, comparison occurs in time, over time; it takes time. Were we to abolish the temporal nature of comparison as a practical discourse, we would lose a crucial factor which makes available to us the significance of the practice we undertake when we perform comparisons.[5] Unlike the (scientific) practice of model-making, an understanding which subsists in the temporality of practice remains attentive to and participant in that shifting set of relationships and procedures, the tensions between the said and implicit, the ordered and disordered, which constitutes practical life. It focuses, as Pierre Bourdieu puts it, on practices' "temporal structure, direction, and rhythm [which are] *constitutive* of their meaning."[6]

Committed to the reinterpretation and rewriting of theology *after* Advaita, this book is also committed to highlighting, taking into account and taking advantage of the time it takes to work through an unfamiliar body of texts, with all the gradually cumulative effects that process has on one's practical (re)organization of previously and newly familiar concepts and commitments. The writing of this book, and by extension its proper reading, are significant as activities one learns from, not merely on the grounds of the conclusions thereby possibly generated. As Chapter 4 indicates in regard to Advaita, the value of patient reading is realized primarily within the person engaged in its practice, and by extension within a community of, or in dialogue with, such persons. Though here too distances may be usefully preserved, the transformation of the comparativist—and her or his resistance to transformation—in the acts of reading and writing are therefore necessary topics of analysis in a comparative project which takes practice seriously.[7]

The perfection of the deeper and often unrecognized ways by which the experienced person relates to the world and continually revises that relationship is the goal of Advaita, because only in that accomplishment is the tension between doing and knowing resolved. To do/know Advaita entails becoming—or being made into—a certain kind of person who makes distinctions in certain ways, thereby transforming all of her or his relations. Analogously, the Christian tradition recognizes in the appropriation of religious knowledge a transformation of one's way of acting, explicitly and in more enduring habitual patterns: what one might term the complex event of conversion. Comparative theology therefore attends closely to the ways in which comparativists' engagement in their materials and response to the new demands articulated during a comparative project reconfigure their religious and theological understanding.

Lee Yearley's recent *Mencius and Aquinas*,[8] an exemplary work which confronts the problems of comparison and which skillfully finds an intermediate path between abstraction and the undigested accumulation of detail, helps us to extend our thinking about comparison as a reflective practice.[9] He identifies three kinds of theory: first, primary theories, which "provide explanations that allow people to predict, plan and cope with the normal problems the world presents;" second, secondary theories, "which differ from culture to culture, [and] are usually built from primary theories in order to explain peculiar or distressing occurrences;"[10] third, practical theories, which "often work on the ideas primary theory produces and can link with notions of secondary theory." Practical theory "presents a more theoretical account than does primary theory and stays closer to normal phenomena than does secondary theory. Moreover, the aim is to guide people toward full actualization and therefore concepts like virtue, obligation, and disposition are utilized. Much of practical theory, then, concerns what we call ethics."[11] In the conclusion of his study Yearley returns to this distinction, again stressing the "in-between" status of practical theories which "aim at a more conceptually precise ordering of human experience than does primary theory; but they stay far closer to the particular, often murky, phenomena that make up much human life than does secondary theory."[12]

Though Yearley's focus on practical theory is finely tuned to the demands of his study of virtue, the notion of a form of understanding which is both concrete and productive of generalization, theoretical and practical, complements our previous comments on practical knowledge and highlights comparative theology as a reflective practice which develops new understandings while preserving the particularities of religious traditions' discourses about themselves.

Yearley's comments on analogy and imagination helpfully mark the balance the comparativist needs to maintain. Staying close to his materials, both respecting and honestly critiquing the ethical positions of Aquinas and Mencius, Yearley rejects univocity, whereby differences are overlooked in order to focus on similiarities, and equivocity, whereby differences are allowed to block any discussion of perceived though elusive similarities in the materials compared; neither univocity nor equivocity helps us to assess and articulate what is actually learned in a comparison.[13] Yearley seeks a middle ground on which to treat more adequately materials which can be subjected to comparison—i.e., which are neither identical nor completely different—and concludes to an analogical mode of thought : "Through analyzing the ordered relationships among analogical terms we can preserve both clarity and textured diversity, and thereby fully articulate similarities in differences and differences in similarities."[14] This process involves "ongoing operations" and "continuing performances," and "does not rest on applying a static structure or a fixed theory to material;"[15] rather, it is rooted in the ability and refined judgment of a skillful comparativist who knows how to make good comparisons and what to do with them:

> . . . I think it clear that comparative studies of human flourishings must engage in a process that necessarily involves us in a form of imagining, in the utilization of the analogical imagination. To say we must use the imagination is not also to say that standards dissolve; it is not to join forces with some of the more radical forms of humanis-

> tic scholarship. Imaginative processes involve standards for judging interpretations and rules that can be followed well or badly... They depend, for example, on the interpreter's sensibilities, they may evoke rather than demonstrate, and they produce inventions . . . these inventions have the power to give a new form to our experiences. The imaginative redescription produced challenges our normal experience of the contemporary worlds in which we live and of the often distant worlds we study.[16]

Though Yearley's work is not explicitly theological, it contributes to a model for comparative theology. It too operates in the same back-and-forth movement between particularity and theory, and is unwilling to surrender either of these; it too depends on the educated imaginative act of the comparativist (comparative theologian) who is transformed by the process of comparison and thus enabled to compare sensitively and to make sense out of particular acts of comparison.

Nevertheless, the present book differs in several ways from Yearley's. First, though practical and ethical considerations are essential to the Advaita material I will be considering, a wider range of epistemological, ontological and cosmological claims are prominent, and all of these involve refinements of reasoning which are distinguishable from ethical judgments and discourse. I will be more concerned than Yearley to trace the path back and forth from practical to secondary theories, and to assess the practical role of the latter within Advaita and in regard to outsiders who may read Advaita and potentially be claimed by it.

Second, Advaita invests heavily in the interpretation of texts, and develops its practical theories through the reflective practices of exegesis. It dwells within a world of texts; though it ventures beyond texts, it does so only through and after them, while justifying these excursions only on textual grounds. Advaita's textual investment has compelled me to focus more narrowly than Yearley on the problem of how believers compose, read, and teach their own religious and theological texts, and how outsiders who are believers in another tradition are to read and write about other communities' texts in relation to theirs, adjusting the margins of both in the process.

Third, while Yearley's stress on the skill and imagination of the comparativist is consonant with my own theological concern about the faith and community of the comparativist, his comments on the issues of faith, truth and community are minimal. I raise these questions more explicitly, exploring the tensions between what one reads and what one writes, between what one believes and how one lives. Consequently, my work is more concerned than Yearley's with the theological implications of the comparison undertaken and with the question of how the tensions created by comparative work can be resolved, in the comparativist and in her or his community.

In the preceding pages I have sketched the contours of a form of comparative theology which remains close to the particularities of the traditions studied, which maintains the prominent position of the practical issues of faith and commitment which characterize theological investigations, and which generalizes in the sense that as a member of a larger community, the comparativist as theologian is required to recount for that community both the details and implications of the comparative project in order to engage the community in the practice or its results. In the remaining sections of this chapter I further specify these indications by attention to the Advaita tradition as a practice of exegesis and commentary (IV), and by a sketch of how a focus on texts, reading and the identity of the reader shape this experiment in theology after Advaita Vedānta (V).

IV. Advaita, Text and Commentary

The following introduction to the Advaita theological tradition, to be amply filled out in Chapters 2, 3, and 4, begins with an overview of the texts relevant to this study. I then situate Advaita, first by examining its understanding of itself as a coherent, organically integrated tradition of commentaries, and then by exploring the significance of the fact that Advaita is at its core an exegetical system, and therefore is heir to the ritual exegesis of the older Mīmāṃsā school of ritual exegesis. I will show that Advaita is fundamentally a practice rather different from the philosophy it has generally been conceived to be, that it is closer to "theology" than "philosophy," and closer to "scriptural theology" than "philosophical theology." Thus characterized, Advaita places a different and in many ways more arduous, yet practicable set of demands on the interested practitioner, the interested hearer and student, whom throughout I describe as the "reader." Advaita thus portrayed loses some of the universality attributed to philosophy; but it also becomes more and not less accessible to the unauthorized but gradually implicated outsider, the comparativist, the theologian who is willing to be (re)educated by the Advaita texts.

1. A Brief Overview of the Advaita as a Commentarial Tradition

"Vedānta" refers generally to a body of concepts and a number of schools of thought which claim as their primary referent and authority the Sanskrit-language upaniṣads, a group of texts from the middle and late Vedic period (after 800 BCE). In the upaniṣads speculation about the orthodox rituals of ancient India was increasingly accompanied by speculation on the nature of the world in which ritual is efficacious, on human nature, and on the nature of the "higher" or post-mortem reality which renders human experience ultimately significant. Inquiries into, and discourses about, the vital breath (*prāṇa*), the self (*ātman*), and the corresponding spiritual and cosmic principle, *Brahman*, are prominent in the upaniṣads. These upaniṣadic explorations proceed by experiment, by question and answer, by exposition and summation; in their rough texture they replicate earlier oral debates and inquiries. The older upaniṣads appear to be only partially homogenized collections of yet older debates and teachings; they are not presented as single works by single authors, and are not complete systematizations. Consequently, Vedānta's theological appropriations of the upaniṣads are marked from the start as acts of careful reading and constructive systematizations which go beyond what is in the texts.

Bādarāyaṇa's *Uttara Mīmāṃsā Sūtras*[17] (perhaps 4th or 5th century CE) is a set of 555 brief, terse aphorisms (*sūtras*)[18] which intend just such an organization of upaniṣadic speculations into a system of thought focused on Brahman, the absolute and transcendent, cosmic and microcosmic principle of life; as interior, Brahman is occasionally equated with that Self/self known as the Ātman. Recalling and revising the views of various earlier and probably contemporary Vedānta teachers, Bādarāyaṇa attempts a descriptive systematization of the upaniṣads, a regularization of their meaning and identification of their main tenets.

His UMS may be divided into two connected projects. In the first half, he organizes the upaniṣads according to their main topic, Brahman (UMS I.1.1–2), and the right reading of texts about Brahman (UMS I.1.3–I.4.) To this he appends an articulation of the implied metaphysics and epistemology of Vedānta, in response to objections portrayed as those posed by other schools of thought (UMS II). In the second though perhaps older half of the UMS, Bādarāyaṇa inquires into the proper regulation of knowledge about Brahman in meditation (UMS III.1–3) as this is practiced by the right people (UMS III.4), and concludes by describing the fruits of meditation and the way in which these fruits are enjoyed by the deceased meditator. (UMS IV)[19]

Bādarāyaṇa's key interpretive judgment is that the upaniṣads describe Brahman in two ways: positively, as possessed of qualities (*saguṇa*), and negatively, as beyond all qualities (*nirguṇa*). According to the former portrayal, Brahman may be imagined as distinct from the meditator; according to the latter, even the distinction between Brahman and the meditator is only a practical, provisional qualification. Though it is not possible to determine completely the nature of Bādarāyaṇa's system, it thus seems to preserve, though without a complete reconciliation, several of the possible versions of the Brahman-self relationship; in turn, it remains vulnerable to further determination.

Advaita, the school of Vedānta which first took form as a tradition of commentary on Bādarāyaṇa's sūtras, sought to provide the required further determination and to resolve the questions related to Brahman by a more exact and final reading of the texts in question.[20] Among the schools of Vedānta, it is distinguished by its consistent and thorough dependence on exegesis, its balance between social conservativism and a radical critique of orthodoxy, and its decision to center its systematization of the complex upaniṣadic discourse on a belief in the final identity, non-dualism, of human self and the ultimate, non-qualified (nirguṇa) reality, Brahman. Though by no means the only school of Vedānta, Advaita's importance is attested by the fact of the many attacks on it by later schools of Vedānta.

Śaṅkara (8th century) is the most prominent of the Advaitins, and his *Bhāṣya* is the first extant commentary on the UMS.[21] Though on most issues he sets forth a traditional interpretation of the UMS, and affords us access to the general Vedānta interpretation of the upaniṣads, he argues distinctively that there is a hierarchy in the teaching of the upaniṣads, the highest position being reserved for the teaching that Brahman alone is the final reality, devoid of anything exterior to itself; according to Śaṅkara, the texts which speak of distinction in Brahman and from Brahman are provisional, prior and intended for different purposes than those texts which deny distinction and which represent the final truth of the upaniṣads.

Śaṅkara's *Bhāṣya* on Bādarāyaṇa invited further commentaries which performed the necessary task of explaining the more difficult parts of the *Bhāṣya*, as well as extending it by refining its pronouncements and exploring its implications; these later commentaries were in turn objects of further commentary. Although the limited intention of this book precludes the much-needed project of a comprehensive study of the development of Advaita as a commentarial tradition,[22] I draw on these later commentaries throughout, particularly the following:

1. Vācaspati Miśra (mid-9th century)—*Bhāmatī*
2. Amalānanda (13th)—*Vedāntakalpataru* (commentary on the *Bhāmatī*)
3. Appaya Dīkṣita (16th)—*Kalpataruparimala* (commentary on the *Vedāntakalpataru*.)
4. Ānandagiri (13th)—*Nyāyanirṇaya* (commentary on the *Bhāṣya*)
5. Govindānanda (end of 16th)—*Bhāṣyaratnaprabhā* (commentary on the *Bhāṣya*, drawing on the *Nyāyanirṇaya*)

6. Prakāśātman (13th)—*Śārīrakanyāyasaṃgraha* (a synthesis of issues at stake in the more ample commentaries)
7. Advaitānanda (17th)—*Brahmavidyābharaṇa* (a direct commentary on the *Bhāṣya*)

2. Advaita as Text: The Flourishing of a Commentarial Tradition

Commentaries are detailed, intricate, often difficult to use and often resistant to the questions modern readers pose to them; often, the older texts which were the subject of elucidation seem easier to follow than the commentarial elucidations of them. Though we may be sorely tempted to ignore the commentarial tradition in assessing the meaning of Advaita, this attempted shortcut is a serious error; we do better to slow down, to learn from and be educated by the commentaries.

If we wish to discover the most pedagogically and theologically appropriate way to read them, it makes sense to heed the announced intentions of the commentaries in question. The earliest texts are not illuminating in this regard: except for the highly important but decidedly laconic *"atha,"* the first word of the UMS,[23] Bādarāyaṇa gives us few clues as to how we are to use his text; Śaṅkara plunges directly into his analysis of the problem of ignorance and is no more helpful.

The later commentaries, however, announce their purpose in passages that are highly interesting and deserving of more careful reading than is usually afforded them. I turn therefore to the introductions of the three commentaries I will use throughout, those of Vācaspati, Amalānanda and Appaya Dīkṣita, in order to indicate how reading commentaries is essential to the project of learning Advaita.

In the verses which inaugurate the *Bhāmatī*, Vācaspati Miśra maps out the spiritual horizon within which his commentary was written:

1. We reverence that immortal Brahman, immeasurable bliss and knowledge, which is manifest accompanied by the two-fold inexpressible ignorance, from which emanate ether, air, fire, water, and the earth, and from which come forth all of this, movable and unmovable, great and small;

2. The Vedas are his breath, the five elements his glance, all that is movable and unmovable his smile, the great dissolution his sleep;
3. To the Veda, eternal and associated with the six manifold imperishable auxiliaries, and to Bhava,[24] we render obeisance;
4. To Mārtaṇḍa, to Tilakaswāmin, and to Mahāgaṇapati, who are worthy of adoration by all and are the dispensers of all fulfillment, we render obeisance;
5. To Vyāsa, the secondary arranger, the composer of the *Brahmasūtras*, the embodiment of Lord Hari's power of knowledge, we render obeisance;
6. Rendering obeisance to that pure knowledge, Śaṅkara, the giver of abundant mercy, we analyze the clear yet deep commentary expounded by him;
7. Just as falling into the current of the Ganges refreshes waters stagnant near the roadside, proximity to the work of the master refreshes the lowly words composed by ourselves and others.[25]

Thus portrayed, the project of commentary implies a close connection among four things: the world in its need and ignorance; the divine power (of Śiva); this power as manifest in knowledge and particularly in the Vedic scriptures; a tradition of authorized teachers of the Veda (*gurus*) down to Śaṅkara who is the principal teacher for the later commentators. The problem of this world is articulated as ignorance, in expectation that the remedy for it is that saving knowledge which is located in the Vedas and made available by proper teachers. The "emanations" of divine power, the unfolding of the world, and the elaboration of the "word" in Vedic speech—in its specific embodiment in certain texts and certain words, and the theories and positions of certain teachers—are parallel, interrelated structures. In practice, knowledge of the Vedic text affords the Advaitic reader access to the spiritual and cosmological components of reality: to know the Veda is to know the world; proper education constitutes the possibility of salvation.

The image Vācaspati uses in verse 7, of the waters falling into the Ganges, is striking: the commentaries are, as it were, above the *Bhāṣya,* and lie stagnant except when purified through a descent into that purifying source. If one can compose a commentary so carefully as to return the reader constantly to Śaṅkara, down into his *Bhāṣya,* then one has written pure, purifying Advaita; were a treatise to present itself as an improvement on or substitute for the *Bhāṣya,* its writing would be only a stagnant pool, a source of disease, confusion. The reader who reads/works through the commentaries is thus guided: commentaries are stagnant if taken as independent treatises, but become purifying waters when they lead us to Śaṅkara; like the holy guide who leads the pilgrim to the Ganges, good commentaries guide to the source the reader previously lost in mere words and mere debates.

Vācaspati's claim is amplified by Amalānanda in his commentary on the *Bhāmatī,* the *Vedāntakalpataru.* His opening verses affirm the characteristic Advaita positions that Brahman is knowledge, ignorance the problem to be faced, and scripture the path to knowledge:

1. That which is unknown by humans, which sustains the unsteadiness of this varied world, which is like the sky that foolish people think to be impure, which is manifest knowledge, expansive joy, the existent Brahman, the highest, which is manifest in hundreds of key scripture passages—to that we render obeisance!

2. By hundreds of rays of awareness he pierces that obscuring covering, the lack of awareness found in the interior space of the heart; he is the moon ever rising which makes rise the ocean of wisdom; he destroys misery born as the thousand rays of this miserable world; his form is auspicious; he is pure, worthy of consideration by the wise, benevolent—to his lotus feet, I attach myself!

3. That man-lion whose form is undivided joy and existence, adorned with the light of liberation, become manifest to shatter the forehead of the elephant of intoxicating delusion; whose praises were sung by Prahlāda, whose divine form came forth most emphatically from

> the pillar: may he be manifest uninterruptedly in the lotus of my heart!

In verses 10–12 of his introduction Amalānanda plays on the title of his commentary, the *Vedāntakalpataru*—"the wish-fulfilling tree of Vedānta"—in order to suggest how commentary liberates, thereby illustrating vividly the integral relationship among the power that gives life, the tradition, and his own work:

> 10. At whose rising the buds designated the various works and their meanings open in lucid explanations; in whom the world's blind infatuation is removed; whose splendor illuminates the highest heaven with the lofty stars as its divine lights; the moon whose light is joy, the teacher of knowledge—to that one I render obeisance!
>
> 11. Vācaspati rendered completely secure the orthodox path; he is victorious, the teacher of the lords of the wise, a demon to adversaries vanquished by his reasoning.
>
> 12. Growing from the Veda, this tree's shoots are made of reason, its investigations form many branches, its countless leaves are of good complexion, its opening blossoms are the realization of the highest Brahman; it gives the fruit of immortality, ready to be plucked by hand; it is the lord of all lords and humans; it is the wish-fulfilling tree which spreads out and skillfully banishes the heat arising due to the sun, this world.

Advaita is a generous, fruitful tree, growing luxuriously with each act of commentary in each generation; rooted in the reality of Brahman and cultivated in the rich soil of the upaniṣads, the *Uttara Mīmāṃsā Sūtras* and the *Bhāṣya* of Śaṅkara, the tradition flourishes and is increasingly fruitful in each successive commentary.

This emphasis on organic growth strikingly reverses a typical attitude toward commentaries: commentaries are not signs of the decay or decline of the original genius of a tradition, its reduction to words, mere scholasticism; they are the blossoming and fruition of that original genius. The "later" is the fruition, the brilliance, of the "earlier," not its deterioration. The later does not supersede the earlier, but what comes after grows out of what comes before. To skip over commentaries in order to read older texts on their own is not to strip away the encrustment of the centuries; rather, it is to examine a gem in a totally dark room, to appreciate a tree by cutting away everything but its roots. The proper way to understand Śaṅkara is to read him as (a distinct) part of a long, rich tradition.

In his comments on Amalānanda's introductory verses, Appaya Dīkṣita articulates, with his characteristic precision and thoroughness, the often merely implied interconnection among the cosmological, epistemological and textual orders of reality. He appreciates and explores fully the rich images Amalānanda places before him, and seeks just the right nuance by which to understand them; for he knows that these words are the path to knowledge of Brahman. Let us note, for example, how he elaborates skillfully the rich meanings latent in Amalānanda's verses 1 and 2. He specifies the nature of the inquiry announced there, correlating it to hearing (*śravaṇa*), reflecting (*manana*) and meditating (*nididhyāsana*), the well-known sequence of steps in Advaitic learning:[26]

> Just as daily the moon rises and, by rays which appear its own and are delimited throughout the various places in the sky, banishes the obscuration of the sky and makes the ocean rise, so too, he drives away ignorance of the meanings of various statements in the mind by means of those reflections of consciousness which take the form of the mind's parts, delimited according to the modes of mind and created by acts of hearing (*śravaṇa*) multiple Vedic statements; he makes arise that wisdom which is in the form of meditation (*nididhyāsana*) by that one-pointedness of mind which is reflection (*manana*), skillfulness in argument and refutation: it is he who always rises, he who is accompanied by Umā who is well-known for giving knowledge of Brahman—as it is said in the *Kena Upaniṣad* 3.12[27] "Let us come to the woman in the sky, Umā, Haimavatī, abundantly shining."

The many words of the Vedic texts cooperate to lead the meditator to knowledge of that Brahman which is always beyond words. Just as the refracted light of the moon illuminates the night sky, the light of the awareness of Brahman illuminates the seeker's mind, and consciousness is gradually uncovered. This light is refracted in the words of the Veda and Advaita; by careful listening to these words, each as it were a ray of Brahman, our understanding of the upaniṣads is gradually clarified. Just as the tide is raised by the moon, Appaya Dīkṣita suggests, critical reflection on what one understands gradually uplifts the mind; just as the eye gradually finds its way to the moon and no longer notices just its rays, the mind gradually traces the path from the words of the text to their source. Expertise in textual knowledge enables the reader to excel in meditation, and contributes to its fruition, as the images, "realities," and the exigencies of interpretation converge harmoniously. The process of textual, verbal knowledge is effective against the strongest of resistances; to know the text is to make progress toward the liberation the text announces.[28]

The commentaries are the communally remembered and passed down wisdom of this pedagogy, the extant form of generations of experience in reading and understanding texts, the accumulated insights of the Advaita tradition into the upaniṣads, Bādarāyaṇa and Śaṅkara. We are thus guided by the commentaries' initial pronouncements about themselves to engage in a larger Text, one written after, around, and upon Śaṅkara's *Bhāṣya*; we read "up" through his thought through a luxuriant commentarial elaboration that grew over generations. We appreciate his importance maximally by learning to be good readers, able to trace later commentarial words back to his; to master this complex commentarial tradition is to become educated in Advaita.

3. Advaita as Uttara Mīmāṃsā: The Pūrva Mīmāṃsā Paradigm

The thesis that Advaita ought to be interpreted as a commentarial tradition is a helpful aid in the initiation of a comparative theological project; but the broader validity of the thesis becomes evident if we recall that Advaita has traditionally been known as the "Uttara [Later] Mīmāṃsā," and thus as heir to the Mīmāṃsā tradition of ritual exegesis.[29]

A few points must suffice to indicate the nature of that Mīmāṃsā background.[30] The Mīmāṃsā tradition gained a definite form in the so-called *Pūrva [Earlier] Mīmāṃsā Sūtras* (henceforth PMS), attributed to Jaimini (2nd century BCE), and thereafter in the first written commentary on the PMS, the *Bhāṣya* of Śabara (2nd–4th centuries CE).

The PMS is an inquiry into *dharma*, which is both the right way of acting and the right order of the universe; this inquiry proceeds by a careful tracing of ritual events to their textual sources, and of texts to their places in ritual enactment: texts are inherently implicated in the world of ritual practice, and careful reading is the necessary prerequisite to coherent practice.

Mīmāṃsā's careful distinctions and connections among words and actions were produced in a mode of exegesis that proceeded by the composition and scrutiny of specific "textual terrains" of introduced, examined and argued "case studies" known as *adhikaraṇas*. Argued out in these case studies according to rules postulated to help the Mīmāṃsakas read and debate properly, the rhetorical and forensic discourse of Mīmāṃsā leads inquirers ever more deeply into a correct and corrected reading, and consequently into more elaborate defenses of the coherence of that reading. In defense of this constructed and argued convergence of text and action, Mīmāṃsā arranges the Vedic world into a sacrificially organized array of center and periphery, with all competing measures of significance—the gods, the author, the ordinary world, truth—relegated to the edge of discourse as merely contributory features. Ultimately, the only thing that matters is the event of sacrifice: dharma, the object of Mīmāṃsā inquiry, is the sum of all right relations, the activated, fully understood and rightly connected set of all the small and large activities and things which together constitute the sacrificial whole.

Later, and in a subordinate fashion, Mīmāṃsā articulates doctrines which stand independent, apart from the texts and rituals that they were first intended to support. Thus, in an important move to which we will advert below, the Mīmāṃsakas argue the authorlessness of the Veda (*apauruṣeyatva*) and the self-validation of language, in order to defend before a wider audience the position that neither the authority nor meaning of texts depends on the potentially unreliable authors to whom they are attributed. Such moves toward systematization always remain intrinsically performative: the meaning(s) of texts and the purpose(s) of (ritual) actions converge; the ascertainment of right meaning entails a gradual ascertainment of what one ought to do; argumentation always retains its "memory" of ritual practice and its rationale, its spatial and temporal valorizations, and truth retains its spatial and temporal identity.

Advaita discourse is modelled on this Mīmāṃsā paradigm. Though claiming to be a step beyond Mīmāṃsā, for the most part it acts in continuity with its admitted predecessor; if it introduces some concepts and practices incompatible with Mīmāṃsā and claims also to supersede it, even these claims are made according to the norms of Mīmāṃsā thinking. Though Advaita argues at length that knowledge is not an action, and that "to know" cannot be necessarily consequent upon "to do," in its emphasis on meditation and the textual path to knowledge, in its modes of exegesis, in its recognition that knowledge is gained gradually through an engagement in the texts which are the subject of exegesis, and even in its treatment of the final realization of Brahman as an event,[31] it shares the Mīmāṃsā concern for performance. Though Advaita may appear much more philosophical than Mīmāṃsā, its articulation of theory and doctrine resides within the confines of Mīmāṃsā's practical emphasis; it too keeps all theoretical and doctrinal pronouncements rooted in textual knowledge, and so persistently orients the understanding reader back into a world of practice.

As Uttara Mīmāṃsā, Advaita extends the Mīmāṃsā practice of reading to a new set of texts. It is most importantly in this sense that it is "after" Mīmāṃsā. Extending the Mīmāṃsā practice to include the upaniṣads, it reads those texts in a Mīmāṃsā fashion, as expressing knowledge of Brahman, the all-inclusive and encompassing reality, and as showing how that knowledge is to be enacted in order to culminate in union with Brahman. Though Mīmāṃsā's refusal to take into account texts like the upaniṣads is strongly contested by Advaita and other Vedānta schools, Advaita is nevertheless most fruitfully thought of as an extension to the upaniṣads of Mīmāṃsā modes of exegesis. Consequently, it is best approached by studying its inscribed Mīmāṃsā discourse; only in that context, and thereafter, should we note how it is distinguished from Mīmāṃsā by certain claims about Brahman and the relationship of knowledge, texts and action.

As a corollary of this decision to describe Advaita primarily as Uttara Mīmāṃsā, I refer to Advaita as "theology," as faith seeking understanding, a salvation-centered explication of the world generated out of an exegesis of sacred texts which seeks to commit the listening (reading) community to specific ritual and ethical practices. These features make the appellation "theology" more appropriate than alternatives such as "philosophy," "mysticism," "ontology," etc., even if an outstanding feature of theology, its focus on the "study of God," is absent from Advaita.

This is so, one must add, even if "theology" has rarely been a term of approbation in the past several centuries. Although the commentarial, theological aspect of Advaita has not been an important object of modern research, scholars have always acknowledged its existence. A century ago Deussen recognized the centrality of the Vedic Scriptures in Śaṅkara's Advaita and he elaborated an explanatory schema which made room for both an exoteric (scripturally based, theological) and an esoteric (philosophical) approach to each of the areas of inquiry he identified: theology, eschatology, cosmology and psychology.[32] Modern scholars such as Nakamura have stressed the profoundly scriptural texture of Advaita, and argued that "the Vedānta is the unique school which tries reverently to follow the Upaniṣads as a whole."[33] Modi, the best modern critic of Bādarāyaṇa and Śaṅkara, argues persuasively that the Vedānta of Bādarāyaṇa grew out of a particular exegetical effort to interpret and arrange Vedic knowledge—and that Śaṅkara was a somewhat capable heir to this tradition.[34]

Nevertheless, in making the commentarial side of Advaita central and in describing Advaita as primarily theological, I distinguish my work from the mainstream of modern approaches to Advaita, which have used an almost entirely philosophical language in their treatment of Advaita, even when it would have been easier to draw on the many theological discourses available in India and the West. There are at least three important reasons why scholars have favored the philosophical approach to Advaita, according to which the textual-exegetical-commentarial side of the tradition is downplayed in proportion to the doctrines of self and non-dualism.

The first reason is of course that such a focus is not entirely inimical to Śaṅkara's estimate of his project, which is much less apparently theological in the ordinary sense than would be Rāmānuja's Vedānta, for example. Though Śaṅkara constantly uses scripture, he will on occasion refer to exegetical concerns as merely indicative of the popular or lower knowledge of Brahman.[35] Though, as we will see in Chapter 3, such claims do not allow us to disregard Advaita's predominantly verbal and scriptural orientation, it cannot be denied that Advaita makes distinctions within knowledge which lend themselves to the supersession of much of what counts for theological discourse. But Indologists, historians and philosophers have appealed to this hierarchization of the exegetical and the "higher" knowledge in order to justify focusing almost exclusively—too much so—on the latter.[36]

The second reason for a nontheological and philosophical reading of Advaita takes us onto more sensitive ground. Some have denied the appellation "theology" to Advaita not because they overlooked its theological aspects, but out of respect for the system in an age when "theology" was not a term of praise, in order to emphasize its relevance by privileging one or another of its aspects, and so calling it "philosophy," "metaphysics," even "mysticism." For centuries theology has been portrayed as a way of thinking which unduly subordinates reason to extrinsic authoritarian structures, authoritarian authors and leaders, and unquestioned priestly norms. Scholars undertook an obligatory search for alternatives which would redeem thinkers and their texts, deemed worthy of retrieval, from their theological context, and have often identified its exegetical portion with unthinking dogmatism or constraint upon the rational mind. At best, theology is "lower knowledge," successful in communicating with a broader, public audience—Deussen's notion of the exoteric—but inferior by comparison with the more nuanced knowledge produced in a thinking that is independent of texts and rites.[37]

In the context of this preference for an alternative to theological thinking, philosophy comes to the fore, and so Śaṅkara is thought to be at his best when he expounds a rarified doctrine of nondualism, Advaita as a kind of profound rational insight. His polemic against mere words and mere rites is taken at face value, narrowly and out of context, and used as a basis for the conclusion that he is adequately understood when his higher, speculative discourse is highlighted and studied exclusively.[38]

Today, if we may presume a more balanced and favorable attitude toward theology, we can understand more properly and fruitfully the relationship between the theological and philosophical domains of knowing. If we take seriously the temporal relationships among these ways of knowing, one may move from one to the other in either direction. One may first engage deeply in sacred texts, and later construct arguments and inquire into the foundations of knowledge that support what one reads; or, one may begin with the articulation of a rational discourse, and at a later point submit it to the demands of sacred texts, perhaps to ground it religiously, perhaps simply to illustrate and explain it. Advaita represents the former of these approaches, while modern readers have tended to interpret it according to the latter.

A third motive for the portrayal of Śaṅkara as philosopher lies essentially in the desire to make his thought accessible to an audience which does not share his faith commitment to the upaniṣads as revelatory and authoritative scriptures. Reason is seen as the bridge which makes cross-cultural, cross-religious communication and understanding possible. Deutsch focuses on this intelligible bridge: "In reconstructing Advaita, we intend to focus on philosophical analysis at the expense of scriptural exegesis. We want to find in Advaita that which is philosophically meaningful to a Westerner and to articulate this content in universal philosophical terms . . . A reconstruction of Advaita

Vedānta is an attempt to formulate systematically one's understanding of what is of universal philosophical interest in it."[39]

Certain themes in Advaita Vedānta do indeed become more immediately, apparently accessible if one abstracts them from their scriptural context: there is an ultimate, nondual self; self-knowledge alone is ultimately liberative; sorrow is due to wrong understanding. Judging by the appearances of what seems to make sense, one can be said to engage in Advaita through a consideration of such claims. But it would be a mistake to isolate these themes and mistake the sum of them for a full understanding of the Advaita. We cannot infer from a successful recognition of reason's distinct role that we have immediate access to Advaita's full meaning.

Quite the contrary: essential to Advaita is its claim that reason is not *the* universal link, *the* complete and adequate bridge. Reason does not operate independently in Śaṅkara's Advaita, though it has a distinctive function; this distinctive role occurs within, and not apart from, exegetical and scripturally-formed thinking; it operates properly when exercised by properly educated, literate persons.[40] Indeed, as we shall see in Chapter 2, the literary and rhetorical characteristics of the Advaita texts make them by design unsuitable for replacement by a summation of their main ideas or the abstraction of their main themes. This is so even if the Advaitins themselves submitted the upaniṣads to constructive readings; as we shall see, the systematizing activity of Advaita has written into it safeguards for the permanent location of those systematized meanings in exegesis, not liable to extraction and independent use.[41]

The task then is to seek an additional point of entrance into Advaita for those who are not believing Advaitins, if we decline to privilege reason and to make some version of philosophical thinking the universal, transcultural bridge. This book intends in part to measure the extent to which the scriptural (textual, exegetical, commentarial) practice of Advaita provides another and theologically more helpful accessibility, in which we can take advantage of the dynamics of reading and so construct a pedagogy which enables the nonbelieving reader to become a partially literate reader of Advaita. In the following chapters I explore the nature of this textual access to Advaita and how it enables a practical transformation of the theologian, not merely through the discovery of an already shared background of views about the world as such, or a shared operation of reason—though these may also be in place—but also through the acquisition of an ampler language in the use of which one can think, read, speak and write differently.

Throughout, the tension will remain between the content and conclusions of reading, and the act of reading itself, and it is the possibilities of this unsettling tension which interest us here. We already know that one cannot become a believing Advaitin simply for the sake of good scholarship. Faith issues aside, we cannot hope to reproduce for our scrutiny the mind of a theologian of a vastly different time and place; study, however prolonged, will not enable us to use the upaniṣads precisely as Śaṅkara does, and in the end we will still not being reasoning from within his version of the upaniṣadic worldview.

Nevertheless, we do read the upaniṣads, and we are able to understand them in part; we do read the Advaita theological texts, and we are able to understand them in part; we check our readings against those of the commentators, and learn to read in ways which approximate the ways in which they read. This partially adequate reading and understanding is a true engagement in these texts and so too in Advaita thinking; it is also an engagement, provisional and partial, but real and rich in implications, in the practice and faith inscribed within those texts. A patient engagement in the commentarial project is therefore a plausible pathway into Advaita, though its price is a reassessment of Advaita which brings to the fore its self-presentation as a commentarial tradition. Some observations on how this textual reading of Advaita will proceed conclude this chapter.

V. *Practical Implications*

1. *Retrieving the Advaita "Text"*

The task of retrieving the possibility of a reflective engagement in the textual, practical and theological aspects of Advaita demands of the reader an attunement to a new set of clues in the Advaita materials, and a rearrangement of what may already be familiar and learned in other ways. We are required to take into account the implications of a textual, as distinct from philosophical, approach to Advaita: how does one read Advaita differently, as an exegetical, commentarial, theological system? In the following pages I identify three shifts which are constitutive of this different reading and which mark the difference which thereafter structures this book: 1. *a commitment to the Advaita Text,* a shift from "texts" to "the Text," to Advaita as constituted in the entirety of its earlier and later texts, the entirety of the commentarial tradition rooted in the UMS and before that in the upaniṣads,[42] and consequently an inquiry into how the significance of texts is inscribed in the demands they impose on the intelligent reader; 2. *a commitment to truth in, through, after this Text*: a shift in the notion of referentiality, away from meanings that are exterior to texts and accessible in textual and other ways, and toward a significance that occurs only after the Text, accessible only to the person who has learned to read, think, understand and write out of, after that Text; 3. *a commitment to the reader of the Text*: consequently, a shift from a notion of the reader as merely the consumer of established meanings, to a notion of the reader as an actively engaged participant who "realizes" the Text's significance, in whom that Text's truth can be said to occur. Let us now examine each shift.[43]

2. From the Study of Śaṅkara to the Study of the Text

To name the set of Advaita texts, from the upaniṣads to the latest of the commentaries, "the Advaita Text," is to insist on the rich integrity of that whole—which we have already previewed in examining the commentaries' own first words—and at the same time on the secondary role of alternative images, strategies, appeals and resources for the comprehension of Advaita. As Uttara Mīmāṃsā, Advaita appropriates the corollaries adopted by Mīmāṃsā in keeping with its steadfast textual commitment. Most notably, Advaita too refuses to invest the author with decisive authority regarding right meaning; with the same minimal discussion which characterizes the (early) Mīmāṃsā defense of authorlessness (apauruṣeyatva),[44] Advaita shifts attention from authors to the way in which texts "in themselves" mean and have a significance which is not fruitfully defined according to the apparatus of authorial intent.[45] In both Mīmāṃsās texts are recognized as possessed of clues sufficient to communicate their significance, and thereafter to indicate what needs to be done in response to the implications of that significance. To read properly is to notice these clues, in accordance with the rules which regulate their ordering and evaluation, and to respond properly in further acts, including those of further reading and writing. The result is what can be legitimately be called a construction of texts' meaning from the "Text itself;" this occurs not because the Text is active and the reader merely an obedient receiver of its commands, but rather because the expectations imposed on a reader by the Text and the results which accrue due to the education of the reader in the process of reading cooperate to compose the locale within which reading transforms the reader into the proper, educated knower of the truth of Advaita; the point of the Text is to ensure that this transformation occurs. The meaning of Advaita is inscribed in the complex whole of the Text, its layers of text and commentary, and to this whole the thought of Śaṅkara is only a single, albeit primary, contributor.[46]

Comparative work is fruitfully understood as a disciplined encounter with the "surface" of the studied tradition, its evident, legible texture and with all that is implied by that textuality. The resultant engagement opens upon a widely disseminated field of language, in which the comparativist is educated, and so in small, expected but also unpredictable ways begins to share the Advaita discourse. We are thus better positioned to take seriously the commentarial project in its full expanse as more than a series of efforts to specify what was articulated clearly somewhere in Śaṅkara's mind; we are therefore more likely to be educated through our study of the Text. In Chapter 2 we will specify the texture of the Advaita Text, and the kind of accessibility that is thereby made available to the skilled reader.

3. From Truth outside the Text to Truth after the Text

The Advaitins insist with great energy that reality is worth knowing, that it can be known truly, and that this knowledge is accessible beyond, through, and after words. One may eventually step beyond texts, but texts form the pathway, along which one progresses toward knowledge of the world as it really is. Advaita resists efforts to dig beneath and behind its Text, as if to uncover the simpler objective truth of which Text is "really" expressive, or "really" talking about.

Essential to the genius of Advaita is the care with which it inscribes the truth of the Text within the Text, making it available, but only to those who commit themselves to the long process of becoming the kind of persons who read properly. However one might finally comprehend the truth of Advaita, and however one might thereafter choose to speak of Brahman's position vis à vis the Advaita texts, that truth occurs in an understanding of Brahman located in the Text, acquired through reading and rereading and not apart from these activities. Though Brahman is neither a fiction (as might be a character in a novel) nor a textual production (as might be a ritual vis à vis the texts which accompany it), Advaita's truth about Brahman does not exist outside its texts, but only after them. Each of Advaita's claims about Brahman or categorizations of it is a practical facilitation of the reader's course toward the event of a final truth elicited through the act of reading; the Text makes possible a definitive comprehension of the truth of Brahman through the particular ways in which it regulates the reader's appropriation of the Text itself.

For these reasons I remain skeptical about efforts to extract from the Advaita texts a set of conclusions or propositions, either as proposed by the Advaitins themselves, or as summarized by ancient or modern compendium-makers, or as rephrased in modern philosophical expression. Though often drawn from appropriate sources, such systematizations frequently replace the Text with its meaning(s), with encapsulated, useful statements of what it really means—and thereby apparently enabling the inquisitive person to get the "gist" of it without having to invest a great deal of time in the daunting Text itself.

The intention of this book regarding Advaita's truth is therefore twofold. On the one hand, it resists the temptation to reduce Advaita to its literary excellences, or to the ever-receding horizon of a completion of the commentarial ascertainment of truth; on the other, it resists the temptation to replace Advaita with a superior text or idea which states its truth more directly and simply than the Advaitins were capable of doing, thereby making the Text superfluous to its own concisely stated meaning. Instead, I seek to trace Advaita's own way of articulating its truth textually, from its preserved and appreciated exegetical basis, and to indicate a way of speaking about that truth which does not abandon its textual basis for the sake of its articulation. This tracing is the project of Chapter 3.

4. From Reader as Observer to Reader as Participant

My final point follows from the preceding two. The resolution of the tension between the complex constitution of the Text and the posteriority to it of its truth requires an active reader who is involved in a series of demanding choices and judgments according to which the relation of Text and truth occurs.

The Vedas and the upaniṣads, as ritual and metaritual speculations, do not lend themselves to neutral assimilation. Bādarāyaṇa's UMS, Śaṅkara's *Bhāṣya*, and the later commentaries all demand the skillful engagement of a committed reader. No welcome is extended to those who wish to be passive consumers, observers, or merely grateful assimilators of neatly labeled conclusions. The Text is useable and performable, it requires use and performance; continually open to novel engagements which are not entirely constrained by authorial intentions or the measures of an external referent, its significance is intimately connected with what the increasingly literate and skilled reader is able to do with it.[47]

Key to Advaita, therefore, are not only its carefully composed Text and rigorously post-Textual truth, but also the proper reader who can enact the Text and so become the location of the realization of its truth. This is why Advaita so carefully writes into the Text definite expectations about the identity of its reader, stating inner and exterior qualifications prerequisite to reading. To use the Sanskrit term, reading is a *saṃskāra*, a (ritual) transformation of the reader. Though "transformation" may suggest purely interior and personal events which pertain to the person's inner capacities, here it needs to be spoken of also as the event of right education, cultivation.[48] The implications of this reconstitution of the reader from the subject matter of Chapter 4.

Advaita's high expectations about the potency of a gradually accomplished literacy and about the event of intelligent reading increase both the difficulties and the possibilities of a true cross-religious understanding which face the theologian who begins to read Advaita without prior restrictions on what and how one is to read or what might be produced by careful reading; skill in reading is at stake, truth is at stake, the identity of the comparativist is at stake. These possibilities and risks constitute the topic of Chapter 5, where I examine how the process of reading and rereading reshapes the project of a desired return to the Christian tradition and the reading, and writing, of Christian theological texts. For although the extended study of Advaita is posterior to the (Christian) comparativist's original knowledge, commitments and literacy, it henceforth precedes reappropriations of that background. The issues taken up respectively in Chapters 2, 3 and 4—the Text, its Truth, its Reader—are thus taken up again in Chapter 5: Part 2 of Chapter 5, where we begin to reconstruct the textuality of the Christian theological tradition in preparation for comparative theology, recalls Chapter 2; Part 3 of Chapter 5, where we recast the question of the truth of theology and the knowledge of God in light of the posttextual inscription of truth in Advaita, and in response to that truth insofar as it is provisionally available to the reader, recalls Chapter 3; Part 4 of Chapter 5, where we recalculate our understanding of the theologian as student and teacher and of the pedagogical and communicative strategies of comparative theology, recalls Chapter 4.

Chapter **2**

The Texture of the Advaita Vedānta Text

I. The Texture of the Advaita Text

To understand Advaita properly is to hear it, listen to it, submit to it, engage in it, practice it—that is, to "read" it properly, to become its approved "reader."[1] Proper understanding includes an understanding of what one is doing when one reads the particular texts and commentaries—from the upaniṣads to the *Uttara Mīmāṃsā Sūtras* of Bādarāyaṇa to the *Bhāṣya* of Śaṅkara and the commentaries on Śaṅkara—which comprise what I am calling the "the (Advaita) Text." In this chapter I investigate the texture of this Text, the particular requirements and expectations written into it which demand of the reader particular responses during the act(s) of reading and then in consequent acts of speaking and writing from and about the Text. Specifically, we need to learn how to leave the Advaita topics permanently inscribed within the Text's margins, to think about and describe its argumentation and conclusions in ways appropriate to its textual modes of progress, textual organization, and reasoning.

Let us begin simply by recalling the distinction between the (extractable and summarizable) content of a text, and the modes of composition in which that meaning is actually available to the reader; and let us emphasize that style, rhetoric and other literary features are the required resources by which we can come to understand meaning—resources we ignore only at the risk of misunderstanding the content to which we would instead devote our attention.[2] Advaita has suffered at the hands of readers who have discussed its themes without sufficient attention to the manner in which these are inscribed in the Text.

In Chapter 1 I have already noted how a too prominently placed thematic or authorial focus may distract us from the full commentarial "flourishing" which constitutes the Advaita project. We must learn to become completely attentive to the way in which Textual meaning comes to us, as we engage in reading the Text and as we learn gradually, on the basis of that activity, to say things about it. The Text resists summation based on major themes, conclusions, or the important intentions of its authors; it resists a (merely) linear reading that moves either toward an expressible conclusion, or from a generally stated theory to its (mere) exemplification. These inscribed acts of resistance can be interpreted more positively by noticing Advaita's insistent imposition of specific demands on its readers, to educate those readers in certain ways of thinking and organizing what is learned from reading, so as to implicate them in ongoing acts of commentary from which the readers cannot simply disassociate themselves.

II. *The Rough Texture of the Upaniṣads*

We begin our review of the complex development of the Text by reviewing in general terms, and using the *Chāndogya Upaniṣad* as an example, the array of possibilities opened up by the upaniṣads as the textual basis on which Advaita composes its interpretive framework.[3]

The upaniṣads embody several attitudes and possibilities regarding learning and what can be known and expressed, and in various ways they present to us modes for the presentation of that knowledge. First, occasionally they report simply the fact—and not the content—of conversations between seekers and wise teachers, and exhort the reader to seek similar conversations, presumably since a text cannot replicate the dynamics of the teacher and student relationship. For example, the story of Satyakāma (*Chāndogya* 4.4–9) moves from an initial dialogue between Satyakāma and his mother (4.4) and the teaching of the bull, the fire, the swan and the diver-bird (4.4–8), to a climactic return of Satyakāma to his teacher for the long desired teaching. But the teaching itself is not given in the chapter, which merely ends by saying, "Then [the teacher] explained to him the same [Brahman]. In that [explanation] nothing was omitted, nothing was omitted." (4.9.3) The set upaniṣadic text is not the appropriate place for the presentation of the needed living dialogue.

Second, an upaniṣad may present the content of teaching, but still not as important in itself; rather, the exposition encourages the seeker to go to a wise teacher for a comparable presentation of knowledge, for the practice of reflective study with the teacher. The knowledge presented in the text is only exemplary. Thus, *Chāndogya* 3.1–11, a richly and elaborately constructed meditation on the "honeys" of the Vedas, each in correspondence to an aspect of the sun and an atmospheric deity, concludes with a record of its own transmission, praise of its unsurpassable value, and directions regarding its future communication to select students: "Therefore, only to the eldest son shall his father proclaim Brahman, or to a trusted pupil, but to no one else, whoever he be." (3.11.5–6)[4] The upaniṣadic text is a record of remembered wisdom, yet thereby still a resource for the active engagement of teacher and student.

Even the portion of the *Chāndogya Upaniṣad* that is most important for the Advaita, the teaching in Chapter 6 on the equivalence (or identity) of the self (*tvam*) and the ultimate principle of the universe (*tat*), is presented as a dialogue in which the boy Śvetaketu is required by his father to perform various exercises by which the knowledge of "You are that" (*tat tvam asi*) is illuminated: to fast (6.7), to split open a fruit (6.12), to examine salt dissolved in water (6.13). The text must be performed in a conducive pedagogical environment if it is to be understood.

Even when the upaniṣads present teachings ostensibly available to the reader, they are still proposing a knowledge which is relational and which requires a conscious repositioning of oneself in relation to the world; their message cannot be passively received or processed as mere information. Thus, as in *Chāndogya* 3, there are passages which require of the student an elaborate positioning of local and larger realities in relation to one another. We may notice also such passages as *Chāndogya* 1.6–7, in which the three kinds of Vedic texts are correlated with cosmological and psychosomatic realities, and 2.2–7 and 2.8–22, in which the parts of sung verses (*sāmans*) are elaborately correlated to referents interior and exterior to the meditator.

There are also inquiries which require the student to trace a path back through time "to the beginning." *Chāndogya* 6.1–8 proposes this kind of analysis of the derivation of things one from another—fire, water, food, and their respective derivatives; *Chāndogya* 7 is comprised wholly of a genealogical search, an analysis of the formal, traditional representation of religious knowledge back into more basic forms: from the Vedic texts as name, to speech, mind, intention, discursive thinking, meditation, knowledge, strength, food, water, heat, ether, memory, hope and breath. The words alone communicate little; they must be properly used, in their proper order, if one is to profit from them.

Let us examine one text in detail, *Taittirīya* 2.1–6a.[5] The passage is structured around five sheaths (*kośa*), each a complex arrangement of parts, accessible only when the prior sheath has been understood; together they constitute the "layers" of the human person: i. food (*anna*), ii. vital breath (*prāṇa*), iii. mind (*manas*), iv. knowledge (*vijñāna*) and v. bliss (*ānanda*). In teaching about the self through a presentation of these sheaths, the passage expends considerable effort in order to say something about Brahman while at the same time regulating how what is said is to be received by the reader. Here is the text:

1. One who knows Brahman reaches the highest. About that there is this verse:[6]

"Brahman is reality, knowledge, infinite; he who knows it concealed in the cavity of the heart and in the highest space, attains all wishes, along with omniscient Brahman."

Out of this self, indeed, emerges ether, out of ether wind, out of wind fire, out of fire water, out of water earth, out of earth plants, out of plants food, out of food man. This one, indeed, consists of the food-sap (*annarasa-maya*); in him this is the head, this is the south side (or wing), this the north side, this the self, this the tail, that on which it rests. About it, there is this verse:

2. "Out of food are born creatures, all these that are on earth; therefore, through food they have their life. Into this food they enter at last. Food is the oldest of beings; that is why it is called all-healing. They obtain all food who adore Brahman as food. That is why it is called all-healing. Beings originate out of food. Through food, they grow. It eats beings, and beings eat it: that is why it is called food."

Different from this one consisting of the food-sap is the inner self (*ātman*) which consists of vital breath (*prāṇa-maya*). With it this one is filled. This now is the human form, and according to its human formation, it is the human form. In it the in-breath is the head, the intermediate breath the south side, the out-breath the north side, the ether the self, the earth the tail, that on which it rests. About it, there is this verse:

3. "According to this vital breath breathe the gods, men and animals. Breath is indeed the life of beings; that is why it is named the all-animating."

Who adores Brahman as the breath comes to the full duration of life; That is why he is named the all-animating. Thus he is the embodied self of that one which is before [the self consisting of food]. Different from this one consisting of vital breath is the inner self which consists of mind (*mano-maya*). With it this one is filled. This now is the human form, and according to its human formation, it is the human form. In it, the Yajus is the head, the Ṛg the south side, the Sāman the north side, the directives the self, the Atharva and the Āṅgirasa chants the tail, that on which it rests. About it, there is this verse:

4. "Before him words turn back, and so too thought, not reaching him; he who knows the bliss of Brahman dreads nothing, now or ever."

> Thus he is the embodied self of that one which is before [the self consisting of vital breath]. Different from this one consisting of mind there is the inner self consisting of knowledge (*vijñāna-maya*). With it this one is filled. This now is the human form, and according to the human formation, it is the human form. In it faith is the head, justice the south side, truth the north side, yoga the self, the great one the tail, that on which it rests. About it, there is this verse:
>
> 5. "He sets forth knowledge as the sacrificial offering, he sets forth knowledge as the rites. All the gods adore Brahman as knowledge, the oldest of all. He who knows Brahman as knowledge and does not deviate from it leaves evil behind in his body and attains all that he wishes."
>
> Thus he is the embodied self of that one which is before [the self consisting of mind]. Different from this one consisting of knowledge, there is the inner self consisting of bliss (*ānanda-maya*). With it this one is filled. This now is the human form, and according to its human formation, it is the human form. In it, what is dear is the head, joy the south side, cheerfulness the north side, bliss the self, Brahman the tail, that on which it rests (*brahma puccham pratiṣṭhā*). About it, there is this verse:
>
> 6. "He who knows Brahman as non-existent becomes as it were non-existent; he who knows Brahman as existent, him they know as existent."

Each sheath is ordered according to the directions, each having i. a head in the east, ii. a south side, iii. a north side, iv. a central "self" (*ātman*), and v. a base to the west. Thus, we have this arrangement of parts for the second sheath, the vital breath:

	i. head/*prāṇa*	
ii. north/*apāna*	iv. self/*ākāśa*	iii. south/*vyāna*
	v. base/*pṛthivī*	

The fifth sheath, bliss, which occasions the Vedānta debate to which we shall refer below, is arranged as follows:

	i. head/*priya*	
ii. north/*moda*	iv. self/*ānanda*	iii. south/*pramoda*
	v. base/*Brahman*	

The meaning of each sheath is illuminated by a mantra, as cited above.

Each individually ordered sheath is placed within a larger ordering; each is said to be interior to the one before it on the list, and presumably is reached after one has encountered and passed through the preceding, exterior one. Only by tracing sheath-by-sheath that path which is marked by the five successive sheaths does the meditator gradually achieve insight into the structure of the person thus layered and, in a self-application and self-appropriation of the sheaths as applicable to the meditator's own self, attains to the self of bliss and knowledge of Brahman.

Yet, though thus complex, rich in meaning(s), and already internally interpreted by the intervening mantras, *Taittirīya* 2.1–6a does not formally fix its meaning(s); in particular, it does not fix the status of the fifth sheath in relation to Brahman, whether Brahman is the sheath of bliss, or still beyond it.

Before turning to the process by which the Advaita goes about determining the relationship between that fifth sheath and Brahman, let us conclude this brief consideration of the upaniṣads. In part, we may simply acknowledge that the early upaniṣads are presystematic and do not complete the process they begin with their highlighting of certain teachings and debates in specified narrative forms; they present without making a definitive choice a number of possibilities as to how to build a more systematic knowledge. But even apart from this unfinished redaction, the *Chāndogya* and other early upaniṣads do not, and do not wish to, present us with complete systematic presentations, versions of knowledge which require only the assent of their readers or only a scrutiny in terms of the accuracy of the correspondence between texts and their announced referents. Upaniṣadic forms of knowledge-as-arrangement require the active engagement of the student, the imaginative reproduction of the proposed structures and a subsequent interior appropriation of them.[7] They thereby maintain a certain ironic detachment from their own formalizing activity, assuring textually that knowledge can never be adequately communicated by its texts: texts serve their proper function when they call into question their own reliability and adequacy.

The uneven and demanding texture of the upaniṣads prompts responses of two sorts. First, the claims and reorientations achieved by the upaniṣads raise questions that they do not entirely answer, and it is important to examine how Advaita preserves and extends the communicative project of the upaniṣads by working out a teaching about Brahman, the world in relation to Brahman, and a position regarding alternative views of the world. This aspect of Advaita, its "truth," will be taken up in Chapter 3.

Second, Advaita takes into account the presystematic and performative nature of the upaniṣads, and we must examine how Advaita retains and inscribes in its presentation of the upaniṣads the ironic, self-conscious and self-critical, upaniṣadic style, how it, like the upaniṣads, resists the reduction of texts to the presentation of already and completely achieved meanings. To this analysis I now turn.

III. The Organization of Upaniṣadic Knowledge in the UMS

In the following paragraphs I discuss several key components which structure the Text: 1. the individual *sūtras*, which by their laconic and minimalist expression indicate from the start that the Text inherently requires commentarial expansion; 2. *adhikaraṇas*, comprised (usually) of multiple sūtras, as the literary and discursive units which set the parameters within which commentary occurs and Advaitic knowledge is accomplished; 3. *pādas*, comprised of multiple adhikaraṇas, made coherent by strategies such as connection (*saṃgati*), coordination (*upasaṃhāra*), harmonization (*samanvaya*) and (occasionally) by the utilization of *siddhāntas* as generalizable rules for reasoning; 4. finally, the division of the whole into four *adhyāyas*.

1. Sūtra[8]

By the Advaita reckoning,[9] the UMS is composed of 555 sūtras, each a succinct statement which is nevertheless likely to imply and expect a massive contextualization if it is to make sense. Sūtras mark arguments about a variety of issues and texts which, to the unaided reader, are often only obscurely encompassed by the sūtras themselves, which are notoriously difficult to interpret. Although they offer some indications of topic and argumentation, they articulate fully neither the issues at stake nor the conclusions to be drawn.[10] From the beginning sūtras necessarily functioned only in the context of (oral, then written) commentary. The multiple, layered commentaries, composed in relation to the stark and simple sūtras, preserve for us the opportunity to trace the stages of their development of the sūtras' meanings. Earlier articulations of the meanings of sūtras, inevitably incomplete, are taken advantage of as indications of ways of proceeding in yet further statements of those meanings. Their intentional incompleteness also requires that the contemporary reader become involved in an ampler oral, or written, explanatory discourse, i.e., in commentary; they invite the reader to become part of a conversation which is available in the Text before us, but never definitively presented in any commentary.

Since these permanently provocative sūtras are marked off in groups which serve as *loci* for argument and inquiry—as adhikaraṇas—and since these adhikaraṇas are the practical units of debate, we must turn to these in order to say anything more about the reception of sūtras in traditional and contemporary settings.

2. Adhikaraṇa

Though it is possible for one sūtra to constitute an adhikaraṇa, an adhikaraṇa is usually several sūtras grouped in order to define the boundaries of a potential exegetical argument about a problematic upaniṣadic text or texts. The UMS Text is divided into almost 200 adhikaraṇas.[11]

The stylistics of the adhikaraṇa are standard. Almost every adhikaraṇa begins with the indication of a text and the posing of a doubt regarding it; even issues which might appear able to be handled just as well without textual reference are framed in that way. Here, by way of example, are Śaṅkara's introductions to the adhikaraṇas of UMS I.1.12–28, the first of which revolves around *Taittirīya Upaniṣad* 2, a text we have already examined:[12]

> I.1.12 After presenting successively the selves consisting of food, vital breath, mind, knowledge, it is stated, "Different from this one consisting of knowledge, there is the inner self consisting of bliss (*ānanda-maya*)" Here the doubt arises: is the supreme Brahman, presented in "Brahman is truth, knowledge, infinite," spoken of here by the word "consisting of bliss," or is it rather some other entity, like the selves consisting of food, etc., other than Brahman?
>
> I.1.20 It is stated in the upaniṣad: "Now, again, he, the Man, that is seen in the sun is golden in colour; his beard is golden . . . This Man that is such, remains lifted above all sins. Anyone meditating thus does certainly rise above sins." [*Chāndogya* 1.6.6–8] . . . Here rises the doubt: is the "Man" a human being who had attained a high eminence on account of the extent of his meditation and action, or is he the ever perfect Lord?
>
> I.1.22 An upaniṣad states: "[Śālāvatya] asked: "What is the goal of this world?" [Pravāhaṇa Jaivali] answered, "Space. For all things certainly originate from space; and they merge by moving toward space . . . " [*Chāndogya* 1.9.1] With regard to this the doubt arises: Does the word "space" mean the supreme Brahman, or material space?
>
> I.1.23 The word *prāṇa* is found to be used in the sense of Brahman in such texts as, "O amiable one, the mind is tethered to the *prāṇa* . . . " [*Chāndogya* 6.8.2] But the more familiar usage, in ordinary life as well as in the Veda, is in the sense of the vital force that is a form of air [energy]. Therefore the doubt arises here as to which of the two should be reasonably accepted here.
>
> I.1.24 An upaniṣad says: "Then that [light] that shines in the excellent unsurpassable worlds above this heaven, above

all beings, and above all the worlds, is this same light that within a human being." [*Chāndogya Upaniṣad* 3.13.7] With regard to this the doubt arises: Does the "light" here refer to the light of the sun, etc., or does it mean the supreme self?

I.1.28 [Śaṅkara cites a series of passages from the *Kauṣītaki Upaniṣad*, which refer to the *prāṇa* ("vital breath"), and says,] With regard to this (*prāṇa*) the doubt arises: Is it merely vital breath that is signified here by the word "*prāṇa*," or is it some divine self, or an individual human being, or the supreme Brahman?

As developed in commentary, an adhikaraṇa responds to the initial, exegetically framed question by distinguishing and exploring its full set of ramifications. It elaborates the initial doubt which is to be explored in all its logical and rhetorical possibilities, and follows through on the set of positions, counter-positions, distinctions, refinements and conclusions, all of which together constitute the adhikaraṇa.

Adhikaraṇas traditionally include these five moments: i. a topic (*viṣaya*), usually defined by reference to a problematic text; ii. a doubt (*saṃdeha*) is usually expressed as an either/or, recognizing two ostensibly possible courses of interpretation; iii. the first, adversarial position (*pūrvapakṣa*) will be eventually superseded—though only after being thoroughly understood—and is usually portrayed as involving a misreading of the text in question; iv. a consequent position (*uttarapakṣa*) which responds to the objection (*pūrvapakṣa*) with a correction that at least partially rectifies the adversarial position; v. the "final, proven" position (*siddhānta*), a conclusion that resolves the initial doubt. The siddhānta, as the accomplished, last position, is only that: it is the argued, defended conclusion to the ongoing debate, final because nothing more can be said—for now. The last voice in a debate, it is for now the best conclusion to appeal to in further discussions; it remains vulnerable, because it is the best answer—thus far. In theory, any siddhānta can be reduced to the status of an uttarapakṣa, or shown to be a pūrvapakṣa. Moreover, the siddhānta never stands independent of the argumentation that precedes it, but rather carries it with itself; the text's right interpretation from among all the interpretations thus far offered, it bears with it the memory of those other interpretations which are only partially wrong and which, in other circumstances, might be shown to apply more aptly than does the siddhānta of this context.[13]

By working one's way through these several positions one learns not only the right reading of the particular text, but also the manner of skillful reading and thinking, and one is thus enabled to make better judgments about the meaning of other upaniṣadic texts too. When the reader undertakes the reading of a series of adhikaraṇas, she or he first masters each by itself, one at a time, worked through as a distinct problem. The reader is thereby enabled to engage in two further projects: a "vertical" and ever-deeper reading which pursues further elaborations of the problem in its commentarially elaborated form—every solution raises new questions—and a "lateral" reading marked by that progress in understanding that is achieved by reading each adhikaraṇa in light of those before and after it. In sections III.2.c and III.3.a below I will consider these two elaborations respectively.

Let us now consider in detail a single adhikaraṇa, UMS I.1.12–19, which focuses on *Taittirīya* 2.1–6a, already introduced above. This is an important adhikaraṇa, for three reasons. First, it asks an important question about Brahman: is Brahman the fifth sheath, "consisting of bliss," or it is beyond that sheath? Second, it is the first in a long series of adhikaraṇas implementing the view, expounded in UMS I.1.5–11, that all soteriologically significant upaniṣadic texts speak of Brahman. Third, it is particularly interesting because in it an apparently fully achieved siddhānta is belatedly judged to be only a provisional position, an uttarapakṣa.

I proceed by examining the following: first, Bādarāyaṇa's regularization of the upaniṣad's exposition of the five sheaths; second, Śaṅkara's adjustments in Bādarāyaṇa's account; third, several ways in which the later commentators continue and develop the earlier discussions.

a. Bādarāyaṇa's Statement of the Problem regarding *Taittirīya* 2.1–6a

We begin with Bādarāyaṇa's sūtras which, as sūtras, are not readily communicative and are difficult even to translate intelligibly. I render each somewhat freely,[14] and to each I append my own comment, relying for the most part on Śaṅkara's first elucidation:

12: On account of repeated references to "bliss," the "one consisting of bliss" must be Brahman.

My comment: "*Ānanda*," "bliss," is frequently repeated in *Taittirīya* 2 and 3, and so identified as its key thematic word;[15] when cited, it is connected with Brahman, which is key in *Taittirīya* 2.1–6a, because mentioned at its beginning (2.1) and end (2.5–6a); hence, it is reasonable to assume that the referent of the conclusive "ānanda-maya," "consisting of bliss," is Brahman, bliss.

13: If one objects that Brahman cannot be ānanda-maya because "-maya" implies liability to change, we say the objection does not hold, since "-maya" can also mean "abundant in."

My comment: *-maya*—"consisting of"—does not always indicate what is changeable and quantifiable, but can also mean "abundance," and so may be applied to Brahman without implying that it is composed of measurable quantities.

14: Moreover, Brahman is mentioned as the cause of bliss.

My comment: *Taittirīya* 2.7 says that Brahman "makes [others] blissful," and it is reasonable for this bliss-maker to have already been called "ānanda-maya."

15: The same Brahman mentioned in the mantra portion is also mentioned in the brāhmaṇa portion.

My comment: The text's first prose (rubrical) section (*brāhmaṇa*) refers to Brahman—"one who knows Brahman reaches the highest"—and so too the first mantra section: "Brahman is reality, knowledge, infinite;" the concluding mantra section refers to Brahman—"He who knows Brahman as non-existent becomes as it were non-existent;" it is therefore appropriate that the concluding brahmana section—about the sheath of bliss—similarly concludes by referring to Brahman; so "consisting of bliss" refers to Brahman.

16: It is implausible to think that the alternative, the human self, consists of bliss.

My comment: If Brahman were not the one "consisting of bliss," the prime alternative would be the human self; but an examination of the plight of the human self shows that it cannot be plausibly identified with bliss.

17: Moreover, the difference between the self and Brahman is clearly taught.

My comment: A subsequent part of the text (*Taittirīya* 2.7)[16] makes it clear that humans acquire bliss; so they cannot be bliss.

18: Because desire is explicitly mentioned, we cannot depend on inference to draw a conclusion.

My comment: In the latter half of *Taittirīya* 2.6, not cited above, the one "consisting of bliss" is said to desire; but desire involves anticipation, and so the one who desires must be able to anticipate, i.e., to be intelligent; therefore the unintelligent material principle (*pradhāna*) cannot be the one "consisting of bliss."

19: In the upaniṣad, the union of this self and that Brahman is clearly taught.

My comment: *Taittirīya* 2.7 teaches that knowledge of the sheath consisting of bliss leads to release; but Brahman is the only object of knowledge which leads to release.

The most straightforward conclusion to be drawn from these eight sūtras is that Bādarāyaṇa holds that Brahman consists of bliss, is the fifth and final sheath, and is reached by the path described in the five steps which comprise this text.

But that conclusion aside, the very fact of Bādarāyaṇa's posing the question has already transformed the text, by using it differently. The effort to fix its right meaning relocates it within an interpretive and systematic framework in which the text is subject to precise determination; as the subject matter of an adhikaraṇa, this relocation gives it a purpose and function which reach beyond those of meditation. However resolved, this interrogation formalizes and makes the conclusion of meditation available in a new way.

b. Śaṅkara's Two Interpretations of *Taittirīya* 2.1–6a

My reading of Bādarāyaṇa's position depends, I have acknowledged, on Śaṅkara's exposition of the same; nevertheless, it is still possible to note ways in which Śaṅkara's interpretation diverges from Bādarāyaṇa's. There are a number of instances here,[17] but I now consider only one, the apparent reversal of Bādarāyaṇa's conclusion.

After explaining UMS I.1.12–19 so as to conclude that Brahman is the one "consisting of bliss," Śaṅkara introduces a second interpretation of the whole text, reading the sūtras anew. In effect, he makes the siddhānta—that "consisting of bliss" indicates Brahman—into an uttarapakṣa in need of further refinement. I note four of his revised readings here.[18]

First, regarding sūtra 13: -maya does mean "consisting of," and is so used regarding each of the first four sheaths and so has a quantitative meaning. If so, one can hardly suggest that it suddenly come to mean "abundant in" when the fifth sheath is reached. For the sake of consistency, we must assume that ānanda-maya means "consisting of bliss" in a quantitative sense, and so refers to a sheath which is not Brahman, some finite reality such as the individual self.[19]

Second, although the sheath consisting of bliss is last among the five, and no sheath is mentioned beyond it, the text does not actually state that this sheath is the supreme reality, Brahman; rather, it states that Brahman is its support: "bliss the self, Brahman the tail, that on which it rests." (*Taittirīya* 2.1.5) The mere fact of being last in the series does not determine conclusively that the sheath consisting of bliss is Brahman.

Third, and similarly, the text clearly says that Brahman is the "tail;" in Śaṅkara's reading, this must mean, "like a tail," i.e., "a support." But Brahman cannot be both the sheath consisting of bliss which has the support, and the support itself.[20]

Fourth, even if knowledge of the sheath consisting of bliss is not knowledge of Brahman, its salvific purpose is preserved, since Brahman is the foundation of that sheath, its support; therefore, the salvific import of the text is not lost if we decide that "consisting of bliss" does not refer to Brahman.[21]

On the basis of these (and other) arguments the previously firm siddhānta—"Brahman is the sheath consisting of bliss"—is reduced to an uttarapakṣa—provisionally true—and a new siddhānta is fashioned: "Brahman is not the sheath consisting of bliss, but lies yet deeper inside that." This presentation of two versions of the siddhānta highlights dramatically, though also exceptionally , the permanent openness of the Text to rereading and the articulation of new positions; every position remains liable to modification, some further word. Advaita desires precision, and considers right meaning an attainable goal; but precision and rightness of meaning occur only within the context of an argument that is never closed, since it will always be possible that a new consideration or a better reading be brought forward. The adhikaraṇa format is the vehicle of that advance, and it ensures that new arguments, and rereadings of old ones, are always possible. When these are advanced, the Text is reopened, and new elements incorporated.

c. The Later Commentarial Contribution to the Interpretation of *Taittirīya* 2.1–6a

As mentioned earlier, each adhikaraṇa can be read more complexly, by tracing "up" through the commentarial elaborations of its meaning further questions and objections and responses to them. Whatever is said in earlier texts will be carefully explained, but each explanation opens up new possibilities. Just as they dutifully explained the first pūrvapakṣa and siddhānta, Vācaspati, Amalānanda and Appaya Dīkṣita dutifully confirm Śaṅkara's second siddhānta, which is not doubted in their elaborations of it.[22] It is not new content that motivates our reading of these later commentaries, but rather their skill in judgment and their ability to negotiate a path through a complex set of arguments. Their careful refinements give precision to Śaṅkara's arguments, elaborating a broad set of subsequent questions which the novice Advaitin must consider, thereby sharpening ever more finely his ability to question and read properly. This pedagogical, literary mode of extended argumentation allows us to understand their commentarial project; the fruit is increasing refinement, not correction or novelty. I illustrate their mode of clarification and complexification by a single example.

Vācaspati shows that it is impossible to preserve the primary meaning of all the key words in the *Taittirīya* text—"Brahman," "consisting of bliss" ([ānanda]-maya,) and "tail" (puccha.)[23] As the text stands, it is impossible for all three words to keep their primary meanings: 1. "Brahman" cannot indicate Brahman if "Brahman" here really means "tail;" 2. "-maya" cannot maintain a single primary meaning, if in the text it first means "consisting of" and then means "abundant in;" 3. "tail" cannot mean both "appendage," a minor portion, and "base," "support" (*pratiṣṭhā*). A decision has to be made then about which of the words are to retain its primary meanings. Why then, Vācaspati asks, is Śaṅkara right in arguing that Brahman is bliss, but not consisting of bliss, and that "puccha" here means "support," and not "tail," "minor part"?

He calculates as follows. There are three ways to resolve the problem. 1. We can take "puccha" as indicating "tail" (meaning "part,") and in the sentence "Brahman is the *puccha*," take "Brahman" figuratively as indicating a mere part of the configuration, not that Brahman which is the object of Advaitic knowledge. 2. Or, we can take the "-maya" in "ānanda-maya" as meaning "abundance," and then we will be able to construe ānanda-maya ("abundant in bliss") as indicative of Brahman, even if this connection is not stated directly. 3. Or, we can consistently interpret "-maya" as "consisting of," allow "Brahman" to keep its proper meaning, and attribute only to "puccha" a secondary significance, so that it means "base" instead of "tail."

Vācaspati argues that 3. is the best option, because it preserves two primary meanings: "-maya" and "Brahman" maintain proper meanings, and only one word, "puccha," loses its primary meaning by coming to mean "base" and not merely "minor part." In alternatives 1. and 2. either "Brahman" or

"-maya" would have lost its meaning: in 1., "Brahman" would lose its primary meaning, and in 2. "-maya" would shift from one meaning ("consisting of") to another ("abundant in") after the fourth sheath. But in all three cases "puccha" would lose its primary meaning, "tail," since no one claims that Brahman is an actual tail; so 3. is best since two of the three primary meanings are maintained and minimal reinterpretation occurs. Hence, by economy of interpretation—without the direct introduction of philosophical claims about what Brahman ought to be—Vācaspati can conclude that Brahman is figuratively referred to as the "puccha," "base," while the "sheath consisting of bliss" indicates a lower, finite reality, not Brahman.

Calculations such as these are abundant in the Text. They are often difficult to follow, they raise further questions, and frequently they are more difficult to follow than the passages they intend to clarify. Since the conclusion will inevitably be a reaffirmation of the siddhānta identified by Śaṅkara, the commentators and their readers have invested in the further inquiry in order to bring Śaṅkara's text to fruition, to show its rich complexity more clearly, and so to amplify its glory—which, as we have already seen in Chapter 1, is their announced goal. Appropriation of the argumentation in careful reading is the goal, not the mere conclusion. To know Advaita is to be able to read it properly, to become able to sort out a complex set of arguments and counter-arguments, to be able to reassess that entire set against the backdrop of other, new sets—and then to see and be differently, transformed by mastery of a portion of the Text. The determination of the right meaning of the *Taittirīya* text is a matter of skill and judgment; for the decision as to right meaning depends on how one reads the text, what one takes for clues, how one assesses these, and how one brings to bear on that reading one's other clues, drawn from other sources, including general conceptions such as how one thinks Brahman is connected with the world—continuously, as in a series of sheaths, or discontinuously, as the basis for such sheaths.

This extended consideration of a single example sketches major features of the functions and uses of adhikaraṇa in Advaita, and of the nature of Advaita argument. Merely passive or merely receptive readings are excluded; the "reader as observer" is replaced by the "reader as participant."

I wish to emphasize that the Text, composed entirely of adhikaraṇas, is *the* privileged vehicle of our entrance into the realm of Advaita, and thereafter into the acquisition of its fruit: refined, discriminate knowledge of Brahman. One goes through the Text, one is changed by it; one cannot go outside it, or around it; there is no outside, and if there were, one would not accomplish anything by going there, or in any useful way become accomplished.

By reading diligently, the modern reader becomes a part of this exchange, involved in the reading and argumentation, taking sides, offering new clarifications and posing new questions. Though one cannot examine every commentarial refinement of every argument, omissions imply choices about how skilled in Advaita we wish to become, how much Advaita we actually want to know, where we will draw the line in our education as Uttara Mīmāṃsakas.

d. Is There a World outside the Text? The Case of World-Renunciation (UMS III.4.18–20)

Though the Advaitins insist that Brahman is an extratextual reality, the debate over whether Brahman consists of bliss is entirely a debate over whether Brahman is indicated by the term "consisting of bliss;" it is couched entirely in terms of exegesis.

Though one may readily concede this on the grounds that the problem in UMS I.1.12–19 is an exegetical one, one may hesitate to make the further claim that all adhikaraṇas mediate what is outside the Text, including Brahman, through the Text. I suggest that we are warranted in making that further claim that the extratextual world is not properly seen or experienced except through the Text, and that this Textual mediation constitutes the only "world" the Advaitins are interested in. If one wants to know the Advaita view of anything, the Text is the way to that knowledge. Nothing discussed in the Text can be understood apart from its appearance in the Text, since everything is transformed by its inscription therein, and is relevant only in that inscribed form.

I illustrate this point with reference to an adhikaraṇa which deals with world renunciation (*saṃnyāsa*). This is a reality that seems to be primarily outside the Text because it, of all things, is supposed to be free of words: It is the state of life of the person who knows Brahman.[24] In the Advaita version, UMS III.4.18–20 asks whether renunciation is a fourth *āśrama* (state, stage of life),[25] distinct from those of the householder, student and forest-dweller. Three important questions are asked: 1. Are there āśramas other than that of the householder? 2. If there are, are these āśramas of equal status with that of the householder? 3. If it is the case that persons who truly know Brahman are unencumbered by the rules which govern the earlier āśramas, are they entirely free of such location, or are they placed in their own, special āśrama—and thus legitimated but also confined?

These are "real life" questions with important social ramifications which could be discussed entirely apart from the Text, and the third question points toward a state of life which should ostensibly be free from all boundaries, which should not be textually circumscribed, and which should not even need the legitimation offered by Bādarāyaṇa and the Advaitins. Yet the Advaita takes the project of textual legitimation seriously, and respond to the three questions entirely by the examination of an upaniṣadic text, *Chāndogya* 2.23.1:

> There are three branches of dharma: sacrifice, study, and the giving of alms form the first; asceticism forms the second; the student who lives in the house of the teacher is the third, provided that he settles down permanently in the house of the teacher. All these [gain] the holy worlds; but he who remains steadfast in Brahman (*brahmasaṃstha*) attains immortality.

The answers to the three questions are made to hinge on how this text is read. The "real life" question of social ordering according to the āśramas is defined by this adhikaraṇa as a question of the interpretation of the *Chāndogya* text; the text is authorized to determine a way of life, even the way of life of people who may not care particularly about texts. It is not just that texts are being used to illuminate an extratextual reality; rather, even in its most radical expression, orthodox society—the society which matters—is subordinated to the proper, orthodox reading of texts. "Renunciation-as-textualized" is presented as the presupposition of "renunciation-in-itself," not the reverse. What might be thought on these issues by illiterate renunciants, or by those who despise the upaniṣads, is irrelevant to Advaita.

The response to the three questions can be summarized briefly. First, it is decided that the *Chāndogya* text at least refers to āśramas beyond that of the householder. Second, it is decided that the text does actually enjoin them: they are spoken of authoritatively here, as if enjoined, and since we do not know of any other text in which they are enjoined, we may legitimately presume that this text enjoins them, even if it does not literally state that injunction. (UMS III.4.20)[26]

The third question—is there a formally recognizable fourth āśrama?—prompts an analysis focused on the meaning of the word "established in Brahman" (*brahmasaṃstha*), asking whether this word describes an established āśrama, by entrance into which one is designated "established in Brahman," or whether the word refers to the group of those who are in fact spiritually advanced, whichever socially recognized āśrama they may occupy, or however they are described. The question is resolved by an arduous textual analysis, in which various subsidiary issues are debated in relation to the question of the meaning of "established in Brahman:" there is, Śaṅkara says, a fourth āśrama, with its own characteristics and rights, which differs qualitatively from the prior three.[27]

This authorization of radical renunciation is immediately restricted. Vācaspati, for instance, comments that the radical act of renunciation is possible only for those who have acquired the requisite textual knowledge: "That ripening of the knowledge of Brahman *which is born of word* is that direct manifestation which is the means to liberation; to it renunciation is enjoined as a subsidiary; but the injunction does not intend persons who are not competent [i.e., who lack the proper textual knowledge.]"[28]

We are not considering "renunciation in itself," nor merely about it, when we read UMS III.4.18–20.[29] The point is not merely that we are compelled to rely on texts to learn about a set of social practices which are unavailable to us now, nor that commentators talk about things in the language of scripture. Rather, it is that even renunciation, uncompromising liberation from strictures such as texts, is meaningful only when inscribed in the Text; as a topic in the Advaita discourse, it subsists in its textual constitution, and its significance is available only in the medium of that proper, literate context.

If we are then to engage in the Advaita discussion of renunciation, we need to understand first of all the close connection between renunciation and exegesis, deferring for the moment our conceptions as to what renunciants give up or what ought to be said about them when they renounce. Then, as readers, we become able to engage the reality constituted in this adhikaraṇa and others like it, as literary places in which certain religious practices are (re)constituted on a textual basis; we are enabled to talk about renunciation in its distinctive and properly Advaitic sense. We learn not only that renunciation is vindicated by the upaniṣads; more importantly, we learn to use upaniṣadic texts properly, reading them according to the proper rules of Mīmāṃsā argumentation, and so learn that renunciation, like everything else, can be properly accounted for.

Of course, one may still talk about renunciation in other ways, perhaps raising a whole range of social and historical issues, seeking too to delve behind the Advaita presentation, to see it in terms of power relationships, etc. But one must still work one's way through the Text, if those other inquiries are to be relevant to Advaita.

3. Weaving the Text Together: Saṃgati and Pāda

Adhikaraṇas are the key units by which Advaita constructs its Text. But we still need to make use of the larger structures of the Text, its divisions into *pāda*s, made of adhikaraṇas, and *adhyāya*s, made of pādas. In the following pages I approach this large task only in a preliminary fashion, showing that the emerging thematization connected with pāda and adhyāya contributes to the construction of the Text as Text, and does not encourage an a-Textual, selective and thematic rewriting of the Text in terms of major ideas.

In this section I examine the construction of pādas. First, I examine "connection," (*saṃgati*) as the primary means of the construction of unity in the Text, the search for the appropriate right connection among adhikaraṇas, and then point to the learned, "textured" reasoning (*nyāya*) that develops from an understanding of the whole Text; finally, by way of illustration I analyze two pāda topics, "coordination" (*upasaṃhāra*), practiced in UMS III.3, and "harmonization" (*samanvaya*), practiced in UMS I.1.12–3.43,[30] to show how they contribute to the construction of the Text primarily as modes of the organization of texts, and not as themes imposed upon them or in replacement of them.

a. Saṃgati: the Connections within a Pāda

The justification of pādas is achieved in part through commentarial efforts to identify themes which distinguish one pāda from another, but more importantly by the internal construction of each pāda by the identification of the connections among its adhikaraṇas. The Advaitins, like the Mīmāṃsakas before them, conceived of each pāda as an ordered series of adhikaraṇas which follow from one another, though in an order that defies simple description: the series of connections, and each part of it, are known by the word "connection" (saṃgati).

As beginners gain skill in Advaita by working through a series of adhikaraṇas, the more the better, they are not left merely with disconnected increments of Advaita learning. Rather, they are then positioned to begin to imitate the commentators by looking for the connections among any two or more adhikaraṇas, and thereby learning the textual, intellectual, rhetorical connections which justify any given sequence of two or more.

The ascertainment of such connections is a difficult task which requires a prior understanding of the rules which govern each adhikaraṇa—i.e., not just its siddhānta, but also the principles and guidelines for its formulation with its particular objections, counter-propositions, solutions. No single line of thought can be found and followed through an entire pāda, since none proceeds simply according to a simple, compellingly clear theme.

Just as adhikaraṇas resist abstraction and summation, the connections among them cannot be set forth as a predictable logical development. The reasoning for each step in the sequence lies imbedded in the details of each adhikaraṇa. The connection, written implicitly into the pāda as we find it, becomes clear only when one adhikaraṇa in all its complexity is read after another in all of its complexity, when both are understood and reread in light of one another.

The connections among adhikaraṇas are articulated by various rationales. A second adhikaraṇa might be said simply to extend a first, either by a continued focus on a single text, or by the application in an almost identical situation of the same rule; the topic of the text considered in one might be taken as suggesting a similar topic or implication to be taken up in the next; a second might be perceived as extending to a new set of circumstances a principle established in the first, with appropriate adjustments in the rules accommodated to the first set of circumstances; a second might be seen as a counter-example or exception to the first; in some cases, an odd clue or verbal echo suggests an educative digression into seemingly unrelated issues.

When the pattern of connections among the adhikaraṇas of a certain pāda becomes clear in the attuned minds of properly educated readers, they gradually accomplish a comparable progression in their understanding, acquiring a sense of the overall project of a pāda within the UMS; this in turn becomes a step toward understanding the whole, and toward comprehending Śaṅkara's project and the accumulated wisdom of the later commentators. Yet this literate comprehension continues to elude ready summation: the person interested in Advaita still has to replicate the process, to keep reading Advaita, for the sake of a further production of insight. There is thus a Textually inscribed coherence to the whole which remains performative, produced through reading and, as the following examples may suggest, otherwise virtually unintelligible.

Despite the problems of summation, it may be helpful to introduce by way of example a simplified rendering of the perceived logic behind one series of adhikaraṇas, from UMS I.1.12 to I.1.31[31] Let us first recall from above the upaniṣadic texts debated in each adhikaraṇa, leaving untranslated the problematic words, each of which can refer to Brahman or some lesser reality:

I.1.12–19 *Taittirīya* 2.1–6a (cited above in full)

I.1.20–21 *Chāndogya* 1.6.6: "Now, again, he, the Man that is seen in the sun, is golden in color."

I.1.22 *Chāndogya* 1.9.1 "What is the goal of this world? The *ākāśa*; for all things certainly originate from the *ākāśa*."

I.1.23 *Chāndogya* 1.11.5 "[The deity to be known] is the *prāṇa*, for all things proceed toward and merge in *prāṇa*, and from *prāṇa* they emerge."

I.1.24–27 *Chāndogya* 3.13.7 "Then that *jyotis* that shines in the excellent unsurpassable worlds above this heaven, above all beings, and above all the worlds, is this same *jyotis* that is within a human being."

I.1.28–31 *Kauṣītaki* 3.2 "I am *prāṇa*, identified with consciousness. You meditate on me, who am of such stature, as long life and immortality."

The focus on difficult *Chāndogya* texts—four of the six—is an important reason for the order of adhikaraṇas; Amalānanda appeals to it directly in UMS I.1.23 as a possible justification for that adhikaraṇa—the next part of the *Chāndogya* is of course to be treated next.[32]

Typically, however, subtler reasons are identified for the sequence of adhikaraṇas. In UMS I.1.12–19 it was concluded—we saw Vācaspati's exposition of the conclusion above—that the primary meaning of words—such as Brahman, -maya, and puccha—ought to be kept, whenever possible; that conservative rule occasions the subsequent adhikaraṇas. Although in every case the question is whether or not an upaniṣadic text refers to Brahman, the basis for doubt and means of resolution keeps changing. I summarize the sequence as follows, relying primarily on Vācaspati:

I.1.20–21 In I.1.12–19, the five sheaths were the topic of discussion, graded means to knowledge of Brahman which is devoid of all specification; but there Brahman alone, and not the five sheaths which might appear to specify it, was the intended object of meditation. Here (in 20–21), by contrast, it is Brahman as qualified—as "inside the sun"—which is the intended topic of meditation and hence of debate.

I.1.22 In I.1.20–21, the presence of an indirect indication which could be attributed only to Brahman—"he is above all evils" (*Chāndogya* 1.6.7)—enabled the Advaitin to decide that other indirect indications, which could refer to Brahman or to the individual self, should be consistently interpreted as referring to Brahman. Here, however, there is an explicit mention of the "ether" (*ākāśa*). Since what is mentioned explicitly takes precedence over what is mentioned implicitly, implicit indications can have no force in determining the topic of a passage when contrary explicit references are available. Therefore, this adhikaraṇa does not replicate the preceding, and new arguments must be presented to fit the new situation.[33]

I.1.23 There are three reasons why this adhikaraṇa follows the preceding: first, it simply extends the reasoning of the previous one, applying its principle to a new text; second, it simply takes up the next difficult section of the *Chāndogya* text considered in I.1.22; third, in the previous adhikaraṇa the fact that the beginning and end of the passage in question referred to the same object—Brahman—helped determine that Brahman was the topic;[34] but the current passage has no single clear topic for its beginning and end, and so its ambiguities have to be handled differently.

I.1.24 In the two previous adhikaraṇas, I.1.22 and I.1.23, indirect indications of Brahman proved decisive in the ascertainment of the meaning of a debated word; here, though there is no such indirect indication of Brahman, there is an indirect indication which points to the light of the sun as the object of meditation.

I.1.28 Here there is no decisive indirect indication as there was in 22 and 23, nor is there any determinative factor such as the relative pronoun which helped determine meaning in 24–27; so the difficulty must be resolved in a yet another way.

Usually a new text is introduced, each new text requires a refinement or narrowing or adjustment of or exception to the rules by which one had successfully defended the preceding siddhānta. Progress occurs in the amplification of one's ensemble of rules, and in the enhancement of one's skill in using them. A series of difficult texts is gradually mastered—we know what they mean, what to do with them, what else to do—and so achieve a more refined and increasingly competent grasp of the rules needed for interpretation.

To know that "Brahman is the chief topic of the upaniṣads," or even that "the aim of the first pāda is to show that the upaniṣads refer invariably to Brahman," is a necessary but merely first step to the comprehension of a pāda. To understand the whole of (a portion of) the Text is to become accomplished in this skilled reading, right knowing and right performance of a reading of the Text. It would be difficult to exaggerate the importance of connection (saṃgati): the cohesion of the Text and the coherence of Advaita subsist in this textual relatedness, and not in the themes, nor even the referent(s), of Advaita knowledge.

b. Textured Reasoning (nyāya)

An allied form of textual knowledge is the reader's gradual internalization of the whole, such that its entire force is brought to bear on the reading of any part of it.[35] This is a wholeness no longer just that of structure or increased skill, but also of a comprehension of the totality. The skilled reader gradually appropriates the Text's wisdom as it appears in each reasoned, wise siddhānta; this achievement of wisdom makes possible a series of rereadings of the whole, each richer than the one preceding it—not just in knowledge about it, but in ever more refined judgments about the proper reading of each of its parts.

A key way in which this larger appropriation is signalled in the Text is the reuse of siddhāntas elsewhere in the Text, in order to illuminate other pūrvapakṣas and siddhāntas. Thus, for example, in deciding in the course of UMS I.1.12–19 whether

Brahman can be referred to as "consisting of bliss," Appaya Dīkṣita cites UMS I.2.3 in favor of the view that this is not possible, and UMS I.3.19 in favor of the view that it is possible.[36] At UMS I.1.23, he cites UMS IV.1.13 in support of the pūrvapakṣin's elucidation of the *Chāndogya* verse under discussion.[37] A striking example from later in the UMS is Śaṅkara's indication that the siddhānta of UMS III.3.58 illuminates the whole of UMS III.3, though one encounters it only at the end of the pāda.[38] In general, an important reason for the density of the Text is the inscription of each commentator's mastery of the whole Text into his commentary on any part of it. The unity of the Text is in part an event which occurs in the memory and learning of its readers, and so the task confronting the student has two key aspects: to appropriate the wisdom of earlier readers of the whole, and to infuse their own reading increasingly with their own gradually achieved sense of the whole.

c. Two Strategies of Coherent Practice

Although a sense of the connection among adhikaraṇas is most effectively gained in the ways described in the preceding section, and although the advantages of staying patiently with individual and then groups of adhikaraṇas are estimable, the reader is also justified in making use of larger features which characterize the Text, including certain strategies which programmatically knit adhikaraṇas into pādas. By way of example, let us consider two examples: UMS III.3 as a pāda dedicated to the practice of "coordination" (upasaṃhāra), and UMS I.1–4 as a group of four pādas dedicated to the practice of "harmonization" (samanvaya).[39]

i. Coordination (upasaṃhāra) in UMS III.3

Modi has shown us[40] that UMS III.3 provides the best starting point for a clear and coherent understanding of the composition of the UMS Text as a project rooted in exegetical and meditational questions. This is so, even if UMS III.3 as we now have it is not necessarily the oldest portion of the heavily redacted UMS. UMS III.3 is concerned with the proper use of texts together in economically unified acts of meditation, wherein texts which remain distinct from one another are used together;

the rules of this coordination are together known by the name "coordination."

Coordination is first proposed in UMS III.3.1–5, which explain that one can and must construct an intricate balance between two facts: Brahman is an extratextual reality; yet, Brahman is, for now at least, only textually accessible. The key sūtras are 1 and 5:

> III.3.1 A more complete text for meditation can be composed drawing on the Advaita texts of all the Vedic schools—for the object of these texts is not distinguished by injunction, etc.
>
> III.3.5 There should be a coordination of appropriate qualifications drawn from various texts, regarding their common referent, since the referent does not differ from text to text . . .

The practical motives underlying the quest for a set of rules to govern the coordination of texts can be illustrated as follows. If Brahman is in one text referred to as "existent," in a second as "bestowing the good," and in a third as "in the cave of the heart," can a person meditating on one of three such texts introduce into meditation the other two qualifications? can the meditator be selective, and introduce just one of those other two? In his comment on UMS III.3.11, Vācaspati explains that one must allow for this selective borrowing since, if Brahman exists, it is neither possible nor necessary to redefine its nature completely in each and every text; certain important qualifications—Brahman exists, is powerful, is unlimited—must pertain everywhere, whether or not they are explicitly mentioned.

Yet, as is stated somewhat belatedly at UMS III.3.58 (according to its Advaita interpretation,) the various texts really do count, and one cannot conflate them into a single theoretical account: one cannot simply compile all the qualities of Brahman, wherever mentioned, into a single whole. One must read correctly, discriminately, and learn to make prudential judgments. Some qualifications, such as "existence," can be applied everywhere; others, such as "in the cave of the heart," apply only where mentioned. One has to acquire facility in judging when to borrow and when not to.[41]

The very possibility of such borrowing suggests that there is an extratextual aspect to Brahman: we can know and can take into account that Brahman is the object of multiple meditations. This awareness legitimately modifies our reading of the texts of various Vedic schools, without rendering that reading superfluous. The questions that need to be addressed in defense of this position include: how are texts to be used in conjunction with one another? how, by implication, are the meanings of texts related to the texts? how is Brahman, which is extratextual, to be known from texts while simultaneously influencing how we read those texts? UMS III.3 thus asks how texts mean, how they determine one another, and how they are their referents mutually determine one another. Its practical goal, however, remains the refinement of the set of rules by which one continues to engage in the act of "reading" Brahman in the Text,[42] yet as efficaciously and coherently as possible.

UMS III.3 is structured by the logic of connection (saṃgati) examined above, by a series of refinements of the basic practice of coordination justified in UMS III.3.1 and 5. I summarize the three adhikaraṇas which demarcate the main lines of the pāda:[43]

> III.3.11–13: Is there a principle by which some qualities attributed to Brahman in one text can be introduced during meditation on another text—while at the same time not introducing all the qualities mentioned in the first text? Yes: qualities which delimit the nature of Brahman in itself must be distinguished from those which configure it for one or another meditation. The former, and not the latter, can be transferred from text to text.[44]
>
> III.3.33: Is the denial of limitations—Brahman is not impure, not measurable, not perishable—likewise applicable by extension, without the meditator being burdened in every case with an unending list of denials of qualities which do not apply to Brahman? Here too the rule given in UMS III.3.11–13 applies: unless the negative qualities are purely contextual, the meditator (who must judge from past familiarity with text and meditation whether or not this is the case) can apply to them elsewhere; but there is no reason to introduce every conceivable negation everywhere.

> III.3.39: A statement from one meditation can be introduced into another, even if that meditation is of a mixed nature, i.e., if some parts of it pertaining to Brahman with qualities (*saguṇa*), others to Brahman without qualities (*nirguṇa*). Even if a few parts do not fit the new context, which may be exclusively about Brahman without qualities or with qualities, one can borrow the parts which fit and omit the others.

Good readers are able to read a text, determine its major points and use it appropriately, and downplay the parts which are there only for some secondary, supporting reason.

> UMS III.3.58: According to the pūrvapakṣin, either all the qualities linked to Brahman should apply to it everywhere—in effect, there should be one large meditation—or none matters, since Brahman is really one and is unrelated to all the mentioned qualities. The siddhāntin argues differently: "Even though the object of meditation is the same, still the meditations of this class ought to be different. Why? Because there are differences in their terminology, etc. "Though the Lord who is to be meditated on is the same, nevertheless different qualities are taught in different contexts." [UMS III.3.58] One of Brahman's qualities is to be meditated upon in one place, and another in another place. Brahman is open to a variety of specifications and is not linked with one to the exclusion of others.

Thus developed, the practice of coordination does not lead the Advaitins to conclude that Brahman can be thought about in general, under a composite form constructed by the harmonization of all upaniṣadic texts. Rather, the practice is designed to safeguard the ongoing act of reading, remembering and combining texts selectively in acts of meditation, so that the extratextual and full nature of Brahman will modify how we read texts while yet not undermining that reading entirely. What is required is not a full understanding of Brahman, but the intelligent reader's insight, the skill to be able to recognize when to combine and when not to combine what is said in different texts.

The practice and its explanation legitimately mark the subject matter of UMS III.3. Yet, it should be clear, knowing that coordination is the topic of the pāda is of little value as an abstract appellation. It is rather a marking which guides the reader as to what kind of practice is under way at this point in the Text; if understood properly, it can be fruitfully used.

ii. Harmonization (samanvaya) in UMS I.1:

In our consideration of the connections in UMS I.1 we have already noticed that the main project of that pāda is to demonstrate harmonization (samanvaya): the effort to show that Brahman is the primary and coherently described key topic of all the upaniṣads in their key passages. Our consideration here can be brief.

Rather than articulating the doctrine of Brahman as a universally available truth demanding assent, the more limited goal of UMS I is to resolve difficulties about the list of texts available for meditation. UMS I.1.12–19 asks whether *Taittirīya* 2.1–6a is a text meant to be used in meditation on Brahman or on the limits of the self in its reach toward Brahman, UMS I.1.20–21 asks about the use of *Chāndogya* 1.1.6, etc. Śaṅkara states the underlying thesis of harmonization in his comment on UMS I.1.4 ("That is known from the upaniṣads because it is their consistent object."):

> "That" means Brahman, which is omniscient and omnipotent, which is the cause of the origin, existence, and dissolution of the universe, and which is known as such only from the teaching of the upaniṣads. How? "because it is [the upaniṣads'] consistent object." All the upaniṣads become fully reconciled when they are accepted as establishing this very fact.[45]

The presupposition behind this identification of a single topic is that the upaniṣads must speak harmoniously, in a single voice, and about a single main topic: if Brahman is the main topic, other objects of knowledge will not be proposed as alternative sources of the desired salvific knowledge. In rejection of the claim of the Sāṃkhya and other schools that the upaniṣads do not consistently identify Brahman as the sole highest reality, Advaita subjects all the contested texts to careful scrutiny in order to verify that Brahman is their single true topic, and so to facilitate the practice of meditation by providing it with a coherent, intelligible foundation in scripture as properly understood.

But the project of harmonization is not merely propaedeutic to the process of meditation; it also has the secondary and (increasingly) significant effect of regularizing the content of the upaniṣads, homogenizing their explorations and stories and experiments into an informative "metadiscourse" about Brahman. It therefore opens the way for a digestion of the upaniṣads into the "best of the upaniṣads," a distilled, useful body of information about an existent reality. Once it is understood that the extratextual Brahman is the uniform and coherently described topic of the upaniṣads, a larger process of formalization and abstraction is under way, and it becomes possible—as an opportunity and a temptation—to use the texts merely as initial occasions or starting points for an ever more independent consideration of Brahman. This shift to knowledge about Brahman, extrapolated from the texts as their meaning, is the beginning of Advaita as Vedānta philosophy.

The challenge for the Advaita as Uttara Mīmāṃsā, however, is to defend and take advantage of the posited homogeneity of the upaniṣads without replacing them with their abstracted content. Harmonization, like coordination, must be preserved as a practice, while yet being allowed to achieve the result of making coherent the diverse meanings present in the upaniṣads. Likewise, the contemporary reader is advised not to mistake harmonization for a simple statement of what UMS I is about, but instead to be aided by it in constructing an overview of the Text, to appreciate it as a practical tool which helps make coherent Advaita's reading of the upaniṣads; harmonization, like coordination, structures a unified approach to the reading of texts, without obviating the need actually to read them.

4. Adhyāya and the Organization of the Whole

The preceding comments on connection (saṃgati), textured reasoning (nyāya), coordination (upasaṃhāra) and harmonization (samanvaya) have helped us to begin tracing a path from the singular details of exegesis through various constructions of a broader coherence in the Advaita, toward a more sophisticated comprehension of the Text that is the basis for a full engagement in Advaita. The larger understanding thus made available remains always a construction posterior to acts of reading, and intended for those who read.

We conclude these observations with a similar view of the whole Text; in light of the preceding textual comments and cautions, it is now possible to view the whole, to outline it. Here is the Advaita description of the Text as divided into pādas and adhyāyas:[46]

Adhyāya I: The harmonization of scripture (samanvaya)

I.1.1–11 Introduction: the object of Advaita, the source of its right knowledge, and its claim about the single, identifiable meaning of the upaniṣads

I.1.12–I.4 Treatment of scripture texts which are unclear on first reading, in order to show that the important major texts unanimously point to Brahman as source of the world, major goal of knowledge, etc.

Adhyāya II: The removal of contradiction (virodha):

II.1 The coherent, reasonable nature of the Advaita system

II.2 The incoherence and unreasonableness of other systems

II.3–4 The consistency of the Advaita view of the cosmos

Adhyāya III: Meditation as the means to liberation (sādhana)

III.1 The cosmology of meditation

III.2 The nature of the self, Brahman, and the connection of the two

III.3 The use of the upaniṣads in meditation

III.4 The implications of the progress of the Advaitin in meditation; the discourse of the renunciant

Adhyāya IV: The result of meditation (phala)

IV.1 The liberation of the self[47]

IV.2 The process of dying

IV.3 Analysis of the postdeath ascent

IV.4 Analysis of the results—endpoints of the ascent

What are the uses to which we may best put this overview of the Text?[48] I conclude with two observations which bear upon how one can profitably appreciate the wholeness of the Text. First, the ordering of the UMS is imitative of the ritual paradigm, and remains oriented to practice and imbued with its logic. Second, the outline presents inversely to the reader the pattern by which it was constructed; what is located first is not necessarily what is to be learned first, but may be the subsequently articulated presupposition of a learning which needs to occur first. Let us consider these in turn.

First, the Advaitins' insistence on the primacy of knowledge does not prevent them from maintaining the analogy, evident in the UMS, between meditative knowledge and ritual knowledge, as two kinds of practical knowledges. It is striking that UMS IV offers no final conclusion as to the nature of Brahman, nor any final refutation of opponents. It is an unapologetically practical consideration of the nature of death, what happens after death, and how the course of the practice of meditation appropriately mirrors the course of the self's postmortem destiny. Nor is there any evidence that it is a mere appendix, or mere application of principles enunciated in UMS I and II; the Text ends where it must, with an inquiry into the practical effects of right knowledge.

UMS III and IV show us that the inquiry into Brahman, the implementation of the desire to know Brahman (UMS I.1.1)[49] is to be accomplished through the practice of meditation—as the ultimately masterful appropriation of the knowledge of Brahman made available in the upaniṣads as these are properly understood in the Text; the pure and absolute nature of the final knowledge of Brahman does not undercut the definiteness, practicality or temporality of the path that reaches there.[50]

However one may use portions of the UMS for purposes more or less extrinsic to Advaita's own purposes, these uses must be subordinated to the full and practical context in which they developed in the first place: the proper practice of purposeful, fruitful meditation (UMS IV) by the right persons (UMS III.4); this meditation upon properly organized texts (UMS III.3) as carried out by meditators cognizant of the ontological and cosmological context within which meditation can be fruitful (UMS III.1, 2), and undergirded by the fact of a coherent truth in the upaniṣads (UMS I) which, though not available to the reasoning mind without an appeal to scripture, successfully surpasses all competing, nonscriptural explanations of the world (UMS II).

It is in light of this practical structure that we best understand the important opening sūtras, UMS I.1.1–4:

I.1.1 Next, therefore, the desire to know Brahman.

I.1.2 "Brahman" indicates that whence derive the origination, etc. of this world.

I.1.3 Brahman is knowable because it is the source of the teachings.

I.1.4 It is known from the upaniṣads because it is their consistent object.

These sūtras are prefatory and regulative indications of how the reading is to proceed. They are not general, informative summations of what comes later in the Text; they are true beginnings, not substitutes for what follows.[51] They set the parameters within which the ensuing analysis is to proceed:[52] a. the UMS inquiry is motivated by a desire to know Brahman (UMS I.1.1); b. the word "Brahman" is minimally designated as referring to "that which is the cause of the world," so as to enable us to use it intelligently, yet without making the ensuing exegesis superfluous by assuming to know in advance all that must be known of Brahman (UMS I.1.2); c. Brahman is investigated according to the exegetical analysis of the UMS, because Brahman is knowable from scripture; d. inquiry into scripture is a reasonable endeavor, because scripture is coherent and has Brahman as its single primary topic.

The four sūtras can also be taken as declarative of knowledge about Brahman, as providing four topics for theological and philosophical analysis: a. Brahman exists, is knowable and worth knowing (UMS I.1.1); b. Brahman is the cause of the world, and is knowable as such (UMS I.1.2); c. Brahman is knowable from scripture (UMS I.1.3); d. the upaniṣads testify to the primacy and salvific efficacy of knowledge of Brahman (UMS I.1.4). The enormity of the commentaries on these sūtras—often named simply the *catuḥsūtrī*, "the section of the four sūtras"—amply shows that they can be taken in effect as "a text in themselves."

While this second and more philosophical reading of the inaugural sūtras cannot therefore be discarded, it must be kept in tension with, and ultimately subordinate to, the first, regulative understanding of them. The tension between knowledge as skill and knowledge as insight grows throughout the Text, and is ever more finely accentuated. Advaita subsists precisely in that tension: it is both Uttara Mīmāṃsā and Vedānta. There is no necessary contradiction between these sūtras as rules for the reader and as statements about Brahman, since, as we shall see in Chapter 3, the latter, positive exposition of knowledge about Brahman is an expected stage and development of the Advaita project of knowledge. Any such development, however, remains later, consequent upon a necessary and persisting engagement in the reading of the Text.[53]

The reader who wishes to engage the Text properly may therefore be advised to use the map laid out by pāda and adhyāya, and the issues spelled out ever more clearly in the initial sūtras—in order to read backwards across the map; possibly, for instance, to begin with the practical issues related to exegesis-for-meditation (UMS III.3,) and then to proceed to a textually constituted examination of the results (UMS IV, UMS III.4) of the presuppositions of the act of meditation, psychology and cosmology (UMS III.1-2,) of apologetics and the removal of doubts about Advaita (UMS II.2,) and finally of the formal rules and practices of the systematization of this knowledge (I).

This reversed path of reading is in part a pedagogical device; the Text is heavily redacted and refined, and one cannot claim merely to be putting its parts back in order. Nevertheless, the advice to read backwards serves as a useful corrective for the modern reader who, eager to engage the philosophical content of Advaita, may be tempted to use the larger divisions of the Text into adhyāya and pāda as an excuse to read selectively, avoiding the discipline of a total and much more prolonged engagement in the Text. Many a reader has missed the point of Advaita by reading only as far as the end of UMS I.1.4.

IV. The Contextualization of Meaning through Engaged Reading

In this chapter I have urged that the learning of Advaita is a primarily textual process, a reader's achievement. This is in part simply the elaboration of the fact that our access to Advaita is for the most part textual: most of us learn most of what we learn about Advaita by reading texts. But it is also the additional insistence that Advaita subsists as this textual composition, what I have termed "the Text," the entire religious-literary act of text and commentary. This Text is a complex literary project—in its practices, in the developments it makes available to us in the form of commentary, and its resultant reinterpretation of the world is a project in writing. The fruits of this Text—what one gets from immersing oneself in it—can be abstracted only at the great cost of severing the vital connection between a Vedānta philosophy and an Uttara Mīmāṃsā. The Text's forward movement in the refinements of commentary is an act of deliberate composition and extension in language and literary form of the rich and ambivalent heritage of the upaniṣads, the *Uttara Mīmāṃsā Sūtras*, and each layer of earlier commentary. One must remain ready to read, to be educated, and so to become differently skilled by particular acts of reading. In addition, one must arduously argue one's way through the Text in its pūrvapakṣas and siddhāntas, patiently becoming learned in the particular refinements by which the discernment of right positions advances; only thereby does one profit fully from the Advaita Text.

Though all of this seems to doom the study of Advaita to the fate of endless reading, pedantic detail, and ownership by a very small, elite audience, actually the opposite is true. The evident, available Textual status of Advaita makes it accessible to outsiders who do not realize the truth of Advaita intuitively from the start, who at the start share few of its premises and expectations. The permanent textuality of the Text ensures the possibility that one can learn Advaita from the outside in, by reading. If the demand that one read is a barrier which excludes those lacking sufficient determination or patience, it is also the school par excellence in which the persistent learner can ever so slowly advance in the desired knowledge of Brahman. For those who learn to perform according to its standards, the Text is the pathway to truth; it is a powerful and generous teacher, whose extraordinary demands allow the persistent few to learn gradually to make the right distinctions and right connections, to begin to know the truth of Brahman.

Or it ought to: the tension between Text and truth remains, and the pathway from becoming expert in the reading of Advaita to knowing the pure, simple, nondual truth of Brahman is not a clear one. How is the extratextual truth of Brahman inscribed within the multiple reading strategies inscribed in the Text? To this question we now turn, in Chapter 3.

Chapter **3**

The Truth of Advaita Vedānta

I. The Problem of Truth in the Text

In Chapter 2 I showed that the study of Advaita entails a prolonged and gradually masterful engagement in a Text composed and complemented for the purpose of reading; the profound and subtle understanding which is the prized goal of Advaita is a reader's understanding. On its multiple levels and in its increasing complexity, the Text is the privileged place of Advaita knowledge, and it is a distortion to reduce it to a (somewhat cumbersome) representation of Śaṅkara's thought, or to identify it as a systematization to which, when properly finished by later scholars, exegesis and argument become mere appendages.[1]

Accordingly, we have already begun to examine the way in which Bādarāyaṇa's UMS, as an organization of upaniṣadic knowledge, includes a series of judgments about what counts in the upaniṣads; we have begun to see how the UMS is patterned after a ritual arrangement of knowledge in which the performative—ritual, meditative, literary—aspects of upaniṣadic knowledge are not sacrificed for the sake of content. In this chapter I comment more closely on the Advaitic construction of the meaning of the upaniṣads and, in particular, on the way in which Advaita moves toward a post-textual truth that never becomes purely extratextual. We thus turn our attention to the "truth of Advaita," the claims Advaita makes about the world as it really is, and the knowledge which liberates the Advaitin from it.[2]

Though permanently textual, Advaita does not portray itself as endlessly about texts, a play of words. It argues that it is true that reality is nondual, that Brahman is devoid of all qualities, that the world has Brahman as its cause—material, efficient and final—and that these positions refer to the actual reality in which not only Advaitins live, but everyone else as well. Like other theological systems, Advaita invests a great deal in this view that its positions are adequate to the real, and that its proposals regarding the human condition are consequently helpful toward salvation. We must now explore, therefore, how the truth claims of Advaita are compatible with its permanent textuality, and how the Text extends itself in its particular, characteristic understanding claim about the world and regarding the truth of Brahman.

In our preliminary examination of the UMS in Chapter 2 we sketched by way of example certain approaches to knowledge in the *Chāndogya Upaniṣad*, glimpsed the rich, complex and richly uneven discourse of the upaniṣads as represented there and in the *Taittirīya Upaniṣad*, and saw how Bādarāyaṇa's UMS moves toward a systematization of the upaniṣads and a regularization of their meaning. His organization of the upaniṣads within the frames of sūtra, adhikaraṇa, pāda and adhyāya, and according to procedures such as coordination and harmonization, is a possible, though uncompleted, move toward a replacement of the upaniṣads with a meaning derived from them, with their subject matter.

Śaṅkara's *Bhāsya* in important ways extends the systematization begun by Bādarāyaṇa. Like Bādarāyaṇa, he holds for a systematization of the upaniṣads although, as I argue in what follows, he declines to follow his predecessor in discovering a doctrine *about* Brahman in the upaniṣads; instead, he retrieves and reinvigorates the system-resistant language that is basic to the upaniṣads. For Śaṅkara, the upaniṣads cannot tell us about Brahman, but they fail in so rich, engaging and persuasive a way that we alter our way of living and realize Brahman in a radical revision of our own identities.

It is on this basis, and in order to articulate the epistemological and ontological stances which underpin upaniṣadic knowledge, that Śaṅkara poses the controversial doctrines which have become synonymous with Advaita: the ultimate nonduality (*advaita*) of the knower and the known; the distinction between Brahman with qualities (saguṇa) and without qualities (nirguṇa); the break with the orthodox Brahmanical tradition on (some of) the prerequisites to knowledge; the view that Brahman is the material and efficient cause of the world—and all of these as pertaining to how language works and what it requires of us. These positions are held to be true, the most plausible articulations of the stated but incompletely explained claims of the upaniṣads. Yet they are also rules as to how to read what is said in light of what isn't being said, or can't be said. The Advaita positions map a horizon within which the performance of reading and commentary can be seen as salvific activities.

The project of this chapter is to examine several important aspects of the Advaita construction of the truth of the Text, and so to trace the construction of a post-upaniṣadic discourse which nevertheless remains true to the particular texture and demands of those texts. We begin by exploring the possibility of a thoroughly, inseparably textual truth.

II. Strategies of Textual Truth

I begin this section with a brief excursus into the writing of Michael Riffaterre, whose observations on truth in fiction are richly suggestive of ways in which one can talk about a truth which nevertheless remains firmly inscribed in its text(s).[3] Presupposing familiarity with the commonplace notion that truth entails a reliable and adequate referential relationship between words and their objects, Riffaterre concedes that by its very nature fiction does not entail that kind of truth. However, he argues that by rethinking key terms we nevertheless can speak of a "truth in fiction:" "the solution to the truth-in-fiction paradox evidently lies in redefining referentiality. Whereas referentiality assumes an actual or potential relationship between language and reality, we have to hypothesize that this assumption suffices only so long as it respects the rules of representation that exist in any language and with which all speakers of that language are familiar. Words may still tell a truth if the rules are followed."[4]

Fiction possesses its own system of referentiality and hence its own truth according to the agreed-upon rules of its own writing: "truth in fiction rests on verisimilitude, a system of representations that seems to reflect a reality external to the text, but only because it conforms to a grammar. Narrative truth is an idea of truth created in accordance with the rules of that grammar."[5] In turn, one can distinguish between a verisimilitude which is a special instance of mimesis, "a sign system based on the referentiality of its components, that is, on the assumption that words carry meaning by referring to things or to nonverbal entities,"[6] and a verisimilitude which is found in consecution, "a special instance of motivation, that is, as a compellingly visible coherence in the sequence of causes and effects."[7] Verisimilitude as consecution "privileges the narrative sequentiality that is entirely within the text's boundaries;" it provides a truth which is thoroughly textual.[8] Though fiction does not proceed by reference to established and perceptible realities outside itself, it is able to extend beyond itself because it has inscribed into it certain tensions and rough textures which compel the reader to reread and to read differently, with a continually shifting attitude toward the text being read. The interaction of the prepared reader with a richly textured whole guides that reader into the space of a narrative truth which can be just as commanding of the reader's attention and response as an extratextual reference might be.

By analogy—and it can only be such, for though textual Advaita's truth cannot be adequately described as a fictional truth—we can understand how truth can be said to reside in the upaniṣads and in the Advaita Text, and how that truth is real, demanding and efficacious—without having also to maintain that there is an extratextual reference for this truth. I now explore the inscription of Advaita's truth in its Text by introducing two of its own textual strategies: 1. the distinction between Brahman without qualities (nirguṇa) and with qualities (saguṇa) as a guide to the proper differentiated reading of the upaniṣads, and 2. the intentionally puzzling and paradoxical upaniṣadic "great sayings" (*mahāvākya*), which express nonduality and thereby make readers reread the entirety of the various upaniṣadic contexts and review their own Textually determined reality.

1. Denying to Brahman its Qualities (nirguṇatva)

Although the upaniṣads frequently characterize Brahman—and the correlate Self, Man, etc.—as possessed of various qualities, on occasion they also instruct us to deny these qualities, portraying Brahman as ineffable, devoid of qualities, properly understood through the negation of qualities, etc. Both kinds of statements command respect, and both need to be read carefully; it is true that Brahman is devoid of qualities, and it is also true that Brahman has qualities. The final truth of Brahman—that it has no qualities—is communicated in the shift back and forth from declarations of the presence of qualities to declarations of the absence of qualities, shifts which bring about a specific kind of attention in the student who takes all the texts seriously. The tension between the two kinds of statements creates an unstable and creative environment for reading, in which the reader is repeatedly repositioned in relation to the texts used in meditation and study.

The value of the tension is witnessed by the fact that Śaṅkara preserves it, resisting formulations about Brahman which reduce the two kinds of statement—Brahman lacks all qualities, Brahman is qualified in various ways—to a single plane of understanding in which the first permanently excludes the second. He insists that the upaniṣads are to be used in both of these ways, for different purposes; a variety of readers are to be engaged according to their intentions, (usually) using first those texts which positively describe Brahman in various ways and (then, later) at other times those texts which declare the absence of qualities. The texts are not contradictory, since they are not about the same thing at the same time; nor are they usable in the same way. However, they inevitably affect the reader who moves between the two kinds of texts without submitting them to a higher viewpoint which would rob them of their productive insistence by locating them on a single level of discourse, as merely two ways of talking about the same reality, saying the same thing.

The Advaita position that Brahman is "really" devoid of qualities even when spoken of as having qualities needs to be understood as a textual strategy which regulates the reading of the nonhomogeneous discourse of the upaniṣads while yet leaving intact their tensive power. That Brahman is devoid of qualities is the truth, but this truth occurs within texts which speak of Brahman in other ways as well, and the claim must not be excised from that context. The truth referred to by the Text is simultaneously the truth of the Text, and these "two" truths—referential and textual—ought neither to be confused nor separated. Were the upaniṣads merely to inform us that Brahman is devoid of qualities, they would be telling us nothing effectively; by compelling the reader to move back and forth from texts which point to qualities and texts which deny them, they prepare the attentive reader to appropriate the truth. Though the upaniṣads cannot have Brahman as their content—Brahman cannot be "said," even by the upaniṣads—the proclaimed ineffability is inscribed within the upaniṣads.[9]

Let us examine how all of this works out in one important adhikaraṇa, UMS III.2.11–21. As we saw in Chapter 2, the commentators term UMS III the section on "means" (sādhana), i.e., on the texts and activity of meditation. UMS III.1 and UMS III.2 explore the horizon within which meditation is possible: the nature of the meditator, the psychological structure of phenomenal and deep self and, in UMS III.2.11–37, the nature of that Brahman which is to be meditated on.[10] UMS III.2 is not expository in the broader sense of proposing a completed theory about Brahman, or the Self, or even about meditation; rather, it is written so as to ensure that meditation will continue to occur within a viable framework.

UMS III.2.11–21 addresses the problem we have already noted: the upaniṣads speak in two ways of Brahman, as possessed of an entire range of qualities, such as wisdom, great strength, attractive color, etc., but also as devoid of all such qualities. The question is, If all of these texts are supposed to have a single referent, how are they to be reconciled?

Bādarāyaṇa's view, insofar as it may be constructed from his laconic sūtras, is that the two descriptions of Brahman in the upaniṣads really pertain to Brahman and not just to its knower; they are not simply imposed on Brahman from the perspective of the human self. Brahman is knowable either as having form, or as devoid of form; how one performs meditation depends on the meditator's preference and the particular text being used for meditation.[11]

Śaṅkara's position is more complex. First, in explaining UMS III.2.14—"Brahman is only formless, to be sure, for that is the dominant point of the upaniṣadic teaching"—he states that Brahman is devoid of qualities:

> Brahman is surely to be known as not having any figure constituted by form, etc., not as having it. Why? "For that is the dominant point of the upaniṣadic teaching," inasmuch as it has been established under the sūtra, "But that is known from the upaniṣads because it is their consistent object," [UMS I.1.4] that texts like the following have for their main purport the transcendental Brahman which is the Self, and not any other subject-matter: "It is neither gross, nor minute, neither short nor long" (*Bṛhadāraṇyaka Upaniṣad* 3.8.8); "Soundless, touchless, colourless, undiminishing" (*Kaṭha Upaniṣad* 1.3.15); "That which is known as space is the accomplisher of name and form; that in which they are included is Brahman" (*Chāndogya Upaniṣad* 7.14.1); "The Man is transcendental, since he is formless; he is coextensive with all that is external and internal, since he is birthless" (*Muṇḍaka Upaniṣad* 1.1.2), "That Brahman is without prior or posterior, without interior and exterior. The Self, the perceiver of everything, is Brahman." (*Bṛhadāraṇyaka Upaniṣad* 2.5.19)

Instead of assigning a metaphorical meaning, Śaṅkara assigns a different intent to texts which attribute form to Brahman: "But other texts, which have as their topic Brahman with figure, do not have as their dominant intention [to expound Brahman as possessed of figure], but rather to express injunctions related to meditation."

The two sets of texts have different intentions—the nature of Brahman, the practice of meditation—and therefore different results. Śaṅkara's appeal is not primarily to the real nature of Brahman, but to the uses to which texts of different kinds are to be put; his argument is an inherently literary one.

At the end of the adhikaraṇa, UMS III.2.21, Śaṅkara shows that he is not trying to replace scripture by an encompassing theory, even the venerable Mīmāṃsā strategy of a ritual reading of scripture, by which all of scripture is subordinated to a single final purpose just as all minor ritual actions are subordinated to the major ritual action of which they are parts. Śaṅkara refuses to allow the texts which attribute qualities to Brahman to be reinterpreted as indirect statements about Brahman devoid of qualities, or to be valued merely as accessory to the texts which deny that Brahman has qualities. The two kinds of texts are not to be placed within a single frame of reference. Because they belong to different domains which are defined by different purposes, audiences and results, they are neither contradictory nor cooperative:

> Accordingly it is wrong to argue, on the grounds that [both kinds of texts] come within the scope of a single injunction, that they combine to impart a single idea [about Brahman] . . . As regards the injunctions about Brahman with qualities and without qualities, no section of the text is available that declares that the competence of the man is identical for both kinds of text . . . It is not logical to accommodate in one and the same substratum such attributes as the sublation of all and the persistence of a part of the phenomenal manifestation. Therefore the division made by us of the [separate] instructions about Brahman with figure and without figure is more reasonable.[12]

Śaṅkara has of course decided which texts are more important, but he bases his estimation in two modes of textual purposefulness, not in a declaration about "reality in itself." He does not claim that texts about Brahman with qualities do not mean what they say, but only that they do not lead to the same result as the others; they need to be read differently and by different readers (or readers at different stages in their reading), for different purposes.

This version of the distinction between the two kinds of texts denies to the reader a higher viewpoint from which to survey all of the upaniṣadic texts at once, offering instead a more refined manner of engagement in the Text; a certain skill is prized, and the means to the acquisition of that skill is proposed. The reader is compelled to approach the upaniṣads in an active and nuanced fashion, by reading the many passages which describe Brahman with various qualities over against, and in tension with, those rarer texts which tell us that Brahman cannot be characterized at all. One does not merely leap to the passages which deny that Brahman can be qualified; one appropriates the whole of the texts and, as an active reader who learns over time, one begins to read differently after making use of the distinctions among them. Then, positioned correctly among texts which proclaim Brahman with qualities, the accomplished reader is enable to move to the assertion that Brahman is devoid of qualities: this is thus a truth discoverable only in those texts as they are situated within the Text, and a truth which guides one in rereading the Text, again and again.[13]

2. *Paradoxes in the Text (mahāvākyas)*

A second way in which Advaita organizes the upaniṣads in order to make their truth evident is the designation of so-called great sayings (mahāvākyas), a number of very brief upaniṣadic sayings which are said to sum up the entire meaning of the upaniṣads—in Advaita, the teaching of nonduality: most important are "I am Brahman," (*ahaṃ brahmāsmi*; *Bṛhadāraṇyaka Upaniṣad* 1.4.10) and "You are that" (*tat tvam asi*; *Chāndogya Upaniṣad* 6.8.7).[14]

This identification of great sayings by Śaṅkara[15] and the later commentators[16] is itself a constructive exegetical move, one neither required by nor in total harmony with the upaniṣads. Insofar as these great sayings are supposed to encapsulate the essential position of Advaita and be the key texts which declare that all dualities are provisional and ultimately superseded, they stand in stark simplicity over against the rich variety of statements found in any given upaniṣad.

As such, the great sayings function analogously to the distinction between Brahman with qualities and without qualities; for here too the point is not to do away with the rest of the Text, but to grade and qualify the way the rest of the upaniṣads are to be read. The effect of the great sayings is perhaps greater, because not only are they concentrated, but they are also paradoxical claims which jar readers by pointing to a truth which they cannot easily locate in ordinary experience. A great saying such as "You are that" (*tat tvam asi*) upsets our reading of the upaniṣads because, in the Advaita reading, it seems to equate two things that ought not to be equated: the phenomenal, finite self (*tvam*) and Brahman (*tat*). It puzzles the reader, demanding an equation without any evident correlate or evident referent in the world, or even in the upaniṣadic texts, for that matter, which for the most part seem directed to a reader who, however estimable, is less than the eternally one, the Self. It is a truth which has no evident reference or confirmation in the world of ordinary experience. Made uncomfortable with what she or he previously took for granted and with prior readings of the upaniṣads themselves, the reader is made to seek a stance in which nonduality can be perceived as true; and the search for this requires a rereading of the rest of the given upaniṣad, in light of its most contentious and difficult portion, its great saying.

Persistent attention to these initially implausible yet demanding great sayings impels the reader gradually into another frame of reference, where what was hitherto unexpected and without referent begins to make sense. Compelled upon the reader by the paradox of the great saying and the consequent reappraisal of the whole of each upaniṣad, this elusive and never forthrightly demarcated new location—a new perspective on reading, a point of realization where notions of "I" and "Brahman" are revised—is where Advaita can be properly said to occur, where there is operative that higher grammar according to which the great sayings now make sense. The truth of Advaita is found in its texts, yet only after the reader has acquired an understanding of these at first puzzling claims. The great sayings are the Text's "other" inscribed within it; they impel the reader into a reader's awareness of the truth of Advaita, a truth not merely present in words such as "You are that."[17]

Riffaterre observes that the truth of fiction is not the sum total of the meanings found within the text, but rather its significance, which he explains as follows: "Significance . . . now appears to be more than or something other than the total meaning deducible from a comparison between variants of the given. That would only bring us back to the given, and it would be a reductionist procedure. Significance is, rather, the reader's praxis of the transformation, a realization that it is akin to playing, to act out the liturgy of a ritual—the experience of a circuitous sequence, a way of speaking that keeps revolving around a key word or matrix reduced to a marker . . . It is a hierarchy of representations imposed upon the reader, despite his personal preferences, by the greater or lesser expansion of the matrix's components, an orientation imposed upon the reader despite his linguistic habits, a bouncing from reference to reference that keeps on pushing the meaning over to a text not present in the linearity, to a paragram or hypogram. . ."[18] He observes too that readers may be tempted to slip onto an easier path to meaning, by searching into the life of the author, etc.; only if they can resist this escape from textuality, they will be confronted with the "truth" of the text.[19] Thinking of truth as this kind of significance can aid us further in understanding how the whole of the Advaita Text can be true, without this truth being the accumulation of the truths of the individual parts or simply a series of single truth statements.[20]

The preceding analyses of the tensions provoked in the reader by the distinction between Brahman with and without qualities, and by the paradoxical great sayings, suggest that one can read the Advaita with an insistence on its profoundly textual, literary communicativeness, while yet continuing to respect its traditional "trademarks," such as the claim that its truth is not a textual product and is truly beyond words, that Brahman is without qualities, that "you" are "that." As a remedy to past exaggerations, these strategies need to be appreciated without the immediate imposition of a philosophical interpretation.

Subsequently, it becomes possible to speak of this Advaita truth in metaphysical and epistemological language. The truth claims posed by the Text on the world can be adequately appreciated, argued, perhaps even proven, if one first sees them as skillfully composed textual achievements, claims on how we read the texts which constitute the Advaita Text.

III. Truth after the Text: The True Meaning of the Upaniṣads and the World of Advaita

The preceding comments, which complement the project begun in Chapter 2, have emphasized the power and indispensability of the Text as a field in which the reader engages the truth of Advaita, which is accessible only by an active reading which confronts it as a finely composed text inscribed in ongoing acts of commentary. With its multiple inscribed strategies, the Text first claims readers through a reformulation of their rules of reading, the proper performance of reading enacted by a trained reader. Though Brahman is not what we say about Brahman, and though reality, utterly simple, does not directly reflect the complexity of ordinary experience and our words about it, Advaita is marked by a subtle, complex and uncompromising commitment to texts and commentaries as the vehicle of this realization of truth within the confinement of language.

Attention to the linguistic and literary strategies of the Text must in turn be complemented by an examination of the Text's content, those claims about Brahman which are by implication claims about the self and the world. The Advaitins invest certain contents with meaning, and articulate a definite position about what the upaniṣads actually say; they intend to identify the arguable, defensible truth of the upaniṣads.

Identified through careful reading, this truth is protected in two ways. First, the Advaitins construct around it a frame of meanings and rules about meaning which favor their interpretation. Second, they preempt efforts to construct meanings outside, or from outside the Text, and inscribe—and marginalize—their competitors in the Text, in a narration which verifies the implausibility of those other positions. In this section (III) I consider the former of these ventures, and in the next section (IV), the latter.

Here I focus on four key texts in order to trace Advaita's construction of the right meaning of the upaniṣads: 1. UMS III.3.11–13, which initiates the project of coordination (upasaṃhāra), is a first step toward bridging the gap between Brahman as described in various texts, and Brahman as knowable simply and immediately, after texts; 2. UMS I.1.5–11, which initiates the project of harmonization (samanvaya), shows that the upaniṣads are unanimous in their identification of the object of salvific knowledge, i.e., Brahman as identified in one key upaniṣadic text;[21] 3. UMS I.1.2, where the word "Brahman," which names the object of the Advaita inquiry, is designated to mean "the cause of the world," but where there is also the additional claim that this cause can be inferred only from the upaniṣads and not from the evidence of the world, the supposed effect; 4. UMS IV.3.7–14, where Śaṅkara moves closest to a systematic statement of his understanding of Brahman.

1. UMS III.3.11–13: Can We Assume that Brahman is Always Bliss?

We saw in Chapter 2 that the primary task in UMS III.3 is coordination, a practical understanding of parallel upaniṣadic texts that enables one to use them together in meditation without reducing them to one text. In order to facilitate more manageable meditation practices, and secondarily (perhaps) to articulate a doctrine of Brahman, the Advaitins argue that the upaniṣadic texts have an "extratextual" reference: texts from different Vedic schools can be used together, since Brahman is the single referent of all of them.

The issue is posed most clearly in UMS III.3.11–13, where the Advaitins seek to distinguish terms about Brahman which apply in every meditation from those which are usable only in one particular meditation. Certain descriptive terms—Brahman is true, existent, blissful, etc.—are said to pertain to the essence of Brahman and are everywhere pertinent, as fundamental to the very rationale for meditative practice; Śaṅkara cites "One only, without a second,"[22] as an example of this kind of statement. Others—"its head is joy, its right side delight,"[23] "uniting all that is pleasant," etc.[24]—are not essential characteristics of Brahman, qualify it only in one meditation or another, and so need not be introduced everywhere.

Once the legitimacy of distinction among kinds of qualities is recognized, the question shifts to how one is to determine which qualities are real, everywhere pertinent, and which are merely provisional constructs for the sake of particular acts of meditation. In commenting on UMS III.3.11, Vācaspati distinguishes qualities which belong to the object in itself, of its own nature, from those which humans posit regarding it provisionally. Real qualities of Brahman "mark" it without attributing to it any kind of finitude; they pertain irrespective of any particular meditational situation. By contrast, provisional characteristics include all those which appear to attribute quantity or change to Brahman and which therefore must be taken as extrinsic and not real qualities. These are warranted only where the upaniṣads explicitly authorize their introduction. In these distinctions, clearly, the composition of a theology of Brahman is beginning to take shape.

Amalānanda's position warrants close examination.[25] He seeks a more refined justification for the distinction among qualities and, consequently, an explanation of why Brahman is better indicated by a series of terms, "true," "conscious," etc., than by just one of them alone. After all, if no word is adequate and if all words are just signs pointing toward a Brahman they cannot express, one might argue that one word suffices as the required though inadequate signifier. He first deals with the problem of why different words deserve different treatment:

> [Objection:] If bliss, etc., should be introduced from all contexts on the grounds that Brahman is one, then why are "uniting all that is pleasant," etc. [which also refer to Brahman] not thus introduced?
>
> [Response:] "Uniting all that is pleasant," etc., are enjoined [only] for the sake of acts of meditation. Because the precise

> demarcation of the result connected with an injunction is not known, then all the details connected with that result must be organized precisely according to the injunction [since there is no other standard by which to make sure that they contribute properly].
>
> By contrast, truth, knowledge, etc. serve to ascertain the essence of the object; wherever the essence of that object is pertinent, there they are to be introduced . . .

He then faces the objection that a multiplication of words is pointless:

> [Objection:] Regarding what is "without qualities" [Brahman] words other [than that single marker "without qualities"] are useless, and so should not be introduced [from other meditation contexts.]

On the contrary, he responds, it is useful to introduce all those words which are judged everywhere applicable, since they cooperate in correcting wrong ideas of Brahman:

> [Response:] [i] Truth, [ii] consciousness, [iii] bliss, [iv] infinity and [v] self are terms which mutually qualify one another, [respectively] overturn the flaws of [i] falsity, [ii] nonconsciousness, [iii] sorrow, [iv] limitedness and [v] lack of self, and so define that single bliss which is the common basis for truth, etc. It is just like when the words "existent," "material thing," and "pot" [all define] a single pot.

If only one term is used to designate Brahman, Brahman may be too narrowly defined, or that one term may be misunderstood merely to indicate a preponderance of that quality in Brahman, and not Brahman's absolute transcendence of the implied limitation:

> The definition that Brahman is of this sort cannot occur due to one word alone, since if only one word is used there will be no conflict [of meanings] and hence no indirect signification. Hence, other words must be used. Insofar as errors are possible, a whole string of words capable of ending the errors must be introduced; in order to end those errors [in every case], the string of word-meanings must be everywhere introduced.[26]

This legitimation of some generalizations about Brahman is a cautious move beyond the precise warrant of any one upaniṣadic text; we thus recognize the constructive role of the skilled reader and theologian, who is able to make judgments based on the variety of texts he or she is familiar with, and not simply on the basis of the single text at hand. Advaita begins gradually to construct its discourse about Brahman.

Yet it retains a practical interpretive focus, insisting on the inadequacy of the words involved; the meditational focus and skepticism about words together deflect efforts to compose a generalized, and then a nonscriptural, discourse about Brahman. Yet while UMS III.3.11–13 neither presumes nor completes a systematic exposition of the nature of Brahman, the construction of that exposition has been inaugurated.

2. UMS I.1.5–11: The Upaniṣads Do Have a Right Meaning

UMS I.1.5–11 completes the introduction to the UMS by giving a specific upaniṣadic foundation to the rules enunciated in UMS I.1.1–4, and at the same time introducing the task proper to the first adhyāya, harmonization (samanvaya): Brahman is the source of the world and object of salvific knowledge, and none of the competing interpretations, such as Sāṃkhya's discovery in the upaniṣads of a material source for the world (pradhāna), is intended by the texts. UMS I.1.12–I.4 is devoted largely to showing that contested upaniṣadic texts all agree with the siddhānta of UMS I.1.5–11. Scripture is coherent because it intends one salvific object.

The argument of UMS I.1.5–11 is encapsulated in I.1.5:

> Because seeing is mentioned, what is not mentioned is to be excluded.

Since the upaniṣads explicitly refer to a cause which is able to see (which has foresight, intelligence), one cannot infer as the implied cause something which cannot see (is not intelligent), such as the Sāṃkhyan material principle. The text at issue in the adhikaraṇa is *Chāndogya* 6.2.3–4, which narrates how the world came forth from the original being:

> The same Being saw [*aikṣata*]: "I will be many, I will propagate myself." Then it created fire. This fire saw, "I will be many, I will propagate myself." Then it created the waters . . . The waters saw, "We will be many, we will propagate ourselves."

The debate hinges on the weight that can be given to the verb "saw" (*aikṣata*): does it imply an intelligent creator, and reserve this ability to Brahman as an intelligent being, or does it confer the same intentional capability on fire and water as well? The attribution of this ability to Brahman alone would support the Advaita position; the attribution of it to the nonconscious elements would support the Sāṃkhyan insistence that creation can be traced back to the nonconscious source—or at least that the upaniṣads do not speak in a single voice, and allow the Sāṃkhyan as well as the Advaita interpretations of the world's cause.

Śaṅkara's argument has two aspects. First, the cause of the world is Brahman, because terms such as "seeing" indicate a conscious knower as the source of the world. Second, alternatives such as the nonconscious material source are to be excluded because they are not mentioned explicitly in the upaniṣads; inferences cannot be made in contradiction to what actually is said. Since Brahman is mentioned, and a material source is not, additional efforts to understand more fully the meaning of the *Chāndogya* text, and thereafter to construct a correct doctrine of creation, need to be worked out on that basis. Śaṅkara's exposition may be divided as follows:

> In the upaniṣadic texts one cannot take one's stand on the insentient material source [*pradhāna*] imagined by the Sāṃkhyas as the cause of the universe; for it is not mentioned in the upaniṣads . . . Rather, the upaniṣads teach thus: Starting with the text, "O amiable one, before its creation, the universe was but existence, one without a second," it is stated "The same Being saw: 'I will be many, I will propagate myself.' Then it created fire." [*Chāndogya* 6.2.3][27]

This seeing indicates that the creator is intelligent, able to plan ahead, etc.

> As for the statement that material source can become omniscient through the characteristic of knowledge belonging to its constituent lucidity,[28] that is not justifiable; for in that state [of the material source as such, when it has not already changed through a loss of balance] there can be no possibility of knowledge as a characteristic of lucidity, because the constituents of the material source are then in balance.[29]

In the state of perfect balance among the three constituents, there is no preference for lucidity, and no basis for it to emerge as predominant and thereby as the basis for the attribution of intelligence to the material principle. In brief, no explanation plausibly supports the unconvincing Sāṃkhyan claim that consciousness originates in an unconscious material source.[30]

Śaṅkara then disposes of problems which call into question the Advaita claim that Brahman is a knower:

> The fact that Brahman is both omniscient and unchanging does not mean that Brahman is therefore not omnipotent, because it lacks the ability to stop knowing; to be omniscient by nature is not a limitation of the freedom of the knower.[31]

> It is not necessary to have a body in order to know, and Brahman requires neither a material source nor any comparable material element; for Brahman "has eternal consciousness by its very nature, so that it has no dependence on the means of knowledge"[32]—no need for a body as an instrument of knowledge. Moreover, the *Śvetāśvatara Upaniṣad* 3.19 clearly states that Brahman can know without a body: "Without hands and feet he grasps and moves quickly; he sees without eyes, he hears without ears, he knows all that is to be known . . ."[33]

There is no problem in maintaining that the world exists only in/as Brahman, even if this seems to imply that the obvious limitations we see around us—ignorance, impurity, etc.—are ultimately flaws in Brahman: "the idea of difference between the Lord and the transmigrating soul is false, having been created by non-discrimination which causes the ascription of the limiting adjuncts—body and the rest. And though the self continues as before [untouched by these flaws], it is seen to remain falsely identified with the body and the rest, the identification having arisen from a series of errors preceding each other."[34]

Although various inferences about a material source for the world seem plausible and consonant with scripture, UMS II.1.4ff. will show that the material complexity of the world is more easily explained by the postulation of Brahman than by that of the material source.[35]

At the end of UMS I.1.5 and in UMS I.1.6 the objection is introduced that since the *Chāndogya* text speaks not only of Being (*sat*) as "seeing," but also of fire and water as doing the same, there is no warrant for concluding that the "seeing" attributed to Being is intelligence—any more than the metaphorical "seeing" of fire is or water is intelligent. Śaṅkara responds that the usage regarding Being is legitimately exceptional: the logic of the passage as a whole points toward the intelligible relation between Being and the human knower, and thus supports an interpretation of seeing as an intelligent operation. Regarding fire and water, there are no comparable persuasive arguments.[36]

UMS I.1.7–11 extends the exposition of the two sides to the Advaita-Sāṃkhya argument in several ways: a. were the material source the object of knowledge, knowing it would not lead to salvation; if effective at all in changing the knower, the transformation would be merely a degradation of the conscious to the level of the nonconscious; such knowledge cannot be intended by the *Chāndogya* passage (I.1.7–8); b. scripture must be unanimous in proposing only one primary topic; it cannot refer to Brahman in some texts and a material source in others (I.1.10); c. there are other texts[37] which speak of Brahman as the omniscient source, and these confirm our interpretation of the *Chāndogya* text (I.1.11).

As a whole, UMS I.1.5–11 defends the theological position that Brahman is the sole intelligent, material, efficient and final cause of the world. The debate which concludes in this position is a matter of right exegesis and, by extension, of the articulation of the implications of that intelligent reading; essential to it are the (controversial) notions that the *Chāndogya* text actually has a single right meaning, and that this meaning is consonant with the meaning of all of scripture. These notions rely on a series of judgments about which parts of texts are more important, how primary and secondary parts are to be sorted out, why other apparently plausible readings are inappropriate and, finally, when and how other upaniṣadic texts and arguments drawn from various disciplines—logic, Mīmāṃsā, grammar—are correctly introduced.[38]

These corollary judgments must be understood, linked, appreciated and eventually accepted, if the persuasion regarding the main doctrine is to be successful. The reader, like the Advaitin, needs to be engaged in making a series of judgments along the way, judgments which in turn need to be reviewed in terms of how much the reader knows of scripture and why the reader's arguments are properly formed and properly applied. The successful reader, able to be persuaded that there is a single meaning to the upaniṣads, that Brahman is the focus of that meaning, and that this Brahman is the sole cause of the world, is a reader who is—or who is becoming—literate and cultured in the "Advaita way."

Nevertheless, as one begins to understand properly the view that Brahman is the material and spiritual cause of the world, one is beginning to say more than the upaniṣads say directly, and one is composing a cosmology, metaphysics, fundamental theology. Increasing clarity about the world and its Truth occurs in accordance with an increasingly perceptive skill in the reading of the Text; but even if this occurs only after reading, it nevertheless takes one beyond the strict limitations of what one has read.

3. UMS I.1.2: Inference within the Margins of the Upaniṣads

By attention to UMS III.3.11–13 and I.1.5–11 I have been sketching a probable genealogy for the systematic exposition of the truth of Advaita; what emerges is a careful balance between a continuing commitment to texts and the articulation of rules about the use of texts and of conclusions that need to be drawn if intelligent reading is to continue.

In its Advaita interpretation, UMS I.1.2 identifies in a preliminary fashion what we mean when we use the word "Brahman" to indicate the object of the Advaita *jijñāsā* (UMS I.1.1). It confirms both the possibility of a discourse about Brahman and the location of this discourse only after and in dependence upon textual engagement. The sūtra is relatively clear:

> "Brahman" indicates that whence derive the origination, etc. of this world.

This designation *(lakṣaṇa)*[39] of "Brahman" as the source of the world is carefully interpreted in Advaita so as to discover and take advantage of an ambivalence regarding what can be said about Brahman, scripturally and reasonably. One wants to be able to speak meaningfully of "Brahman" and thus to know what one is talking about in reading the Text: to be able to read it coherently, yet without claiming a foreknowledge which would make the actual reading superfluous. As in the case of UMS III.3.11–13 and UMS I.1.5–11, the decision that when we speak of "Brahman" we mean the source of the world, is portrayed as a practical decision regarding the use of texts, and not as a deduction from their content or an allied appeal to a reasonable explanation of how the world came about.[40]

By itself the sūtra appears to describe Brahman in terms general enough to allow for inference, and opens the way to such reasoning. Śaṅkara accordingly declares that only Brahman, the Lord, can be an adequate source for the complex and varied world we observe around us:

> The universe as described cannot possibly be thought of as having its origin, etc. from anything other than the Lord who is possessed of the qualities already mentioned; [it cannot originate from] the non-conscious material source, or from atoms, or from non-existence, or from some human person; nor can it originate on its own, since in this world, things have causes specified according to space and time.[41]

But then, one might argue, if Brahman is in fact the cause of this observable world, one should be able to draw an inference from the world, the effect, regarding Brahman as cause: "Those who stand by God as cause rely on this very inference alone for establishing the existence etc. of God as distinguished from a transmigrating soul."[42] Śaṅkara rejects this inference, though he has no problem with its conclusion. He insists that there is a unique textual basis for saving knowledge; UMS I.1.2 does not mean that Brahman is a source that can be inferred; rather, it tells us that the word "Brahman" is designated to the useful name of what we learn from the upaniṣadic texts. In other words, the sūtra reinforces our dependence on the upaniṣads:

> The sūtras are meant for stringing together the flowers of the sentences of the upaniṣads; for it is precisely the sentences of the upaniṣads that are referred to in these sūtras. The realization of Brahman is accomplished on the basis of a firm conviction arising from deliberation on the texts and their meanings; it is not accomplished on the basis of other means of knowledge such as inference, etc.[43]

The commitment of Advaita is to textual knowledge of Brahman, and not merely to conclusions one might draw on the basis of texts, or in some other fashion. Reasoning, Śaṅkara adds, can help *after* one has learned of the source from the upaniṣads, but not before, because "Brahman's relation with anything cannot be grasped, since it is outside the range of sense-perception."[44] All inferences which argue from the effect to the cause are unreliable and inappropriate circumventions of the required engagement in the Text.

In place of an inference available to reason as the basis for sure knowledge, *Taittirīya Upaniṣad* 3.6, which decisively excludes alternative views about the source of the world and establishes that all comes from and returns to Brahman ("bliss"), is identified as the upaniṣadic text the sūtra has in mind: "From bliss certainly all these beings originate; they live by bliss after being born; and towards bliss they proceed, and into bliss they get merged." Inference is thus set firmly within the realm of textual expertise, where one learns first to recognize what texts mean and how to use them properly, and thereafter to extend one's knowledge of the upaniṣads by reasoning properly.

UMS I.1.2 previews the judgment about the upaniṣads made in UMS I.1.5–11 and lies in deliberate tension with it: we find Brahman spoken of in the upaniṣads; we know Brahman from the upaniṣads; the Brahman we know is the Brahman spoken of in the upaniṣads. Everything we need to know is in the upaniṣads—and the upaniṣads inform us truly and adequately about the real world in which we all live. It might seem plausible, then, to reverse the emphasis and argue that the upaniṣads confirm and legitimate what we can know by other means, particularly inference. The purpose of Śaṅkara's deliberately awkward reading of UMS I.1.2 is precisely to reserve to exegesis the advent of truth, foreclosing all competing avenues.[45]

The juxtaposition of textual definition and persistent incomprehensibility found in UMS I.1.2 enhances the importance of UMS I.1.5–11 as determinative of how the upaniṣads speak of Brahman, yet without overdetermining that expected knowledge. The ascertainment of the truth of *Taittirīya* 3, that Brahman is the world's source, does not make superfluous the rest of the upaniṣadic claims about Brahman, and does not give us a handy inference by which to replace the upaniṣads. Nevertheless, we do in the end know more than the words of the Text: we know the truth, we know Brahman. Accessible deep within the Text and only to the committed reader, it is still universally pertinent, the truth of their reality, available to all those who can and do learn to read properly.

4. UMS IV.3.14 and the Systematization of Advaita

Advaita articulates a truth which extends beyond its texts, a truth which is reasonable, world-encompassing, open to inquiry; yet this truth is firmly situated after textual knowledge, as available through an appropriation of the Text. As a final test of this thesis I call our attention to UMS IV.3.14 (and so to the entire adhikaraṇa, UMS IV.3.7–14), an important instance in the Text of an extended discussion of Brahman in its provisional (*apara*) and higher (*para*) forms. Deussen was perhaps the first modern scholar to emphasize this important discussion: "As regards the esoteric doctrine [of the higher (*para*) Brahman] . . . there is found at the end of his work a passage in which his consciousness of its inner necessary connections comes out as clearly as possible, and which [is] a compendium *in nuce* of Śaṅkara's Metaphysics . . ."[46] His translation of Śaṅkara's comment on UMS IV.3.14[47] divides it into six parts: i. an initial statement about the manner of liberation through knowledge of Brahman; ii. the esoteric cosmology; iii. the esoteric psychology; iv. the esoteric morality; v. the esoteric eschatology; vi. the esoteric theology.

His claim, that here at last we find a statement of Advaita doctrine in a positive form and not imbedded entirely within the "exoteric" truth of commentary, deserves serious consideration. But I suggest that as a systematization, UMS IV.3.14 is but one more instance of the effort to define as precisely as possible how texts lead us to Brahman, and to identify the rules governing this approach. The distinction between Brahman as provisional (*apara*) and as higher (*para*) is not in itself liberative knowledge nor is it liable to external scrutiny as to its truth. It is true in the Text, about the Text, wherein alone liberative knowledge resides; if we engage the Text properly, liberative, higher knowledge does then become possible.

Let us consider several aspects of the whole adhikaraṇa and sūtra 14 within it. Like UMS I.1.12–19, UMS IV.3.7–14 is an instance of Śaṅkara's decision to read the Text "against itself." The journey that the deceased takes after death is the topic of a discussion couched in terms of the statement, "The one who is not human takes them to Brahman;"[48] at issue is the identity of that "Brahman" which is the destination.

The adhikaraṇa reads most naturally if we take 7–11 as a pūrvapakṣa presented in the name of Bādari (7): his view is that the post-mortem journey of the soul can be only a movement toward the provisional Brahman. 12–14 then represent Jaimini's siddhānta (12): the destination of this journey is nothing but the higher Brahman itself.

Śaṅkara turns the argument around, to make Bādari's position the siddhānta: in a provisional form Brahman can be a destination, though one totally unrelated to realization in its higher form. The position of Jaimini, though given second, is the pūrvapakṣa, "presented [last] merely as an apparent, alternative view by way of helping the [student's] development of the power of intellect."[49]

This striking rereading sets the stage for Śaṅkara's lengthy exposition of UMS IV.3.14 as a lengthy defense of the Advaita version of the adhikaraṇa and a rebuttal of the proposal that Bādarāyaṇa is in fact supporting the view attributed to Jaimini. His comment is a rich and complex example of how attention to the (re)reading of texts is affected by positions based on (earlier) readings, and hence of how Brahman is to be rightly thought about and texts rightly read.

Śaṅkara says that Jaimini's view cannot be the siddhānta, on the grounds that "Brahman cannot logically be a goal to be attained. The higher Brahman which pervades everything, which is inside everything, which is the self of all . . . can never become a goal to be achieved."[50] Texts which portray movement toward Brahman must be understood as referring to the provisional Brahman, to which spatiality and locality still apply. Texts which deny distinction in Brahman must be given priority over those which indicate distinction, on the pragmatic grounds that it is only the former which lead to a knowledge lacking nothing: "when one has realized that the Self is one, eternal, pure, etc., one cannot want anything else, because of the plausibility that by this understanding one has thus accomplished the human goal."[51]

After expounding the nature of the self which can be liberated by knowledge,[52] Śaṅkara offers an instruction on the proper, limited and propaedeutic use of texts which seem to talk about Brahman as the destination of the post-mortem journey of the self,[53] and concludes with a summary statement about Brahman in its provisional and higher forms. He asks, "Are there then two Brahmans, one higher and the other provisional?" He offers this scripturally framed answer:

> Quite so; for we come across such texts as, "This very Brahman, Satyakama, higher and provisional, is [the sacred syllable] Om." (*Praśna Upaniṣad* 5.2) What then is the higher Brahman and what is the provisional Brahman? Where Brah-

> man is described by words such as "not material," etc. in order to reject those specifications such as name and form which are constructed on the basis of ignorance, there the higher Brahman is taught; where Brahman is specified by various specifications such as name, forms, etc . . . there the provisional Brahman is being taught for the sake of meditation.[54]

Even this determination of the meaning of "Brahman" does not excuse the reader from returning to the Text; it is a reminder of the previously enunciated principle[55] that different texts have different purposes and must be used accordingly. Though the tendency toward a systematization of the knowledge of Brahman becomes most evident here, in which the tension between a permanent engagement in reading and a conclusive gleaning of the results of reading is resolved in favor of the latter, the complete accomplishment of this tendency is nevertheless not found in the Text. As will become clear in Chapter 4, the final resolution of the tension between the Text and its truth, between reading and the products of reading, cannot be expressed as the content of a text; the truth remains a well-guarded and exhaustingly prepared-for event which can occur only in the practiced, educated reader. The "system" of Advaita is a well-planned event, not a theory.

Before turning to that topic of the reader, however, one important aspect of Advaita's truth remains to be explored. Advaita invests great energy in the task of locating its position on Brahman within a larger textual and general intellectual framework which takes into account the claims of outsiders. This defense is an aspect of Advaita's practical, communicative truth, and it requires our attention.

IV. Defending Brahman: The Fragmentation of the Other in the Text

Profoundly exegetical and pedagogical, Advaita doctrine is also a (re)description of the world. It occurs throughout the Text, and its force accumulates in a series of individual defenses against competing views of the world. The exegetical issues addressed in each adhikaraṇa cumulatively imply a fuller Advaita narrative of the world.

Thus, for example, the following specific arguments all contribute to the overall defense of the Advaita narrative as it moves through "local" arguments toward a complete accounting for its world: the debate with Mīmāṃsā opponents in UMS I.1.4 over the necessity of ritual action; the exposition and defense of the preexistence of effects in their cause in UMS II.1.14; the issue of theodicy in UMS II.1.34–36 and in UMS III.2.37–41; the partial defense and then rebuttal of the notion of agency in UMS II.3.41–42. Inevitably, these claims imply something about competing worldviews—not by stepping outside Advaita's Textual framework, but because their articulation includes the inscription of those competitors within the scripturally ordered and exegetically regulated worldview that Advaita develops.

Two texts are particularly helpful in showing us the characteristic Advaita way of anticipating objections and defending itself against competing worldviews. First, UMS II.1.1–11 defends Advaita's explanation of the world as derived from Brahman by showing it to be "less unreasonable" than the competing Sāṃkhya view. Second, within UMS II.2, the pāda in which various competing positions are organized, inscribed and described as deficient within an Advaita narrative of the world, UMS II.2.1–10 illustrates how even "argumentation by reason alone" occurs only within an upaniṣadic framework. Let us now consider each in turn.

1. UMS II.1.4–11: The Relative Reasonableness of the Advaita Position[56]

In UMS II.1 and II.2 Advaita defends the view that Brahman is both the material and efficient cause of the world. The goal of UMS II.1 is to show that though derived solely from the upaniṣads, this position is consonant with tradition (UMS II.1.1–3) and reason (UMS II.1.4–11). UMS II.1 does not attempt to reproduce the scripturally achieved results by reason alone, but only to show the conformity of right reasoning, exercised by a right person, to the right reading of the upaniṣads. As such, it has a specific function to perform in the overall "plot" of the

Text: to confirm the Advaita interpretation of the upaniṣads, to reassure the Advaita community of the truth of its reading.

There is really no chance that the system will turn out to be in conflict with correct reasoning: the Advaitin is both judge and jury, and the other systems, paraphrased and rarely quoted, are allowed to speak only within the norms of Advaita's predetermined conversation. Exegesis and reasoning had been exercised together in Advaita long before the completion of UMS II.1, as a finished narration, made the relation of Brahman to the world an explicit topic of controversy; Advaita exegesis had from the start been informed by correct reasoning, and Advaita reasoning has been educated by exegesis. However useful and important the demonstration which occupies UMS II.1, it will bear no unexpected results; it is not an exercise of independent reasoning.

As in UMS I.1.5–11, Sāṃkhya provides the pūrvapakṣa in UMS II.1.4–11. According to UMS II.1.4–5, Sāṃkhya introduces two arguments. First, reason has a legitimate role to play in delineating the objective reality Advaita claims to point to. Therefore, the Advaita position, like any other, should be submitted to rational critique. Second, that critique will show that the Advaita position fails the test of reason, since one cannot plausibly argue that Brahman, characterized by the Advaitins as intelligent and pure, is the material as well as efficient cause for a world which is demonstrably neither intelligent nor pure.

In UMS II.1.11 Śaṅkara agrees with the proposition that reasoning is legitimate, inevitable and necessary for life, and that it is at work even during the practice of exegesis. But he also claims that unless it is the reasoning of the scripturally literate person, it cannot provide an adequate view of reality as a whole; indeed, it is most inadequate on the topics of the most importance—the knowledge of Brahman, and what counts toward salvation.[57]

Independent reason is inherently inadequate for several reasons. First of all, Brahman is not an ordinary object of knowledge:

> As for the argument that because Brahman is an existent thing, other means of knowledge should apply to it, that too is wishful thinking. For this entity is not an object of

> perception, since it is devoid of form, etc. And it is not subject to inference, since it is devoid of all grounds of inference, etc. But like the religious acts (producing virtue), this entity is known from the scriptures alone . . . Mere empty logic cannot find any scope here; only logic conformed to the upaniṣads is resorted to here as a subsidiary means of realization. (UMS II.1.6)[58]

Second, the reasoning of the uneducated person is notoriously unreliable:

> One should not on the strength of reasoning alone challenge something that must be known from the scriptures. Reasoning that has no scriptural foundation and springs from the mere musings of the human mind lacks conclusiveness; for such musings are uncontrolled. Thus we see that an argument discovered with great effort by experts is falsified by other experts; and an argument hit upon by the latter is proved to be hollow by still others. So nobody can rely on argument as conclusive, since the human mind is so variable in its ways. (UMS II.1.11)[59]

Third, we all know that "reasonable argumentation" never lead to a definitively right viewpoint:

> . . . Although reasoning may be noticed to have foundations regarding some topics, in the present context it cannot possibly be immune to the charge of inconclusiveness; for this extremely sublime subject-matter, concerned with the true nature of being, the basis of liberation, cannot even be guessed at without the help of the scriptures . . . (UMS II.1.11)[60]

Brahman is an objective extra- and posttextual reality; legitimate, upaniṣadic statements about Brahman do not contradict properly exercised reason. But Brahman is beyond reason's grasp in the sense that it places before reason truths it cannot combine into a single, overarching explanation; reason may recognize various points correctly, but never reaches a vantage point from which to envision the whole. The purpose of argument is to show that there are no reasonable grounds for seeking an explanation of the whole other than that indicated by the upaniṣads.

This moderate and restrained estimation of reason is at the heart of Śaṅkara's response to the Sāṃkhyan charge that Brahman as portrayed by Advaita cannot be the cause of the perceptible world. He argues that it is not inconsistent to say that Brahman is the cause of the world, even if Brahman and the world differ in many evident ways; causes and effects frequently differ in important respects, and it would be pointless to speak of cause and effect were the two alike in every respect. The fact that material reality is not conscious and is imperfect does not prove that it has a non-conscious, imperfect cause. In any case, there is at least one important continuity: the world does exist, and every element of it shares at least the fact of existence with Brahman. (UMS II.1.6)[61]

Here, and throughout the rest of UMS II.1,[62] the Advaita strategy is to demonstrate that its viewpoint does not contradict reason on any given issue, but also that reason never achieves a broader systematization according to which everything the upaniṣads say can be organized reasonably. It is here that the superiority of the upaniṣads is shown: only to it, in all its textuality and indirection, can one attribute an adequate, practical narration of what the world is really like.

UMS II.1 thus helps its readers to mediate the tension between the world which reason constructs on the basis of what it can understand, and the always more complete worldview expounded by scripture. There is never a place from which to examine reason's and scripture's claims impartially; one does not decide eventually, at some point, that scripture is more reasonable than reason. Only after one submits to scripture and is imbued with its way of constructing the world can one think properly about the possible, limited and never entirely systematic contributions of reason exercised without reference to scripture.

2. *Arguing the Advaita Position: UMS II.2.1–10*

a. The Structure of UMS II.2

Before considering our second example, II.2.1–10, let us view the general project of II.2. The agenda of UMS II.1 was to demonstrate that every vexed issue (cause and effect, the agency of the self, the problem of evil) could be analyzed rationally, and that the Advaita position would in each case be shown to be the most adequate, not surpassed by any other. Neither the upaniṣads nor a close scrutiny of Advaita positions lead to the conclusion that Advaita is inadequate; the only comprehensive system is that inscribed in the Advaita Text as the combination of the upaniṣads and their right reading in the tradition.

The positive argument for Advaita's plausibility in UMS II.1 is balanced in UMS II.2 by a presentation of the implausibility of selected opposing views. The goal of UMS II.2 is to show that competing worldviews cannot stand rational scrutiny, but also thereby to educate the Advaitin in the "refutability" of opponents and so to strengthen his confidence in the truth of Advaita—but without shifting the analysis to a forum where reason would be the primary standard.

The pāda is particularly interesting because of the claim that in it the argument against adversary positions proceeds by reason alone: now, says Śaṅkara, there follows "a refutation of their reasoning independently of the texts; we are going to refute their arguments in an independent manner, without any reference to the upaniṣads."[63] On this basis, one might expect that members of the identified adversarial schools could conceivably be persuaded by straightforward and convincing Advaita reasoning.

But not only are such conversions rare, they are not the goal of UMS II.2. We do not have here a "real-life debate" in which we can hear Advaita debating its opponents, or by which we can enter Advaita through the shortcut of reasoning, but only a carefully scripted series of Advaita adhikaraṇas that fit the Text's already established overall narrative.

I begin with an overview of the succession of the pāda's adhikaraṇas, as counterpositions are named and described by the Advaitins.[64] It divides into two groupings of positions. First, there are positions which reduce the conscious to the nonconscious, or vice versa:

1–10 Sāṃkhya: the material source (pradhāna), composed of the three components (guṇas,) is the nonconscious cause of the world;

11–17 Vaiśeṣika: the atomic basis of reality

18–27 Sarvāstivāda Buddhism: aggregates of momentarily composed objects;

28–31 Vijñānavāda Buddhism: the construction of non-conscious reality by consciousness alone;[65]

31 Śūnyavāda Buddhism: the total denial of nonconscious reality;[66]

Second, there are positions which subordinate the non-conscious to the conscious, but without denying the role of the former:

33–36 Jainism: the status of the nonconscious dependent on consciousness, in all of its diverse positionings;

37–41 Maheśvara Śaivism: a conscious lord who is the efficient cause, but not substantial cause, of the world;[67]

42–45 Pāñcarātra Vaiṣṇavism: a lord who both efficient and substantial cause, but only in a series of differentiated forms.

Third, overshadowing the pāda though not restated in it, is Advaita, according to which Brahman alone, in its utter simplicity, is the efficient and substantial cause of the universe.

Let us summarize the apparent rationale for this line-up, while readily conceding that the represented schools might well have other views of the issues involved or of how to present themselves. In the first series, the movement is from "materialism," exemplified by the gross nonconscious principle of the Sāṃkhya, in which the appearance of consciousness in the world is explained as a derivative of matter, to "spiritualism," the gross intellectualism of the Śūnyavāda in which nonconsciousness is entirely explained away; in between lie Vaiśeṣika atomism and the forms of Buddhism which allow for momentary forms of material nonconsciousness. Despite their differences, these positions have in common their failure to present a true causal relationship between the conscious and the nonconscious, as one or the other is explained away simply as a version of the other. Either the material or the spiritual gets lost.

In the second series, the unexpected juxtaposition of the Jainas (33–36), Śaivas (37–41) and Pāñcarātra Vaiṣṇavas (42–45) can be explained as the portrayal in series of three increasingly successful efforts to explain how the nonconscious is caused by the conscious. In the Jaina position, matter is dependent upon the Jaina dialectic of many-sidedness (*syādvāda*) and takes multiple forms in dependence on that dialectic; in Śaivism, there is a conscious lord who is the efficient but not substantial cause of the world; in Pāñcarātra, there is a conscious lord who is both the efficient and the substantial cause of the world, though the latter only in a series of evolved forms. All three are superior to the preceding Sāṃkhya, Vaiśeṣika and Buddhist positions, because they recognize the real dependence of a real world on a real conscious principle. Only in Advaita, however, is the pure and simple causality of Brahman as pure consciousness adequately recognized.

The two series of errors which comprise UMS II.2 therefore constitute a topography of error, from its larger to its more subtle and less egregious forms. The systems have been scripted so as to play their parts in the drama of the Advaita Text, as foils to the truth Advaita finds in the upaniṣads. Though the arguments against each are declared to proceed without reference to the upaniṣads, the presentation from the start surrounds the adversaries with the presuppositions and conclusions of Advaita's scripturally based thinking.[68] The Advaitins take into account all their competitors' views, writing them up so as to confirm the view of an already convinced Advaita audience that there really is no other way to see the world than Advaita's way.[69] Although a simple analysis of the correctness of the Advaita reading of the upaniṣads might suffice for a narration of Advaita's truth, censure of conflicting views must also be considered a legitimate addition to that narrative, added to confirm the Advaitin's faith in Advaita. Liberation depends on knowledge of the real, and efforts must be made to make sure that seekers are not misled by superficially pleasing positions. UMS II.2 thus serves an intracommunity, pedagogical purpose; it is neither a report of actual arguments with opposing schools, nor is it primarily a manual for use in argument with those schools. Its accounts reveal both a commitment to a true and efficacious knowledge—such as endures no contradictions—and the recognition that this account, including its disposal of contradictory views, affirms the faith of those who are already Advaitins. UMS II.2 suggests that its apologetics are intended to confirm a truth already acquired, not to persuade or convert outsiders—even if the stray outsider might convert on the basis of UMS II.2. One does not find in UMS II.2 the point of encounter between Advaita and the world outside its Text, but rather a further step in the inscription of that world into the Text.[70]

b. The Refutation of Sāṃkhya in UMS II.2.1–10 and the Scriptural Reasoning of Advaita

The encompassment of reason and its arguments by upaniṣadic faith in the course of the refutation of Sāṃkhya in UMS II.2.1–10 illustrates concisely the general project of UMS II.2; the adhikaraṇa amply illustrates that the debates with "outsiders" occur entirely according to the premises of the "insiders'" position, and do not indicate a qualitatively different, less upaniṣadic moment within the Text.

The general critique of the Sāṃkhyan material source (*pradhāna*) proceeds along the lines we have already seen in UMS I.1.5–11, where the material source is shown to be inconsistent with the data of the upaniṣads, and UMS II.1.1–11, where it is shown to have no advantages over the scripturally confirmed Advaita viewpoint. Here the inquiry advances by moving from the question of the cause-effect inference to the question of the claims required for the possibility of purposeful activity.

The attack is thorough: i. the unconscious is never seen to transform itself, especially in the highly complex fashion which would be required to account for the world, except if guided by some conscious agent (UMS II.2.1–2);[71] ii. natural processes must depend on some intelligently perceived finality (UMS II.2.3,5); iii. the material source and its three constituents (guṇas) either never begin to interact, or never cease to interact (UMS II.2.4,6–

9), since no freely acting intelligence is involved; iv. the categories of the Sāṃkhyan analysis are arbitrary, variable and never quite clear. (UMS II.2.10)

Though the distinguishing feature of this series of arguments against Sāṃkhya is supposed to be that the refutation proceeds independently of texts, in fact the declaration of reliance on reason alone marks no real divergence from the general pattern of Advaita's narrative, in which the virtues of Advaita and its "others" are considered only as they are inscribed within a scripturally constituted horizon.

There are five main points at which the argument "based on reason alone" is thoroughly informed by the upaniṣads.

First, when the pūrvapakṣin argues that Advaita's Self, supposed to be pure and unchanging consciousness, cannot be expected to cause action, the siddhāntin responds as follows:

> On the analogy of the magnet and form, etc., something bereft of any tendency to act can still impart this to others. For instance, a magnet, though possessing no tendency to act by itself, still induces that tendency in iron. Objects of perception like form, etc., which by themselves have no tendency to act, still impart this tendency to the eye, etc. Similarly, it is but logical that the Lord, who is all-pervasive, the Self of all, omniscient, and omnipotent, should be the impeller of all even though He is Himself free from any tendency to act. (UMS II.2.2)[72]

The Lord mentioned here is of course the Lord who can be known adequately only from the upaniṣads.

Second, the upaniṣads show that all action has God for its source; this position is more logical than the attempt to attribute the stimulation of action to the nonconscious. For instance, the illustration of milk flowing spontaneously from the mother, without conscious direction, was cited previously[73] only "from an everyday point of view, to show that action can take place in a thing itself without the aid of any external means. But from the upaniṣadic point of view, it is known that all acts take place under God's bidding." (UMS II.2.3) In other words, the actual state of things—as opposed to what merely seems to make sense on the basis of extrapolation from a common sense view of the world—is known from the upaniṣads; extraneous appeals to instances, such as the generation and flow of mother's milk, are ultimately judged to be unconvincing.

Third, it is impossible to understand how a material source either starts or stops moving—what is there to prompt such changes? But "since the Lord has omniscience, omnipotence, and marvellous power (*māyā*), his engagement in or disengagement from activity presents no contradiction." (UMS II.2.4) Of course, this hypothesis of divine power (māyā) is a hypothesis prompted by the upaniṣads, not the achievement of reason working alone.

Fourth, and similarly, a purely material source cannot work like the magnet mentioned in UMS II.2.2—unmoving but causing movement—since its nonconsciousness and lack of intention would mean that its activity would either never start or never stop; "in the case of the supreme self," by contrast, "there is the greater advantage that it is inactive from its own point of view, but is a driving urge, from the standpoint of divine power (māyā)." (UMS II.2.7) Again, the rejection of the Sāṃkhyan hypothesis is based on a position, the māyā thesis, which ultimately has upaniṣadic roots.

Fifth, the Sāṃkhyans vainly attempt to use the theory of a purely material source to sort out the set of impossible relationships they have entangled themselves in:

> This thesis of the Sāṃkhyas is self-contradictory. For sometimes they enumerate seven organs and sometimes eleven; similarly sometimes they teach about the origin of the subtle elements from the great one [*mahat*], and sometimes from the ego; so also sometimes they mention three internal organs, and sometimes one. (UMS II.2.10)[74]

The construction of explanations is not a problem for Advaita, since the Advaitins do not claim to offer an alternative theory that is compelling solely on rational grounds. Advaita exegesis has established that all is one; the troubling elements and relationships simply do not exist. The Sāṃkhyan efforts at explanation can be rejected without having to present totally convincing alternatives, since their doctrines contradict the upaniṣads. But "from the upaniṣadic point of view, one cannot even dream that there is no liberation, because here [in the Advaitic reading of the upaniṣads] it is known certainly that the self is one, that the one cannot be both subject and object, and that all the different modifications are mentioned in the upaniṣads to be based on mere speech." (UMS II.2.10)[75]

Such argumentation is a reasonable discourse voiced by and for those who are educated in the upaniṣads, and it may impress the believer, as it is intended to do; but others, who are not the intended readers of the Text, will surely find this appeal to the upaniṣads not quite a demonstration based on reason alone. They may come to accept it, but only if they first submit themselves to the upaniṣads—as these are properly read in Advaita. Reason is not decisive.

Reasonable argumentation occurs in Advaita, and outsiders to the Advaita tradition need not abandon the prospect of reasonable inquiry; but this reasoning occurs only deep within the UMS Text, deep within Advaita's textual progress toward a right understanding of the world as a soteriologically attuned whole. In UMS II.2 one learns more about Advaita's informed reasoning, not about reason itself, nor about which of the described positions might turn out to be correct on the basis of rational scrutiny alone. To excerpt UMS II.2 (or any part of it) for separate consideration may be a tempting shortcut into Advaita, but it is an ultimately misleading exercise that fails to enlighten.

V. Truth, Text and Reader

In the preceding pages I have described several basic methods by which Advaita articulates its real truth claims: i. the double discourse about Brahman with qualities and without qualities, and the intrusive and paradoxical great sayings, as two strategies by which the reader is forced constantly to reread the Text, and so realize a truth that cannot be stated, even in the Text; ii. the permanently exegetical genealogy of doctrine of Brahman; iii. the accompanying decomposition of competing positions through a Textual narration of them. Advaita strives mightily and succeeds, I suggest, in narrowing to certain, specific textual avenues the way of access to its truth, while yet announcing that truth vigorously. In defending its positions, Advaita precludes access to these positions from any neutral position that might appear independent of the claims of the Vedic world on those who would investigate it. The truth is available, yet only within the confines of a demanding Text and consequent upon engagement in it.

When the Advaitin writes that Brahman is devoid of qualities, that the identity of the human person is Brahman, and that these claims are those which are most consonant with the way the world really is, these are indeed claims which, though not easily accessible to all, cannot be dismissed as merely local, merely textual strategies. But they are articulated in and from sacred texts as understood by a believing community; those who have access to these texts have access to a truth which comes to the fore after the Text but not apart from it. Though not open to immediate judgment because they bear with them an elaborate set of rules about their reception and use, neither can they be taken as elusive or as so imbedded in detail that judgment becomes impossible; the claims are true, and the right persons, rightly educated, will be able to judge them so. "Outsiders" are such because of various obstacles between them and the Text; they remain prone to read it the wrong way, and so to think incorrectly.

Almost all contemporary readers are, of course, outsiders. Yet it is precisely here, on the margins of the Text, and not in speculation about the rational claims of Advaita or in a search for the experience to which it points, that a point of access appears. Though demanding, the Text is a teacher. It instructs the interested inquirer in the skills of approach to Brahman; it encourages the reader's engagement in it, and if properly learned, it guides the reader to a truth which can be cognized after it. The more we read, the more we become insiders. The truth of Advaita is as near as the Text itself.

As near as the Text itself—i.e., in the approved school, in the approved teacher's mouth, received by the approved student born into an approved family; Advaita may seem, after all, to keep its Text securely, hopelessly at a distance. The promise of access to the truth of Advaita through its Text may be prematurely offered, for thus far we have taken for granted that accessibility is either easily granted, or limited only by the demands of literacy. We have not yet examined the interior and exterior limitations imposed by Advaita on those who would seek access. The remaining question, after those of the Text and its truth, pertains to the reader of the Text, the realizer of the truth. This is the subject matter of Chapter 4.

VI. A Concluding Note on Advaita and Intertextual Truth

Advaita's truth as presented in the preceding pages needs to be considered carefully, in a way that does not reduce its truth to a "mere'" understanding of texts. Earlier references to Riffaterre's "fictional truth" have already indicated a way to think about a truth that is constitutively a truth of and in texts. Before concluding this chapter I offer a complementary indication of how religious truth, as a community's doctrine, can be understood consonantly with the exegetical and practical emphases enunciated here.

To do this, I appeal to the work of a modern Christian theologian. In his *The Nature of Doctrine*,[76] George Lindbeck identifies three types of theories of religion and doctrine: an "experiential-expressive model," which holds that religions have a common core experience which is expressed differently by different religions,[77] a "cognitive-propositional model," which "emphasizes the cognitive aspects of religion and stresses the ways in which church doctrines function as informative propositions or truth claims about objective realities,"[78] a "cultural-linguistic model," the topic of the book, according to which "a religion can be viewed as a kind of cultural and/or linguistic framework or medium that shapes the entirety of life and thought . . . it is similar to an idiom that makes possible the description of realities, the formulation of beliefs, and the experiencing of inner attitudes, feelings and sentiments. Like a culture or language, it is a communal phenomenon that shapes the subjectivity of individuals rather than being primarily a manifestation of those subjectivities."[79] Advaita's Text-truth-world relation conforms to this third model in which propositions and experiences, though not excluded, are subordinate to the exigencies of a formative Text.

Lindbeck develops his third model at length, with important and helpful observations on how theological language works, how one acquires skill in it, and how communities articulate a world "out of" their sacred texts.[80] Here I introduce only his observations on truth. In an "excursus on religion and truth" Lindbeck addresses the problem of the categorial truth of religious claims, such as go beyond the demonstration of the coherence of those claims for the sake of believers, to claims about the world as such.[81] Thus, Christian believers "assert that it is propositionally true that Christ is Lord: i.e., the particular individual of which the stories are told is, was, and will be definitively and unsurpassably the Lord."[82]

Lindbeck makes several points that are pertinent to our understanding of the Advaita model of truth and of the way in which outsiders actually encounter this truth. First, he distinguishes "intrasystemic truth" from the "ontological truth" of statements: "The first is the truth of coherence; the second, that truth of correspondence to reality which, according to epistemological realists, is attributable to first-order propositions."[83] Regarding the former, he observes that the expected coherence of the system includes not just "axioms, definitions, and corollaries," but also "a set of stories used in specifiable ways to interpret and live in the world . . . a religious system is more like a natural language than a formally organized set of explicit statements . . . the right use of this language, unlike a mathematical one, cannot be detached from a particular way of behaving."[84]

The latter kind of truth includes ontological correspondence and reference to the "real." Here, though coherence is necessary, it is not a sufficient basis for religious truth. The ontological truth of religious utterances is linked to a way of life, since that truth "is not an attribute that they have when considered in and of themselves, but is only a function of their role in constituting a form of life, a way of being in the world . . . a religious utterance, one might say, acquires the propositional truth of ontological correspondence only insofar as it is a performance, an act or deed, which helps create that correspondence."[85] Reference is a practice, a construction, not an innate or merely available correspondence.

Recalling Aquinas' insistence that "although in statements about God the human mode of signifying (*modus significandi*) does not correspond to anything in the divine being, the signified (*significatum*) does," Lindbeck observes that when, "for example, when we say that God is good, we do not affirm that any of our concepts of goodness (*modi significandi*) apply to him, but rather that there is a concept of goodness unavailable to us, viz., God's understanding of his own goodness, which does apply."[86] Our statements about God do not express directly what God is; rather, they shape the way in which believers are to think and then to act, for the narrative about God implies a narrative about human beings too.

He then discusses the skill required for one to understand and speak this analogous, propositional-performative language about God. He argues that an affirmation or denial of the religious truths requires familiarity with the implied way of life, that one become the kind of person who can recognize what is true: "one must be, so to speak, inside the relevant context; and in the case of a religion, this means that one must have some skill in *how* to use its language and practice its way of life before the propositional meaning of its affirmations becomes determinate enough to be rejected."[87]

Despite Advaita's awareness of the limitations of language and its concern for experience, it insists on the mediation of the knowledge of Brahman through textual knowledge, and so engages the Advaitin in acts of skillful reading. At the same time, and not contrary to this emphasis on language, it formalizes its positions as propositional claims intended to refer to realities outside the Text.[88] Lindbeck's model helps us to understand why it is important and useful that truth claims are thus situated in language, and why this situation need not be a reduction of truth to textual meaning(s). His emphasis on how doctrines begin in scriptures which create the world in which the community lives, and then help to formulate real-life behavior, illuminates the way in which Advaita discovers and makes use of the truth of its positions.[89]

Chapter **4**

Advaita Vedānta and Its Readers

I. The Tension between the Text and Its Truth

In Chapter 2 I attended to the constitution of Advaita as a Text comprised of upaniṣads, sūtras and their continuing fruition in commentaries, a Text (formidably) accessible to us in the broad and rich variety of its textures; in Chapter 3, I traced the careful, cautious, but gradually decisive and effective enunciation of a post- and extratextual truth that is not only a right understanding of the upaniṣads and of the world, but also a right enunciation of an event of realization that is always more and yet also simpler than the words in which it occurs, and I resisted the implication that Advaita is exclusively textual knowledge, or merely "words about words about words." Together, these chapters sharpened the paradox of Advaita: there is an evident, universally available truth which commands assent, but it is available only under certain pedagogically prescribed circumstances, after the Text is read, mastered, accomplished. The "outside" of the Text as truth—its reference, its universalizable meaning—is nevertheless located "after" it, discovered when reading is properly undertaken and when the Text's inscribed truth is carefully and patiently articulated without the breaking of those threads of contextualization by which it remains permanently a Textual truth.

Though it demands to be read, the Advaita Text never makes the truth merely present to the reader, for mere presence would make it possible to consume that truth, or to excise it from its contexts, reducing it to one more thing a reader may care, or not care, to know; it would also undercut the Advaita teaching on the ineffability of Brahman and the Text which is supposed to be the vehicle of the communication of Brahman.

If the truth is posterior to the Text, achieved after and through it, then the Text must be seen both as a place where the expenditure of time and energy is likely to be fruitful, and as a place which yields fruit only to the person willing to invest in it, reading skillfully toward a moment of accomplishment, realization. Anyone can approach the truth, but almost no one will make, or be able to make, the effort required for that approach: that there actually is a truth to Advaita becomes evident only in the event that there in fact happen to be authorized and accomplished readers. In this chapter I turn my attention to this required reader of the Text, the Advaitin as student *(jijñāsin, Uttara Mīmāṃsaka).*

Though signalling in advance that privileged moment when insightful reading is finally accomplished by the reader, the tension between truth and Text also has a more immediate, practical expression: its features are delineated in the requirement of competence (*adhikāra*), inscribed by Advaita into its Text as the measure for the training of proper ones and as the barrier against improper readers and improperly trained ones. As Vedānta philosophy, Advaita insists upon a universal and unrestricted knowledge available to all knowers. As Uttara Mīmāṃsā, it links the accomplishment of this knowledge to the act of the competent knower who achieves knowledge in discriminate reading.

Great importance is invested in identifying that reader, who is inscribed within a set of intellectual and social expectations that deliberately exclude most potential readers. Only the right kind of people can benefit from Advaita; such people are marked off by the Text which, by its demands regarding competence—its self-regulating prescriptions, its difficulty—ensures that the "Advaita event," pure realization, can occur authentically and without any constraints whatsoever. Though Advaita on occasion presents itself as Vedānta, thoroughly and nonideologically available in self-knowledge, it is always also Mīmāṃsā, available only to a privileged group of educated upper-caste men:

the elitism of Advaita which often discomforts the modern student is essential to it as the practical discipline which it fundamentally is.

In the following pages I explore the extension of the tension between truth and Text to the description of the reader and the manner of proper reading. First, in section II, I show that the accomplishment of Advaita's simple nondual goal occurs only within the dispersed and temporal realm of reading, and that the accomplishment of perfectly skilled reading and the accomplishment of Advaita knowledge are both skill in discernment (*viveka*), the perfectly discriminating "reading" of self and world. The subtle mastery of the Text by its reader occurs simultaneously with the accomplishment, the event, of its truth. Second, in section III, I explore the desire to know Brahman (*brahmajijñāsā*) as a free, unqualified and unpredictable event which nevertheless always implies the intention to learn to read in a skilled, prepared fashion. I show too how this specification of knowledge and its originatory desire cooperate to narrow the set of competent readers of the Text, particularly through the strictures of caste, and so predetermine the set of those competent to achieve Textual knowledge. Finally, in section IV, I indicate how this determination of the reader serves also as a prescription of the progress and destiny of the person who moves toward release and achieves it. The expected reader does become the indescribable, perfect, liberated person—but only within the boundaries of definite expectations: indescribability must occur in just the right way. Section V concludes the chapter with reflections on the consequences of the preceding findings for the comparativist.

II. Timeless Truth, Timely Reading: The Truth in Reading

1. The Simplicity and Temporal Complexity of Liberative Knowledge[1]

Advaita expectations about the reader of the Text must be studied in light of its analysis of the process of reading and understanding texts as a gradual and temporal process which nevertheless yields a knowledge of a Brahman which is perfectly simple and beyond time. I sketch this process by noting the Advaita analysis of *Bṛhadāraṇyaka Upaniṣad* 2.4.5, a text which the Vedantins of various schools use to explore the tensions between knowledge and text:[2]

> The self, dear, must be seen, must be heard, must be understood, must be meditated on, Maitreyi. By seeing and hearing the self, dear, one understands; by this knowledge, all this is known.

The text marks, and seems to enjoin, moments in a process that (apparently)[3] begins in seeing (*darśana*) and culminates in true vision (*darśana*): seeing, hearing, understanding, meditating, vision.

The manner in which knowledge of Brahman can be said to arise textually is the core question the passage occasions for the Advaitins. Once they admit, as they readily do, that texts neither contain nor constitute that which they communicate—even upaniṣadic words are not the reality they articulate[4]—the Advaitins are required to explain how knowledge of Brahman, which is perfectly simple, beyond qualification and time, can be acquired through a gradual mastery of texts over a period of time. In the very long adhikaraṇa composed under UMS I.1.4,[5] the question of whether knowledge can be enjoined, as ritual is—it cannot, from the Advaita viewpoint—leads to the question of what is actually enjoined when one hears an injunction such as, "Know this."

The pūrvapakṣin argues that texts such as *Bṛhadāraṇyaka* 2.4.5 clearly indicate that knowledge of Brahman is enjoined—it *must* be heard, understood, meditated on—just as ritual is enjoined according to the Mīmāṃsā tradition. The siddhāntin responds that knowledge of Brahman cannot be enjoined. Why? because knowledge is never an activity:

> Since [when an object is known, the knowledge of it] is determined by a thing coming within the range of perception, it is surely knowledge and not action. Thus also it is to be understood in the case of all objects coming within the range of the valid means of knowledge.

Knowledge of Brahman is no exception:

> That being so, knowledge of the true relationship between Brahman and the self is not subject to injunction. Though verbs in the imperative mood etc. are seen to be used with regard to this knowledge, they are dulled, like a razor striking against a stone, for they are aimed at something which cannot be the object of compulsion; for knowledge has as its object something that exists, not something to be done or avoided.[6]

Apparent injunctions, such as "must be seen," etc., serve another and auxiliary purpose: they bring to an end various preoccupations, and turn the Advaitin away from the world, toward the inner self.[7] They prepare the way for knowledge of Brahman, contributing to the construction of the environment in which knowledge can occur—an environment which is comprised essentially of the prepared, competent reader.

The steps of knowledge can be enjoined insofar as they are the exterior activities related to knowledge; but the knowledge that occurs is not the guaranteed result of those activities, even if they are well performed. By its nature, knowledge eludes reduction to the predictable availability of either repeatable statements or imitable actions; at no stage can it be enjoined, since at the very moment that injunction becomes possible—when the object is clear and the activity definable—that clarity and definition make the enjoined activity superfluous. Knowledge is always an event, occurring only as the increasingly clearer apprehension of the intended object at each stage in the assimilation and clarification of what is initially perceived, heard or read.

Nonetheless, it cannot be practically disassociated from those accompanying steps. Advaita's refusal to characterize knowledge of Brahman as an activity which can be carried out is not a wholesale denial of the component activities which normally precede knowledge; rather, it is a nuanced distinction between knowing and its ordinary context, a precise apprehension of the implications of what we mean when we say that we have come to know something.[8] The position thus relies on these nuances as to how knowledge occurs purely and simply while yet occurring within various adequate environments; it skillfully balances the considerable activities of learning, including those of reading, with an irreducibly simple moment of realization. But, as we shall see below, what is characteristic of Advaita is not these nuances—which may be inevitable in any analysis which attends to the practicalities of how knowledge comes about—but rather its utilization of them in order to balance an insistent identification of the knowledge of Brahman as absolutely simple with a highly specific set of expectations about how one goes about knowing, and who the skilled knower is.

UMS IV.1.1–2 addresses again the tension between the purely cognitive understanding of knowledge and the practical, textual location of knowledge, and this time the focus is even more specifically on texts. The pūrvapakṣin argues that if texts are of any salvific use at all, they will immediately, upon first reading, tell us what Brahman is, and will therefore immediately have their liberative effect—if they are ever going to have it. If they are not immediately effective, no amount of repetition will bring about this proper understanding and effect.

Śaṅkara's two versions of the siddhānta[9] show how texts which enjoin meditation presuppose progress from an initial introduction to a text through a potentially prolonged process of meditation, to a final, true knowledge. In general, "repetition may be resorted to even where the instruction occurs only once; a repeated instruction indicates repetition as a matter of course." (UMS IV.1.2)[10] In regard to the problematic issue of the relation between texts and the knowledge of a Brahman which is neither temporal nor extended in "moments" of knowledge, the siddhāntin observes that it is a simple fact known from ordinary experience that one moves from an incomplete and vague knowledge to an increasingly precise knowledge; this requires no special justification: "It may also be argued that reasoning and [attention to a] text can [on a first effort] only produce a knowledge of the general features of the object, but not so of its special features . . . Since the latter more intimate knowledge is what removes ignorance, repetition serves that purpose." (UMS IV.1.2)[11]

While texts are unchanging—in the sense that their words are fixed—repeated meditative readings gradually change the reader's understanding of these words: "It is a matter of experience that though the meaning may be vaguely apprehended from a sentence uttered only once, people understand it fully as they progressively remove the false ideas standing in the way." (UMS IV.1.2)[12] If one already has clear knowledge of Brahman and of one's self, repeated readings meant to contribute to the acquisition of that knowledge are obviously unnecessary; but if one lacks that knowledge, rereading brings one gradually to it: "one false constituent may be discarded by one attempt at comprehension, and another by another. In this sense understanding is gradual." (UMS IV.1.2)[13]

Vācaspati elucidates the process of learning that comes about due to diligent, repeated reading: "It is true that the immediate manifestation of Brahman is not the immediate fruit of scripture and reasoning; nevertheless only the consciousness which is prepared by knowing its object with the help of scripture and reasoning finally is able to reach that state of understanding which achieves the immediate manifestation of Brahman;[14] cognition does not come quickly regarding the meaning of any sentence; and when we deal with a sentence such as 'You are that,' in which the meanings of the words are exceedingly hard to grasp, [cognition of] the sentence's proper meaning, which must be preceded by [apprehension of] its word meanings, will certainly not come quickly; rather, the knowledge of the word meanings will come most slowly. . . "[15] After the adversary concedes that comprehension in ordinary reading may be improved by repetition, Vācaspati adds that knowledge of the self is no exception: "Although the [essentially] manifest self has no parts, it appears as if it has parts due to superimpositions and their [partial] removal, and so appears very much as if unmanifest. Hence, cognition occurs gradually, by means of [a gradually achieved comprehension of] the meaning of the sentence."[16]

No amount of repetition guarantees that one will understand the text one is reading; the words are unchanging, and do not become clearer unless one understands them. Nevertheless, repeated readings do in fact lead gradually to a clearer understanding; the achieved knowledge is "all at once," and is not burdened permanently with the arduous slowness of the process of acquiring it. The knowledge of Brahman is gradual not because Brahman is a temporal reality, but because knowledge's venue is textual. Like other acts of reading, the reading of the upaniṣads generates a knowledge which reaches beyond the texts; but the reading of the upaniṣads too does not result in an immediate and simple apprehension, because they too are mastered only gradually. Whatever one's theology of Brahman may be, knowledge of Brahman is achieved through the appropriation of upaniṣadic meaning—and that takes time. It requires a bright and patient reader, who is persistent in reading and also able to learn from it, gradually making the transition from the necessary words which speak of Brahman to a pure and simple knowledge of Brahman.

2. Two Analogies: Music and Yoga

I conclude this opening consideration of the location of the reader between the simplicity of knowledge and the temporality and complexity of coming to knowledge with two helpful analogies introduced by the Advaitins. The first, introduced by Vācaspati,[17] is drawn from music: the refinement required to realize the truth of Brahman in the Text is like the refinement of one's ability to hear musical notes:

> Just as through the sense of hearing, aided by the impressions brought about by the repetition of the knowledge gained from the science of music, one experiences directly the different musical notes, *ṣaḍja*, etc., in their different cadences, even so the human person, prepared by the impressions brought about by the repetition of the meaning of the Vedānta texts, through the internal organ experiences its own nature as Brahman. (UMS I.1.1)[18]

Amalānanda comments that just as the gradual mastery of the art of listening to music enables one to hear differently and so to appreciate what one previously missed in music one may have heard frequently, the subtle and unchanging truth of the

Self—which is always present—is gradually manifest—to one who has studied the upaniṣadic statements about the unity of the self and Brahman and so become skilled in hearing the upaniṣads.[19] The purification and preparation of the inner self is achieved gradually, by mastery of upaniṣads which are the spiritual "score" which one practices in order to become skilled in the subtleties of the truth.

The musical notes are already being played distinctly even when one still lacks the capacity to distinguish them; the acquisition of a refined ear for music is a possible and plausible project, more necessary for some than others, and more practicable for some than others. Similarly, the upaniṣads are already perfectly conformed to Brahman, and the rare, subtle path to a proper apprehension of Brahman is perfectly inscribed in those texts; though the novice Advaitin will at first be unable to decipher what the texts present, over time he or she masters the texts and notices what was previously unheard.

The second analogy compares reading with yoga. As we have seen, the fact that the delicate and subtle Advaita understanding can be achieved in a skillful understanding of the upaniṣads poses to us the paradox that the absolutely simple is achieved in a temporal process. At UMS II.3.39, Śaṅkara spells out the correlation between the steps of meditation and the steps of yoga: "Concentration (*samādhi*),[20] taught in the upaniṣads as a means for the realization of that Self that is known from the upaniṣads alone, is spoken of in such texts as 'The self, dear, must be seen, must be heard, must be understood, must be meditated on,' . . ." (*Bṛhadāraṇyaka Upaniṣad* 2.4.5)

Vācaspati picks up on this reference to concentration (*samādhi*), the last step taken in Patañjali's classical yoga, and correlates the four steps in meditation to the last three of the eight steps of yoga:

> [The word] "Concentration" (*samādhi*) indicates constraint (*saṃyama*); fixed-attention (*dhāraṇā*), contemplation (*dhyāna*) and concentration (*samādhi*) are meant by the word "constraint." As it says in the [in Patañjali's *Yoga Sūtras*], "This same contemplation, shining forth [in consciousness] as the intended object and nothing more, and as it were, emptied

> of itself, is concentration."[21] Here, fixed-attention is indicated by the words, "it must be heard, it must be understood." Contemplation is indicated by "it must be meditated on." Concentration is indicated by "it must be seen."[22]

Earlier, in his elaboration of the *Bhāsya* comment on UMS I.1.4, while insisting on the necessarily gradual achievement of verbal knowledge,[23] Vācaspati had already compared it with the gradual nature of progress in yoga:

> Hence, after one has comprehended that the human self is the supreme self, through knowledge of the nature of hearing texts like "You are that" [*Chāndogya Upaniṣad* 6.8.7], and confirmed this by reasoning based thereon, there results intuition of Brahman through the contemplation [otherwise known as focused apprehension (*bhāvanā*)] of that [truth] practised at length and unintermittently; sacrifice, etc., serve in this [contemplation]. As it says [in *Yoga Sūtras* I.14], "But that [discipline of meditation] practiced for long, unintermittently and with care is the firm basis [for realizing the truth]."[24]

The slow, painful, patient mastery of one's body in yoga culminates in an absolutely simple and perfect moment of realization; so too, the discipline of mastering the Advaita Text culminates in a simple realization of Brahman.[25]

Reading, like yoga, is a complex set of practices which results in a realization greater than the component activities. In neither Advaita nor yoga is realization caused by anything: twisting one's body this way and that does not cause realization, words uttered or written on a page do not cause knowledge of Brahman. But in both, practices are essential to the achievement of what can never be the result of practices. If one were to despise bodies or to avoid texts because of some desire for a higher spiritual knowledge, one would be left with an undisciplined and unrealized desire; only through the physical and textual does one acquire a knowledge which is reducible to neither.[26]

Reading, music, yoga: knowledge takes time, and one must use one's time properly. The result is the ability to discriminate, the skill to make the required subtle distinctions which constitute a correct reading of reality. It is a skill practiced and perfected over time. Nonetheless, the resultant realization is not temporal and is not merely the product of certain actions effected in a certain order. This mediation of the simple and eternal through the complex and temporal is explained, authorized and defended by the Advaitins in the variety of direct and indirect ways we examined in the previous chapter; but it is finally validated only by the example of an accomplished Advaitin, a properly trained and supremely discerning reader who sees the wordless simplicity of Brahman through and after the many sacred words of the Text. We must now trace the genealogy of that reader in the textually mediated desire for Brahman (*brahmajijñāsā*).

III. Becoming a Reader

1. The Desire to Know Brahman and the Desire to Read

The tension between the simplicity of knowledge and the complexity and temporality of the reading process by which that simple knowledge is attained is replicated in Advaita's twofold discourse about the expected background of the potential Advaitin. On the one hand, there can be no prerequisites for knowledge of Brahman; the desire to know Brahman has no cause, and the knowledge of Brahman cannot be produced; both are free and unconstrained by textual or other constraints and are simply, always possible. On the other hand, Advaita has very high expectations about who can become such a desirer and knower; it proposes a list of qualifications ranging from calmness and other virtues which flourish in the mind trained, or as if trained, by Mīmāṃsā, to a set of external qualifications which include both the right manner of learning—after initiation, with a recognized teacher—and by extension the right social identification.

The discussion starts under UMS I.1.1 with an exploration of the prerequisites which make one eligible to take up the study of the Text, particularly in the exploration of possible meanings for the word *jijñāsā*, which indicates both "the desire to know" and the activity which brings about the desired knowledge.[27] In PMS I.1.1 ("Next, then, the desire to know dharma" [*atha ato dharmajijñāsā*]), and in UMS I.1.1 ("Next, then, the desire to know Brahman" [*atha ato brahmajijñāsā*]), the discussion of jijñāsā is placed within a discussion of the significance of the opening "next" (*atha*), a word which can possibly, though not necessarily, mark the beginning of an activity or text or ritual as a radical new departure vis à vis that which precedes it.

Śaṅkara expends considerable effort in finding a way to interpret "atha" in this latter sense, so as to minimize any precedent for the new enterprise of brahmajijñāsā which comprises the Advaita Text. After rejecting four alternative readings of "atha" which discern various precedents to brahmajijñāsā,[28] he finally settles upon a series of interior qualities as the sole prerequisites of the desire to know:

> They are: discrimination between things that are eternal and things that are noneternal; a loss of taste for the enjoyment of objects here and hereafter; perfection in such practices as control of the mind, control of the senses and organs, etc.; the desire for liberation.[29]

There is nothing specific to Advaita, nor to Vedic orthodoxy, about these interior prerequisites, nor do they bear any necessary textual component. Yet Advaita characteristically locates them firmly within the Text and interprets them entirely in keeping with the expectation of attention to it; it narrows their domain and identifies a textual pedagogy as the basis for their acquisition. How this textualization occurs is best illustrated by following the Advaita debate over the meaning of "jijñāsā" in *atha ato brahmajijñāsā,* and over the way in which this desire is established in continuity with and distinction from the dharmajijñāsā of Mīmāṃsā. This is the debate over why the unprecedented and pure desire to know Brahman, accompanied only by the four prerequisites, should be linked to other prerequisites implied by a demanding commitment to the reading of the Text.

Advaita draws on the Mīmāṃsā version of the debate. In locating dharmajijñāsā vis à vis its background at the beginning of his *Bhāṣya* on PMS I.1.1, the Mīmāṃsaka Śabara links it to the Vedic command, "One must study one's proper portion [of the Veda]" (*svādhyāyo 'dhyetavyaḥ*);[30] he argues that after one has properly received and learned one's appropriate texts, only then (*atha*) can one begin the necessarily subsequent (though optional) process of inquiring into the meaning of the memorized texts, in order to gain a perfect understanding of dharma. The vast PMS Text is a justifiable enterprise because it builds on that earlier memorization yet adds to it the new component of complete understanding.[31]

In probable imitation of Śabara, Śaṅkara asks if there can be any precedents to the Advaita desire to know. It is evident, he says, that the desire for Brahman has no expected or necessary precedents; whichever prerequisites one might name can never guarantee that the desire to know actually arises. In particular, it is erroneous to propose prerequisites which demand continuity with the Vedic tradition, if this means the prior performance of ritual, or a knowledge of how to perform ritual, or even a knowledge of Mīmāṃsā as a "metaknowledge" of ritual,[32] since the desire to know has as its object none of these, but Brahman alone.

Since Brahman is an existent reality, we also cannot presume that the desire to know Brahman stands in immediate correlation with a desire to read texts. Indeed, Śaṅkara insists that the desire to know cannot be equated with an inquiry which can be inaugurated, for the act of inquiry requires as its prior motivation the desire to know.

He thus privileges "jijñāsā" as desire, and relegates to second place "jijñāsā" as inquiry, including that inquiry which is reading. This insistence on the unprecedented originality of the desire to know is sensible, and is verifiable from ordinary experience; one cannot predictably instigate in someone the desire to know, nor can one determine precisely the sufficient grounds for this desire. It is also evident that the desire to know Brahman does not depend upon the desire to know how to perform rituals, and that wanting to perform rituals is not the same as wanting to read texts about Brahman. It also serves to distinguish Advaita as the Uttara Mīmāṃsā from the prior (Pūrva)

Mīmāṃsā, preserving the distinctness of the Advaita project as a new response to a new desire, oriented to a new object of knowledge.

But the claim for the originality of the desire does not entail a complete break with Mīmāṃsā. In both Mīmāṃsas the desire is satisfied through a disciplined engagement in the investigation of texts, and the uniqueness of the desire need not entail the uniqueness of the methods of inquiry. In fact, the Advaita insistence on the (theoretical) exemption of knowledge from the material constraints accompanying actual ritual performance does not extend to a rejection of Mīmāṃsa's mode of investigation, which was constructed in the context of ritual practice. Though the reading practice is correctly distinguished from ritual practice, the rejection of a requirement for ritual performance does not dissolve all formal and genealogical links to the ritual view of the world, and one reads toward a knowledge of Brahman with much the same methods of exegesis that were operative in regard to ritual materials and for the sake of a knowledge of dharma.

Hence, the opening of a path beyond works is spoken in a language intelligible primarily, perhaps exclusively, to those familiar with ritual and the Mīmāṃsā language about ritual activity. Though the relationship of brahmajijñāsā as desire to brahmajijñāsā as inquiry is unique, and though neither bears exactly the relationship that dharma and dharmajijñāsā bear in Mīmāṃsā, nevertheless brahmajijñāsā is not independent of texts; as an inquiry it is profoundly and massively implicated in the Mīmāṃsā discourse, and expects practitioners who can become adept in that discourse.

In making the distinction between "jijñāsā" as the instigating desire to know and "mīmāṃsā" as the activity of inquiry—equivalent to jijñāsā as inquiry—Vācaspati explains how the purely unoriginated jijñāsā inaugurates Mīmāṃsā activity:

> Nor is the desire to know (jijñāsā) the same as inquiry (mīmāṃsā,) so that, like the treatise on yoga, it might be something that one undertakes; the word "Mīmāṃsā" . . . signifies an inquiry (*vicāra*) that commands respect, while

> the word "jijñāsā" signifies the desire to know. "Desire to know" is indeed what makes one undertake the inquiry.[33]

The distinction and connection are legitimate, and the clarification of terminology is possibly helpful; the word "mīmāṃsā" is used to distinguish the activity of inquiry from the originative desire, and the word "jijñāsā" is reserved for the desire. As desire, brahmajijñāsā may come at any time; but as a project that needs to be undertaken, it is just like dharmajijñāsā, and is necessarily posterior to knowledge of the pertinent texts—both versions of jijñāsā as inquiry are reading activities. The claim of Advaita's independence from ritual is thus balanced by the admission that one must be like a Mīmāṃsaka, an Uttara Mīmāṃsaka, in order to "do Advaita." The kind of skill one gains from Mīmāṃsā is required, however one may achieve it.[34]

This specification is surprising only if we mistakenly define Mīmāṃsā as ritual rubrics. Mīmāṃsā itself is not so much about the performance of rites as it is about the proper understanding of rites, their texts, their actualization and the extended set of related issues—an understanding acquired by a sophisticated probing of language, ritual and their presuppositions. By distinguishing knowledge about how to do rites from the ability to discern connections and differences in a ritual/textual context, Vācaspati sorts out "mere Mīmāṃsā" as that detailed knowledge of rites which is decidedly not necessary for Advaita, from the skills of making proper distinctions which the Advaitin as Uttara Mīmāṃsaka assuredly must acquire. Though the desire to know and its satisfaction cannot be caused, the skill through which knowledge is accomplished can be learned, and needs to be taught properly to proper students. Though content[35] and the manner of relationship between texts and object of inquiry differ in Mīmāṃsā and Advaita, and though such differences entail differences in epistemological, metaphysical and cosmological structures, they do not mark radically different textual commitments and methods. Neither differences in content nor the consequent differences in structure indicate that Advaita is performed differently; the Advaitin must be an Uttara

Mīmāṃsaka in order to do something new and different from the Pūrva Mīmāṃsā.

Though indirect, Advaita has a real (though not total) dependence on skilled reflection on ritual performance; consequently, there is also a real (though not total) practical identification of the Advaitin student with the Mīmāṃsaka student. If one is not the heir to the skills entailed by Mīmāṃsā's reflection on ritual, one can desire Brahman but not perform brahmajijñāsā properly, and so will be unable to satisfy one's desire. This is so even if one concedes, as a point on an ever-receding horizon, the possibility of an immediate realization in a totally uneducated person. In every case short of that ideal, to be a Vedantin without being a Mīmāṃsaka is a fruitless identity. The true Advaitin is a careful reader of texts and the articulator of a truth of Brahman out of and after texts.

Two positions thus reach expression simultaneously: on the one hand, Advaita originates solely in the pure and mysteriously originated desire to know, a desire which cannot be fixed in any frame of reference, nor guaranteed by any sort of preparation, and which is satisfied by Brahman alone, not by the knowledge of anything else; on the other hand Advaita is also a specific, privileged enactment of that desire, a well-defined skill and activity which is learned in a certain proper fashion. As desire, Advaita is unconditioned and unprecedented; as practice, it simply extends the older practices and pedagogy of Mīmāṃsā to new material. In the next section, we shall examine how these tensions combine to define the Advaitin as a skilled reader of texts who only thereafter becomes entirely free.

2. Authorizing the Reader: The Prerequisites of Knowledge

Advaita's emphasis on the textuality of knowledge entails the identification of a competent readership, comprised of those skilled enough, or able to become skilled enough, to engage in reading the Text with the sophistication it demands. The necessarily original and requisite desire to know and the path toward its satisfaction are situated as posterior to a sophisticated ability to read "like a Mīmāṃsaka."

This expectation of literacy is coupled with a set of less obvious restrictions about who is permitted to acquire this literacy; these accentuate the tension between the simplicity of Advaita in general and the elaborate prescription/description of those who are, or can become, competent in the Text, between its universal though rare availability and its arduous but practicable textual approachability. In UMS I.3.26–33 and UMS I.3.34–38 this competence (adhikāra) is explored. In the preceding adhikaraṇas of UMS I the relationship between desire and reading has been established, as has been the content of that reading. With these adhikaraṇas the question arises: what are the boundaries of the group of those competent to read? UMS I.3.26–33 deals with the contested competence of the gods, who will be allowed membership in that group, and UMS I.3.34–38 with the contested competence of the śūdras, low-caste males, who will be excluded from it.

As usual, the question is argued in terms of the right reading of specific texts, with a precise estimation of the implications of various readings for the coherence of the orthodox viewpoint. As usual, too, the problem is differentiated into a number of arguments in each adhikaraṇa.

On the general issue of competence the Advaitins follow the Mīmāṃsakas who, in the parallel discussion which occurs in PMS VI.1,[36] proposed first an almost unrestricted profile of those competent to perform sacrifices, but then severely restricted that profile by a series of further specifications. In the Mīmāṃsā discussion, the preliminary proposal is that any person who is intelligent enough to learn the requisite texts and who has a desire for the results of sacrifices is competent to perform them; for desire is the motivating force behind intelligent human actions, of which ritual action is but an example. Subsequent adhikaraṇas restrict this broad definition by denying competence to women apart from certain activities they share with their husbands,[37] and by limiting competence to twice-born males who are sufficiently wealthy and healthy.[38] The Mīmāṃsā exclusion of śūdras is based simply on the claim that the Veda excludes them in its self-regulation of its readership;[39] the Mīmāṃsakas do not argue that śūdras are inferior intellectually or otherwise. Since rituals and their designated performers are formed and finished entirely within a world constituted by the Veda, the search for another, anthropological basis on which to found competence or lack thereof would be pointless.[40]

The same presuppositions and positions remain operative in Advaita: competence is restricted to conscious, intelligent beings, and whoever lacks the desire for the promised results—now, the results of meditation—is not competent to undertake the action of meditation. One must have the physical and mental capacities required, e.g., well-functioning senses, the ability to remember, the will to concentrate, etc.

But by the same process of gradual exclusion, this broadly defined competence is gradually restricted to the twice-born males—just as the Veda is interpreted to indicate. One might have expected the dynamics of knowledge and access to it to function rather differently in Advaita, which is distinguished by the fact that Brahman is not, like ritual, a construct of texts, but rather a real though posttextual reality. One might rightly expect that deities, and humans of all castes and both genders,[41] would be potentially competent students of Advaita, just by virtue of intelligence, an inherent ability to know. Nevertheless, the Advaitins remain very much Mīmāṃsakas, constricting their audience by the demands and expectations of reading as a skilled, cultured practice, as they concede competence to the gods but deny it to śūdras.

The reason the gods might appear incompetent is that they do not receive the sacred thread in the investiture ceremony (*upanayana*) and do not study the upaniṣads in the approved fashion with a proper teacher. Knowledge must come in the right way, one might argue, and no amount of impressive divine knowledge should matter, unless it has been gained in the right way. Śaṅkara disposes of this objection swiftly: "Nor can it be said that they are barred by the scriptures about the investiture with the sacred thread; for investiture is meant for the study of the Vedas, and to [the gods] the Vedas get revealed spontaneously." (UMS I.3.26)[42]

According to Vācaspati, the fact of this "spontaneous revelation" does not free the gods of a need for the Veda, to which they have their own manner of access:

> It is not that the Veda learned from the mouth of the guru in the proper fashion is the cause for a fruitful understanding of ritual and Brahman; rather it is that in the time after study, [that properly learned Veda] is recollected by a man who has gained an understanding of reality according to word and reasoning, because he has understood the connections between words and their meanings, according to logic, etymology and grammar. As the sacred tradition is thus recollected by men in this birth, so it is recollected in this birth by the gods who learned it in the proper way in a previous birth. It is on this basis that it is possible that the Veda is spontaneously revealed to them.[43]

This explanation cuts two ways. The real point of Vedic study is obviously the acquired knowledge of words and their meanings, particularly insofar as Advaita stresses the acquisition of knowledge as an intellectual endeavor. As long as this knowledge has been gained, there should be nothing magical about hearing the words from the guru's mouth at the present moment. But what might be construed then as unrestricted accessibility—the gods have the knowledge, so they must be competent—is refined so as to reaffirm allegiance to the Text: the gods have the knowledge, so they must have learned properly previously, in an earlier existence.

In UMS I.3.34–38, śūdras are denied competence on the grounds that it is not enough to read intelligently and understand the upaniṣadic texts: one must engage in proper study (*adhyayana*) of one's properly "assigned" and memorized texts (*svādhyāya*).[44] In defense of the competence of śūdras, the pūrvapakṣin argues the simple and straightforward view that even if śūdras cannot receive the thread in the upanayana ceremony, they are nevertheless able to learn in other ways. It is evident, he argues, that śūdras have the same capacity for knowledge of Brahman as other humans, by the simple fact of their birth as human beings.[45] Since Brahman is not merely the product of an esoteric body of texts, Brahman should be knowable even to śūdras. Moreover, even if one were to concede on the basis of the Mīmāṃsā siddhānta that the śūdra is precluded from an acquirable capacity—i.e., from initiation and the accompanying rights and privileges pertaining to ritual—and so unauthorized to perform rituals, one could still object that this does not affect the capacity for knowledge since, as Advaita has insisted from UMS I.1.1 on, one does not need to perform sacrifices in order to be able to know. The pūrvapakṣa concludes by noting that even if one wishes to deny to the śūdra the privileges of the brahmanical style of learning, there is no reason to exclude other means for the śūdra's acquisition of knowledge, such as learning from books.[46]

Insofar as Advaita consists of knowledge, pure and simple, the criticism is on target; the pūrvapakṣin is simply following through on the logic of the Advaita exposition of what the radically simple knowledge of Brahman implies. But the siddhāntin stresses the status of jijñāsā as a mode of inquiry, not simply the desire to know, and focuses on the importance of the manner of access to the Text. The circumstances of learning are important, for by them knowledge is made properly available to the right kind of people. Only after proper learning can the simple and suppositionless nature of knowledge of Brahman emerge.

Śaṅkara presents a simple, stark version of the Mīmāṃsā argument that śūdras are to be excluded, simply because the Veda excludes them:

> The śūdra has no competence, since he cannot study the Veda; for one becomes competent regarding things spoken of in the Vedas after one has studied the Vedas and known these things from them. But there can be no study of the Veda by a śūdra, for study of the Veda presupposes investiture with the sacred thread, which is restricted to the three castes. (UMS I.3.34)

Vācaspati's initial statement of the siddhānta balances the dynamics of reading against their contextualization within the strictures of the Veda itself; he responds more directly to the pūrvapakṣa:

> Let us concede that the injunction to study, "One must study one's proper portion [of the Veda]", is not recorded in the context of any fruitful ritual action, and that it is not connected invariably to any ritual just by the meanings of its

> words; for this proper learning is not connected invariably to any ritual as are the sacrificial ladles, etc.[47]

Proper memorization of one's proper texts is not obviously the only medium of liberative knowledge. Nevertheless, he continues, "the injunction to study as the proper preparation of one's proper texts makes it clear that this study is the approved means of sacred learning."[48] Mere study, based on other means of access to texts, cannot be fruitful, and it must be assumed that there is some fruit to gaining knowledge in this particular way only.

Vācaspati then traces a dense Mīmāṃsā-style argument as to whether study can have the desired result—realization of Brahman—even if undertaken independently of the approved mode of study in regard to the proper texts. Drawing on several Mīmāṃsā siddhāntas as examples, Vācaspati's pūrvapakṣin argues that the intelligent appropriation of texts study can have the desired result, even if none is explicitly mentioned. It should therefore be recognized as a practice distinct from ritually- and caste-inscribed approved study, and even if śūdras are deprived of the right to the approved form of study, the intelligent practice of reading will still be available to them.[49] The siddhāntin rejects this line of reasoning, insisting that only that proper study performed in relation to one's properly learned sacred texts is efficacious:

> A fruitful understanding of ritual or of Brahman, resulting respectively in reward and liberation, is brought about by one's proper texts refined by proper study. If so, we can say that only to that person who has undertaken proper study will come that fruitful understanding of ritual and Brahman which brings about reward and salvation respectively, and not to anyone else [i.e., to others who study without the proper preparation.][50]

Moreover,

> Proper study is possible only for him who has been prepared by investiture, and this person can come only from among the twice-born. Without investiture, that proper

> preparation which constitutes proper study cannot occur; therefore that understanding which śūdras get by studying books, etc., cannot be fruitful. It is therefore proven that because the śūdra lacks the scripturally authorized capacity, he is not competent for meditation on Brahman.[51]

Though intending a universally pertinent domain, Brahman, salvific knowledge is nevertheless mediated by the Text, and access to the Text is mediated by the approved set of Textually articulated preparations and refinements. As in the Mīmāṃsā argument, the exclusion of the śūdra is argued entirely in terms of an argument about the Veda; nothing is said about the natural abilities of the śūdra, nor about knowledge "in itself."

The argumentation is pure Mīmāṃsā, and these judgments about access to knowledge of Brahman are made only by those who are masters of Mīmāṃsā; the arguments rely on judgments by the Advaitins as Uttara Mīmāṃsakas who decide what is an appropriate reading of the debated texts. It is only within the shared horizon of Mīmāṃsā normativity that Mīmāṃsā examples are judged apt by the pūrvapakṣin, but then judged irrelevant, in these particular adhikaraṇas, by the siddhāntin.

It is no surprise then that not only is the desire to know Brahman mediated through Textual knowledge, but also that access to the Text is judged possible only in an intelligent reading which is mediated through the proper channels of initiation and relationship to a teacher. Once the link of knowledge and Text is established, the simple nonduality of knowledge is submitted to an ever broader and more complex set of qualifications pertaining to readers and their reading. If ultimately the accomplishment of Advaita as Vedānta rests on an event of pure and simple understanding, in Advaita as Uttara Mīmāṃsā this event is inscribed within an entire set of claims about who is in the position to make such judgments.

It is quite likely that the contemporary reader will remain unpersuaded by the Advaita decision to exclude śūdras from proper knowledge of Brahman, and there are many arguments for a different conclusion. But the dissatisfaction points to the tension that lies at the heart of the Advaita discourse, the tension between the Advaita insistence on the centrality of the Text and its appropriate reception, and its equal insistence on the simplicity and unrestrictedness of its truth. According to the latter, śūdras ought to be included; according to the former, they cannot be. Advaita could not be easily freed from this tension, were it to persist as a productive form of textual, liberative knowledge; it is partially on this basis that some modern versions of Advaita recast it entirely as Vedānta philosophy, excising both the tension between Text and truth and the exclusions connected with it.

IV. The Constraints on Liberation and the Cessation of Reading in UMS III.4: Description as Prescription

In the preceding sections we have traced the "fault line" between Advaita as Vedānta and as Uttara Mīmāṃsā, the series of tensions between the simple and the complex: between purely nondualist knowledge and skilled mastery of the Text; between Brahman as knowable in itself and extratextually, and as available only after the Text; between jijñāsā as an inherently free and unpredictable desire, and as a prolonged and patient process of skilled reading that proceeds in a manner tantamount to training in Mīmāṃsā; the identification of the reader as simply an intelligent, interested person, and as the right kind of person, who can in fact be educated in the right fashion. These tensions extend consistently the fundamental tension between the Text and its truth, safeguard that tension against reduction, and describe the kind of person who is able to negotiate, in the singular event of personal realization, the irreducible but productive gap between Text and truth.

We turn now to a final instance of this tension between the interior configuration and the exterior constraints of knowledge, by considering the person who is in part and then completely the "product" of the study of the Text, the desirer (jijñāsin) who possesses the desire for liberation (*mumuksutva*) and acts accordingly. Here too we see the uneasy but creative juxtaposition of complete freedom and indescribability—for the liberated person cannot be described—with a thorough inscription/prescription of that person within the legitimating structures of the Brahmanical life.

The main features of this analysis are already in place: on the one hand, the person who seeks liberation departs radically from the confines of ordinary Brahmanical life, and is by definition beyond prescriptions and expectations; at the same time, however, the right kind of person, the proper Advaitin who is engaged in the Text within its ritual location, is the only one who can achieve this radical freedom. In the following overview of the simultaneous prescription and description of the seeker I restrict my attention to UMS III.4, of which the description of this seeker is the primary topic.

1. Expectations about the Person Who Will Renounce

The careful and orthodox legitimation of the completely free person begins in a spare but decisive form in UMS III.4.1–17, where the knowledge found in and gained through the upaniṣads is identified as pertaining to the "human goal" (*puruṣa-artha*) and not as subordinate to the "ritual goal" (*kratu-artha*). The independence of knowledge is thus ensured: knowledge is utterly free, neither dependent on nor subservient to any of the lesser goals which comprise the range of orthodox religious practice.

However, this insistence on the independence of knowledge relies on the Mīmāṃsā description of how two measures for the cohesion of ritual—the goals of the performer (puruṣa-artha) and the finality of the rite itself (kratu-artha)—relate to one another.[52] In PMS IV.1.1–2, Jaimini distinguished between the human goal and the ritual goal. The former was characterized as the perspective of the "pleasure" (*prīti*) of the performer (*puruṣa*), while the latter was characterized as the perspective of the wholeness and integration of the ritual (*kratu*), irrespective of connection with the performer's pleasure. The human goal characterizes a ritual from its performer's viewpoint, the ritual goal from the viewpoint of its internal coherence. The two perspectives are generally juxtaposed without the identification of one as superior to the other; they exist in the same time and space, constituting two frames of reference on the same ritual event.[53] In the body of the PMS IV, Jaimini uses the distinction to sort out an array of complex textual and practical complications according to their contribution to the finality of the ritual, intrinsically (kratu-artha) or from the performer's perspective (puruṣa-artha). In various circumstances, one or the other perspective is found to be more useful in helping to adjudicate ambiguities in ritual performance. Both perspectives are organizing markers, and they do not designate different levels of reality; two perspectives on a single event, they are not in competition.

When Bādarāyaṇa identifies knowledge as the human goal and chooses to define this by its distinction from the ritual goal, the distinction therefore need not be taken as sharply disjoining two realms of reality, nor need it imply that the two are entirely independent of one another, or that knowledge definitively supersedes action. Indeed, the very fact that Bādarāyaṇa frames the debate on the status of liberative knowledge in terms of these two goals strengthens rather than undermines the connection of knowledge and the larger orthodox milieu represented by the ritual goal; the designation of upaniṣadic knowledge as the human goal affords it a distinct identity, while yet situating it intelligibly within the boundaries of other orthodox goals and perspectives. The identification of knowledge as the human goal does no more than to create a distinct, albeit in Bādarāyaṇa's view privileged, place for upaniṣadic knowledge.

The rest of UMS III.4 explores the implications of marking knowledge as one in a pair of perspectives; a practical theory of meditation is articulated through a series of admissions and restrictions whereby Advaita, in its by now familiar balancing act, defends the idea that ritual is a de facto prerequisite to the acquisition of knowledge, though in no way a necessary precedent to the event of knowledge. UMS III.4.18–20, which we examined in Chapter 2 in terms of the inscription of the debate over renunciation entirely within the world of the Text, asks how the knowledge of Brahman changes its "performer" and his relation to ritual knowledge and practice: if the knower's position is changed as he moves beyond the boundary of his state of life (āśrama), is he then repositioned within a new but still determinative set of constraints—i.e., within another state of life? By elaborate textual arguments UMS III.4.18–20 concludes that there are states of life other than the householder's, which are subject to textual legitimation and schematization: renunciation itself becomes a fourth state of life, and the renunciation of rites is scripturally authorized.

2. The Ritual Background to Renunciation

The establishment of a fourth state of life makes it possible to question further the balance between that absolute, unique state of life and its textual/ritual determination. The location of the renunciant's life vis à vis the tradition is examined in UMS III.4.25, 26 (and 27), in 32–33, and in the consequent description of the renunciant which is the predominant topic of the adhikaraṇas which comprise UMS III.4.36–52. We now consider these in turn.

The Advaita explanation as to why the performance of ritual is not a necessary background to knowledge is a careful balancing act which leaves the ritual apparatus entirely in place. UMS III.4.25—"Therefore the renunciant does not need the installed sacred fires, and rites dependent thereon"—points to the simpler and starker side of the Advaita position: since Advaita knowledge is not subordinate to rites (i.e., is not kratu-artha), this knowledge does not require for its achievement or maintenance the performance of rituals. Just as knowledge of rituals is not an obvious prerequisite to brahmajijñāsā, there is no obvious way in which the performance of certain ritual actions is necessarily accessory to the realization of Brahman.

In UMS III.4.26–27 the constraints of tradition are quickly reasserted:

> III.4.26: On the strength of the upaniṣadic sanction of sacrifices, etc., all religious activities as well are necessary—in the way the horse is.[54]

> III.4.27: The renunciant must be endowed with control of the mind, control of the sense organs, etc., since these con-

trols are enjoined as subsidiaries of knowledge; and hence have to be practiced.

Although rites are not necessary for the person who already has knowledge of Brahman, and although rites cannot cause knowledge, they are nonetheless necessary for the person whose desire to know Brahman is inchoate, inarticulate and therefore not yet constructive of a program of inquiry. Śaṅkara explains that they help make the person into the right kind of person who can inquire properly: ". . . knowledge does not at all depend on the performance of the duties of the various stages of life for producing its own result . . . [But] knowledge needs the help of all the duties of the various stages of life, and it is not a fact that there is absolutely no dependence on them . . . once knowledge has emerged, it does not depend on any other factor for producing its result, but it does depend on others for its emergence."[55] Both the internal virtues of self-control, etc., and the performance of rites are required for the seeker.[56]

Vācaspati pays close attention to the temporal process of change in the knowing person, and to how helps such as ritual performance play their part in knowledge's emergence:

> Therefore, like control of the mind, control of the sense organs, etc., ritual actions are required for knowledge, with respect to its emergence. According to the text, "One who thus knows,"[57] control of the mind, control of the sense organs, etc., are interior subsidiaries regarding the origin of knowledge, because they are connected with the proper form of knowledge. Ritual actions are exterior subsidiaries, because they are connected with the desire to know. By the performance of the obligatory rites prescribed for the various states of life, therefore, dharma arises, and due to that sin is destroyed. For [sin] deeply soils the mind by the confusion of the permanent, pure, happy, etc. with this world, the non-self which is essentially impermanent, impure, unhappy, etc.; these confusions are connected with adharma . . . [The student] learns from his teacher's words and from scripture that the means [to the destruction of sin] is the thorough understanding of the nature of the self. Ritual actions are a help in the origination of this knowl-

> edge of the self, by means of aiding the desire to know. The one who desires to know becomes single-minded in his direction to that one goal, and desires to perform the hearing and understanding [which lead one there].[58] Certain knowledge arises from the statement, "Then, you are that . . ."[59]

UMS III.4.32–35 builds on the siddhāntas of UMS III.4.25 and 26–27[60] by asking a question which tests and fixes the interior boundaries between the potential renunciant and his "this-worldly" compatriots: if it is agreed that rites help the person who desires liberation, are rites optional for the person who does not desire liberation? As in the older ritual calculus shared by Mīmāṃsā,[61] intention (*saṃkalpa*) matters. A rite can lead to different results, depending on the announced intention of the performer. Here too, rites ordinarily serve the mundane and heavenly purposes of the person who does not desire liberation, but the same rites, performed in the same way, will help toward salvation the special person who intends liberation as an at least longterm goal. The rites themselves flexibly allow for this diversity of effects due to the performer's intentions. They help toward the origination of knowledge, and yet without contradiction they still bind the person who does not seek knowledge. The obligation to performance remains in force, whatever the intention of the performer vis à vis knowledge and other results.

These key adhikaraṇas—1–17 on the distinction between the human and sacrificial goals (puruṣa-artha and kratu-artha), 18–20 on the legitimacy of a renunciant state of life, 25 on the independence of knowledge from rites, 26–27 on the subordinate but real role of rites, and 32–35 on the importance of intention vis à vis the nature of the efficacy of rites—together compose the framework within which the independence of knowledge from ritual can be articulated in a fashion consistent with the ritual and Mīmāṃsā precedents of Advaita.[62] The intersecting, differing but not entirely separable purposes and results of ritual and meditation are carefully distinguished and ranked—and both are properly inscribed within Advaita's overall description of reality.

3. Prescribing Renunciation

As might be expected in light of the Mīmāṃsā position on the interconnection of word and ritual which shapes the Vedānta discourse, the balance between the unrestricted simplicity of Vedānta knowledge and the complexity of the Uttara Mīmāṃsā's Textual knowledge is thus replicated in the balance between that simple knowledge and the complex ritual context within which someone is readied for the renunciation of action: the competent performer of rituals is the person for whom independence from ritual becomes a real possibility.

The rest of UMS III.4 (28–31, 36–51) prescribes/describes the indescribable, unlimited renunciant; it is devoted to drawing boundaries—of definition, legitimation and limitation—around the life of the Advaitin who desires to know Brahman (who is brahmajijñāsin), and around the life of the renunciant who has already attained knowledge (who is *brahma-jña*). This boundary-drawing protects the radicality of fully realized knowledge while at the same time determining what is appropriate to the achieved state of knowledge and the moments leading up to it. I summarize the adhikaraṇas as follows:

1. UMS III.4.28–31 There is a text, "For the man who thus knows the vital breath, nothing is uneatable." (*Chāndogya* 5.2.1) Against the prima facie view that this abrogates the usual restrictions on food, Śaṅkara argues that the text is not injunctive, and hence lacks force. In emergencies, all foods are acceptable, whether or not one is a renunciant. Otherwise, the seeker and the renunciant must both abide by the accepted restrictions.

2. UMS III.4.36–39 Widowers and others who are not competent for the normal practice of the means which help toward knowledge may still meditate and so reach the goal, full knowledge.[63]

3. UMS III.4.40 Once one has progressed from one state of life to the next, there is no possibility of reversion to a prior state of life. Realized renunciants too are bound by

this rule, even if for them the obligation is based in an irreversible interior transformation.

4. UMS III.4.41–42 Two views are presented as to whether a student who "falls" from celibacy—who reverts to an earlier state of life—can perform expiation and be restored to his renunciant state.

5. UMS III.4.43 extends 41–2; however the lapse from celibacy is evaluated, the lapsed person is to be expelled from ordinary society and from all transactions with respect to "sacrifice, study, and matrimonial ceremony."

6. UMS III.4.47–49 The state of silence, mentioned in the *Bṛhadāraṇyaka Upaniṣad* 3.5.1, is judged obligatory for those who seek Brahman.

7. UMS III.4.50 The same text says that the renunciant should live as a child. But this does not indicate complete irresponsibility, which would be indecent; rather, the injunction intends the childlike virtues of humility and lack of pretension, etc.

8. UMS III.4.51 The successful satisfaction of the desire to know Brahman and the consequent inquiry into that knowledge of Brahman which is liberation may occur in this lifetime, or in another birth.

9. UMS III.4.52 When knowledge is attained, the consequent liberation is always one and the same for all those who acquire it.

These nine adhikaraṇas map the life of the Advaitin according to specific and limited differences, and establish important continuities with the orthodox tradition as a whole. The renunciant is totally free, but is located deeply within the orthodox fold; restrictions still apply, sanctions are still enforced, and the achieved knower is expected to behave responsibly, *not* like a child. Though the liberated state is beyond words it occurs, like Advaita's truth, after the Text, after its words and procedures of reading and arguing, its intellectual and social practices, and not apart from it. One reaches wordlessness through words, after them, according to them.

The extent to which these prescriptions bind the fully liberated renunciant as well as the seeker of renunciation is not entirely clear. One can argue that while Bādarāyaṇa fully intends to establish the restrictions which govern the life of the liberated renunciant (while still alive) as well as that of the seeker, Śaṅkara perhaps limits the domain of these prescriptions to the latter. But even for Śaṅkara, the domains would not be merely juxtaposed, since the unrestricted liberated state—theoretically possible at any time—occurs in practice only after the seeker's disciplined submission to the rules of the search. Just as the ineffable truth of Advaita occurs in practice only after a thorough appropriation of the Advaita Text, the state of life in which one is completely free from restrictions occurs only after the inner appropriation of those restrictions. The elusive and ever-receding moment of transformation, where one "leaps" from a life governed by rules to a life in which rules are impossible, from a life of renunciation as a means to knowledge to renunciation as the event of knowledge, is a tension which finds no systematic resolution in the Text. It is only in the realized Advaitin, who reads and does everything correctly, that liberation from inscription, description and prescription can occur, that the brahmajijñāsin becomes brahmajña.

V. Advaita Elitism and the Possibility of the Unauthorized Reader: Finding a Loophole

Truth is the event of true discernment, the subtle ability to sort things out and see them as they are. Skilled reading is the practical school of this learning, and perfect reading culminates in perfect discernment. The perfected competence of the properly determined reader always hearkens back to his (or her) original capacity and desire, which cannot be produced, and yet it depends on his (or her) proper training by the proper people. In its simplest version, Advaita sees knowledge as a pure consciousness not bound by words and in no way a form of agency; its truth is simply the utterly liberative knowledge of Brahman.

But in its complexity as Uttara Mīmāṃsā, it thoroughly inscribes this truth in the Text and designates knowledge as the accomplishment of right reading, in order to ensure that some at least might realize the truth.

In turn, this right reading is qualified by all that right reading entails, including the identification of skills, approved pedagogical settings, and approved behavior for those who are reading and for those who have read. Thus, while the universality of Advaita's truth is available to all, it is mediated through the tightly restricted and ever more technically articulated confines of the Text. This curious convergence of knowledge and text, availability and constraint, is the defining characteristic of Advaita: truth, skill in reading, and competence are mutually determining concepts, each confirming yet also contesting the boundaries established by the other.

This tension is deeply imbedded in Advaita; it is productive of the massive achievement of the system as Text and truth, and it constitutes the temporal-spatial rendering of the truth of Advaita in ways that, over a range of topics from the requirement to read to the specification of how the person who has finished reading is supposed to act, are increasingly complex, specific, demanding and exclusive. The positive intention of Advaita is to ensure that its truth be actualized in at least a few people, by providing at least for them the maximal education, and in a fashion that promises maximal fruitfulness. Yet by severely restricting and intensely preparing an elite audience for this knowledge, Advaita in practice severely limits its own universality. Its barriers of difficulty, demands on time and energy, and more direct exclusions of the "wrong kind of people" make it formidable, local, defensive; actual competence is extended to just about no one. Expectations regarding the reader are thereby intensified to the highest degree; only in the rare, right reader who carries out the project of reading properly and with perseverance is the supersession of the tension between Text and truth finally achieved. The transition from Uttara Mīmāṃsā as practice to Vedānta as simple knowledge is never a given; it must occur, and occurs only when the proper person comes along.

At the conclusion of Chapters 2, 3, and 4 the contemporary reader and comparativist is compelled to stand in an analogously tense and precarious situation. On the one hand, these chapters cumulatively effect a powerful exclusion of access to Advaita through experience alone or knowledge alone; they insist on channeling access through the narrow door of the Text and its rigors, according to the sheer demands of reading it and the elaborately constructed safeguards which determine potential readers. On this basis, we seem to have made it impossible for outsiders, theologians or others, to participate in Advaita.

On the other hand, however, this understanding of Advaita and this exclusion of the paths of experience and reason in favor of the Text has been a successful intrusion upon the Text; it is articulated only in the persistent act of (mis)reading the Text, violating its margins, comprehending and then losing sight of its truth, uncompromisingly shaping and reshaping each and every question an outsider might bring to the Text. Though discovering ourselves barred, we have nevertheless insisted on becoming readers of the Text, however inelegant and improperly prepared our reading might be. The ideal of pure Advaita insight is thus revered at the very moment it is violated, as we cross the boundaries of Advaita and intrude upon its inner spaces, thereby beginning to make available to every patient reader of English the Text's power to transform those who read it. Though the truth of the Text may elusively conceal itself behind the complex demands of proper reading, our (mis)reading nevertheless provides a simple rejoinder to that complexity, and so cooperates with the Advaita to express once more its characteristic tension between the complex requirements of reading and the simple event of insight.

We are quite far removed at this point from a discussion of the principles of Vedānta philosophy, and we have quite arduously rendered ourselves unready to compare Vedānta theology with Christian theology. We have managed to lose our exteriority to Advaita, and now stand outside neither tradition; we are equipped only for those words which come after the continuing, persevering act of engaged reading. Yet, immersed in this increasing host of interpretive issues which threaten at every turn to exclude us altogether, and so to subvert our project, we are at the same moment finally ready to consider how one might progress to a retrieval of theology after Vedānta: to the rereading of a Christian Text, with all that is thereby implied regarding texts, truths and readers. This is the inquiry which makes up our final chapter.

Chapter 5

Theology after Advaita Vedānta: The Text, The Truth, and The Theologian

I. *The Practice of Comparative Theology*

The previous chapters have taught us the importance of careful reading, and the necessity of discovering Advaita's truth after and through that Text which reaches from the upaniṣads to the latest of the commentaries, and not despite it. Even if one desires a simpler truth beyond the complexities of texts and commentaries, and a rupture with the elitist strictures of the tradition, in Advaita these are deferred to a posttextual moment of insight, in which the practiced and accomplished reader resolves the tension between Advaita's texts and its single referent, Brahman.

Comparative theology as theology after Vedānta proceeds in the same fashion. I therefore begin by reemphasizing the practical and temporal nature of comparative theology, as a rereading and subsequent retrieval of one's prior theology after an appropriation of Vedānta. Theology after Advaita Vedānta is not a theology that chooses from among the ideas of the Advaita and Christian traditions, but is one in which a Christian theologian begins to think again the entire range of problems and possibilities in the (Christian) theological tradition, after a serious engagement in the Advaita Text: after, posterior, in imitation of, according to Vedānta.

Time is of the essence, and the significance of time cannot be replicated, nor its fruits identified, in the abstract; though the progress one accomplishes over time can be talked about and its contours sketched, it must be enacted in order to be properly understood. This chapter therefore preserves a studiously practical tone; it is primarily concerned about how one might read theology and articulate theological truth after one has become at least initially familiar with Advaita.

By design, this chapter fails to draw firm conclusions based on the comparison of Advaita and Christian theology, for the goal is rather to uncover the important activities and changes which necessarily precede any such conclusions. Later, on the basis of this delineation, and as it is amplified in further experiments in reading, it will become possible to draw more specific conclusions on what a theologian is to read, or write, in a comparative context, and how one might best identify that theologian. Moreover, as stated in Chapter 1, it is only one particular form of Christian theology that is really at issue here—my own particular appropriation of late 20th century American Roman Catholicism—and this as (re)articulated after the study of Advaita, which is only one particular form of Vedānta. Any larger insights into comparative method must be carefully derived from a comparison which, though in a certain way ambitious, is studiously narrow in content and concerns; and, as indicated in Chapter 4, such insights are likely to be the achievement of skilled readers, those who apply this (mere) example properly.

The particular exercise in comparison which comprises this chapter selects the *Summa Theologiae* of Thomas Aquinas as the Text[1]—inscribed in its tradition, adorned with its commentaries—which is to be reread after Advaita Vedānta. There is no single compelling reason why this choice is the best or the most productive, or necessary. Comparison is a creative procedure, in which the comparativist's construction of new meanings begins with her or his partly arbitrary choice of texts to compare. Comparison forges a link which was not previously there, a link which (usually) cannot be justified on the basis of historical connections or of similarities so striking that they compel comparison.

Even if some preliminary sense of similarities or differences guides a comparativist in constructing the comparison, a potentially unlimited set of possible starting points presents itself. Even if one becomes aware of intriguing similarities, and legitimately (or not) theorizes about common structures of human reason or action or experience or language which can be called upon to justify these similarities, the comparativist remains first and foremost the active, creative composer of the text/context in which any of these points might be considered.

The dynamics of this constructed and creative situation must be remembered and respected by the comparativist, since after the initial choice the new context does not remain entirely in her or his control. She or he must be willing to submit to the possibilities of the newly composed context, to allow unexpected meanings to occur in the course of rereading, new complications—an entire array of further issues which she or he may not have had in mind at first. If the comparativist uses texts differently than they were intended to be used in the first place by their authors and communities and traditions, she or he must also admit that the newly constructed comparison has possibilities not entirely under the control of this comparativist; initial intentions do not govern completely the fruits of comparison.

If one takes seriously the experimental, constructive nature of comparisons, then both the comparativists and their communities will have to be patient with practices that do not yet have refined theoretical justifications. These practices lack such explanations precisely because they are new, and because they need to occur, repeatedly, before it is worthwhile to spend time trying to justify them and reduce them to a smoother, habitual form. When measured against other areas of theology, long established and refined over centuries, comparative theology will seem ill-defined and ill-evaluated. Rather than denying this incompleteness, we need to note carefully the early stage of its development at which comparative theology stands—it is only now identifying its texts and how to read them— and to insist that this inaugural practice is not—ought not to be—turned quickly into perfect(ed) theory.

This chapter mirrors the pattern which was identified at the end of Chapter 1 and which structured the intervening Chapters 2, 3 and 4: corresponding to the consideration of the Advaita Text in Chapter 2, section II of this chapter examines the texts/traditions/Text which the comparativist constitutes in the return to his or her own tradition after comparison; corresponding to Chapter 3, section III inquires into the truth of the theology composed by such a theologian; corresponding to Chapter 4, section IV examines the reader-theologian who rereads theology after Advaita Vedānta, who writes out of the posteriority and who, ultimately, is the location where the resolution of the tensions between theological comparison and theological truth occurs.

II. The Composition of the Text for Comparative Theology: Reading the **Summa Theologiae** *and the* **Uttara Mīmāṃsā Sūtras** *Together*

Our reading of the Advaita Text—the *Uttara Mīmāṃsā Sūtras* and its commentaries in the Advaita tradition—has been a fruitful experiment due in part to its specificity and detail. Its fruition can now be enjoyed in a comparative context, insofar as the comparative project is carried forward with the same care for detail and specificity. To inaugurate this mode of specific comparison, I draw on one of the great classics of the Christian theological tradition, the *Summa Theologiae* of Thomas Aquinas (1225–1274). The *Summa Theologiae*[2] is finely reasoned, elegantly argued, and pedagogically attuned, a classic contribution to the articulation of the Christian faith—as doctrine, practice, behavior, understanding. A very brief outline of this large work must suffice:

Part I God
- Quaestio 1:[3] (theology as) sacred teaching (*sacra doctrina*)
- Quaestiones 2–26: the divine essence
- Quaestiones 27–43: the three divine Persons
- Quaestiones 44–119: the procession of created beings from God

Part II.1 Virtue and its structure in general
Part II.2 Virtues in particular

Part III Christ
Quaestiones 1–59 the Incarnation
Quaestiones 60–72 the sacraments[4]

This monumental theological achievement, in some ways a European analogue to the Advaita Text, is introduced here by way of example. Parts of it are chosen for a selective reading, without any pretense that this selection follows that full reading and rereading which will be required to bring the present experiment in reading and rereading to completion.

Time spent in the reading of Advaita prompts us to reconceive of the *Summa Theologiae* as a "Text," in the sense introduced at the end of Chapter 1 and explored in detail in Chapter 2: a series of (written) acts of language which are irreducible to any author's or authors' intention(s) or to the announced and practiced purposes of any particular later tradition, but which are read as intertextually composed into a larger whole comprised of a series of related texts: e.g., a text along with those which are inscribed in it by citation, and those which exist in the form of commentary upon it. It is this larger Text of the *Summa Theologiae* which is fruitfully read along with the Text composed in relation to the *Uttara Mīmāṃsā Sūtras*.

As mentioned above, we are already engaged in an important constructive activity when we construct this, or any other, particular comparison. The rereading process begins well before the act of comparing one or another part of the *Summa Theologiae* with one or another part of the Advaita Text, and much has been effected merely by our decision to read the *Uttara Mīmāṃsā Sūtras* and *Summa Theologiae* Texts together. The *Summa* is put to a new use, reconstituted by a reader who intends to look at it from a new angle, for new purposes. Instead of using it simply as an instance of medieval theology, or as a vantage point from which to assess a variety of issues related to medieval Christian thought in connection to Aristotelianism, Jewish and Islamic theology, etc., or as *the* text of Catholic theology, or as the best introduction to Christian theology—instead of these (and other) traditional uses, the comparative theologian uses the *Summa Theologiae* to clarify the changes that occur in the Christian reader who has engaged seriously in the reading of Advaita.

One may find that the *Summa Theologiae* is thus enhanced, because it is now privileged to exemplify the Christian side of comparison, as a superior, articulate version of the Christian faith. Placed in a new context by being reread after Advaita, it is given a new and prominent position vis à vis both sides of the comparison. It is as if Aquinas has now been identified, by experiment, as the "Śaṅkara of Europe," the *Summa Theologiae* as the "Christian *Uttara Mīmāṃsā Sūtras*," etc. But we may also find that the *Summa Theologiae* is thereby reduced to a (mere) example; it becomes "one important Christian text," important—at least at the moment—less for its content or its success as an authoritative articulation of the Christian worldview and its knowledge about God, than for its function as a vehicle for the clarification of issues not contained directly in the *Summa Theologiae* itself. The relationship between a very important Christian text and the comparativist as reader has been radically revised, as the text becomes a mere tool in the comparativist's hands: it is marginalized, for one has stepped outside it, instrumentalized it. It now occurs in a larger world than it could have imagined, it no longer entirely constitutes a world, it is reused in a way that is strikingly divergent from the intention of its author and from the tradition's habitual handling of it. The comparative reader sees not only how the *Summa Theologiae* presumes and entails a complete Christian worldview, but also how that worldview reaches no farther than its margins, what it has been able to say in its vocabulary, rules of language, and accumulated set of references. All of this is so, even if one wishes to avoid, as I do, a reduction of the compared texts to mere materials for consumption in a comparative project which seeks a tertium quid, some wisdom which reaches beyond both the UMS and *Summa Theologiae* Texts.

The general transformation of the *Summa Theologiae* as Text is further specified in the comparativist's selection of examples by which to highlight similarities and differences, to uncover and accentuate the implicit presuppositions of the text, details which, however small, are crucially important in conveying its texture. This process of finding examples need not be a matter of identifying those parts of the *Summa Theologiae* which are considered (by contemporary Thomists) to be the most important, most representative of Aquinas' thought, most original, most traditional, most brilliant. It is in part an act of resistance to such habitual choices and evaluations that one retrieves the whole of the Text by the circuitous route of reading Advaita first. It may even turn out to be a reading which goes against the consensus of Aquinas scholars as to what counts most in Aquinas—a resistance practiced not merely for the sake of novelty, but in order to uncover possibilities hidden by centuries of familiarity.

Let us begin by examining two examples in which parts of the *Summa Theologiae* are read differently after the study of Advaita. My first example uses ST I.13.4 in comparison with UMS III.3.11–13 and Amalānanda's comment thereon (already considered in Chapter 3). I have chosen them because both texts address the problem of theological language, and together pose an interesting set of similarities and differences about how one can speak of what is not adequately captured in words. By contrast, my second example raises the issue of how one might handle a possible case of incomparability: the Passion of Christ as treated in ST III.46–49.

1. *Rereading* Summa Theologiae *I.13.4 after UMS III.3.11–13*

a. Setting the Comparison

In Chapter 3 we examined UMS III.3.11–13 as part of our project of tracing the development of an exegetically rooted discourse about Brahman in the UMS Text. UMS III.3, we saw, is devoted to the question of how one is to use in meditation different texts from different upaniṣadic traditions which may speak of Brahman in the same way; in that pāda the Advaitins develop the practical strategy of coordination (upasaṃhāra). The Advaitins presupposed that the upaniṣads, which are a series of texts-for-meditation, all refer to the same Brahman; they asked whether the information given about Brahman in each text was pertinent only when that text is being used in meditation, or whether it was permissible—indeed required—that one carry over from one text to another certain qualifications of Brahman. Śaṅkara's response was that those qualifications which pertain to the essence of Brahman—that it is true, existent, blissful, etc.—are everywhere relevant, while others qualify Brahman only for the sake of one meditation, and so apply only there: "its head is joy, its right side delight," "uniting all that is pleasant," etc.

As we saw, Amalānanda articulated the necessary distinctions which allowed for an articulation of a way of speaking—a theological grammar of Brahman. Here, again, is the core of his comment:

> [Objection:] If bliss, etc., should be introduced from all contexts on the grounds that Brahman is one, then why are "uniting all that is pleasant," etc. [which also refer to Brahman] not thus introduced?
>
> [Response:] "Uniting all that is pleasant," etc., are enjoined [only] for the sake of acts of meditation. Because the precise demarcation of the result connected with an injunction is not known, then all the details connected with that result must be organized precisely according to the injunction [since there is no other standard by which to make sure that they contribute properly].
>
> By contrast, truth, consciousness, etc. serve to ascertain the essence of the object; wherever the essence of that object is pertinent, there they are to be introduced . . .
>
> [Objection:] Regarding what is "without qualities" [Brahman] words other [than that single marker "without qualities"] are useless, and so they should not be introduced [from other meditation contexts.]
>
> [Response:] [i] truth, [ii] consciousness, [iii] bliss, [iv] infinity and [v] self are terms which mutually qualify one another, [respectively] overturn the flaws of [i] falsity, [ii] nonconsciousness, [ii] sorrow, [iv] limitedness and [v] lack of self, and so define that single bliss, which is the common basis for truth, etc. It is just like the words "existent," "material thing" and "pot" [all define] a single pot.
>
> The definition that Brahman is of this sort cannot occur due to one word alone, since if only one word is used, there will be no conflict [of meanings] and no indirect signification. Hence, other words must be used. Insofar as errors are possible, a whole string of words capable of ending those errors must be introduced; in order to end those errors [in

every case], the string of word-meanings must be everywhere introduced.

Though each word is in itself inadequate, and though the meaning of "Brahman" is not merely the sum total of the meanings of words spoken alongside it, the inadequate words taken together are mutually corrective and serve to define, if not Brahman itself, a correct and useful way of speaking about Brahman, a correct usage of the word "Brahman."

We can now read ST I.13.4 against this background. The introductory section of the *Summa Theologiae* is a defense and exposition of the possibility of doing theology. Within this larger topic, I.13 deals with the possibility of naming God, and the status of the (largely scriptural) names used with reference to God.

ST I.13.1–3 establish three points of particular relevance for our understanding of 13.4: a. although God is infinite and not subject to limitation, names can be legitimately used with reference to God (article 1); b. these names refer to the substance of God, and do not merely exclude erroneous conceptions (article 2); c. the words which we use regarding God's perfections apply more appropriately, and not less so, to God than they do to human realities to which we also apply them. Thus, it is appropriate to say "God is good," although we have no other example of perfect goodness that would justify this use of the word "good" (article 3).

In ST I.13.4, Aquinas rejects the view that all names applied to God are synonymous since God is totally simple and therefore by his very essence the referent of all names. If the referent of all names is a single, simple reality, how could they *not* all mean the same thing? The response is as follows:

> On the contrary, all synonyms united with each other are redundant, as when we say, "vesture clothing." Therefore if all names applied to God are synonymous, we cannot properly say "good God," or the like, and yet it is written, "O most mighty, great and powerful, the Lord of hosts is thy name." (*Jeremiah* 32.18)
>
> I answer that, These names spoken of God are not synonymous. This would be easy to understand, if we said that these names are used to remove, or to express, the relation of the cause to creatures; for thus it would follow that there

> are different ideas as regards the diverse things denied of God, or as regards diverse effects connoted.
>
> But even according to what was said above (ST I.13.2), that these names signify the divine substance, although in an imperfect manner, it is also clear from what has been said (ST I.13.1,2) that they have diverse meanings. For the idea signified by the name is the conception in the intellect of the thing signified by the name. But our intellect, since it knows God from creatures, in order to understand God, forms conceptions proportional to the perfections flowing from God to creatures, which perfections pre-exist in God unitedly and simply, whereas in creatures they are received, divided and multiplied.
>
> As, therefore, to the different perfections of creatures there corresponds one simple principle represented by different perfections of creatures in a various and manifold manner, so also to the various and multiplied conceptions of our intellect there corresponds one altogether simple principle, according to these conceptions, imperfectly understood. Therefore, although the names applied to God signify one thing, still, because they signify that [one thing] under many and different aspects, they are not synonymous.[5]

Our namings of God are many, and each is justified because all perfections properly pertain to God. Yet they are significant only as mediated by our understanding of finite realities, and so none is in itself adequately expressive; hence we learn better by using more and not fewer of them.

Thus far the two texts. Rather than the proposal of a theory of theological language which would then be exemplified with reference to the texts, the practice of comparative theology is first of all a patient and prolonged reading and rereading of the texts together. Indeed, it would be ideal for the studious reader to memorize both passages before proceeding further with analysis; one would then more accurately replicate the sequence of proper memorization and study to which we referred in the preceding chapter.[6]

But for our consideration I simply repeat the texts here, this time juxtaposed for the sake of a comparative reading.

Amalānanda

[Objection:] If bliss, etc., should be introduced from all contexts on the grounds that Brahman is one, then why are "uniting all that is pleasant," etc. [which also refer to Brahman] not thus introduced?

[Response:] "Uniting all that is pleasant," etc., are enjoined [only] for the sake of acts of meditation. Because the precise demarcation of the result connected with an injunction is not known, then all the details connected with that result must be organized precisely according to the injunction [since there is no other standard by which to make sure that they contribute properly].

By contrast, truth, consciousness, etc. serve to ascertain the essence of the object; wherever the essence of that object is pertinent, there they are to be introduced . . .

[Objection:] Regarding what is "without qualities" [Brahman] words other [than that single marker "without qualities"] are useless, and so they should not be introduced [from other meditation contexts.]

[Response:] [i] truth, [ii] consciousness, [iii] bliss, [iv] infinity and [v] self are terms which mutually qualify one another, [respectively] overturn the flaws of [i] falsity, [ii] non-consciousness, [ii] sorrow, [iv] limitedness and [v] lack of self, and so define that single bliss, which is the common basis for truth, etc. It is just like the words "existent," "material thing" and "pot" [all define] a single pot.

The definition that Brahman is of this sort cannot occur due to one word alone, since if only one word is used, there will be no conflict [of meanings] and no indirect signification. Hence, other words must be used. Insofar as errors are possible, a whole string of words capable of ending those errors must be introduced; in order to end those errors [in every case], the string of word-meanings must be everywhere introduced.

Aquinas

[Objection: It seems that all the names which are used for God are synonyms.]

On the contrary, all synonyms united with each other are redundant, as when we say, "vesture clothing". Therefore if all names applied to God are synonymous, we cannot properly say "good God," or the like, and yet it is written, "O most mighty, great and powerful, the Lord of hosts is they name." [*Jeremiah* 32.18]

I answer that, These names spoken of God are not synonymous. This would be easy to understand, if we said that these names are used to remove, or to express, the relation of the cause to creatures; for thus it would follow that there are different ideas as regards the diverse things denied of God, or as regards diverse effects connoted.

But even according to what was said above (ST I.13.2), that these names signify the divine substance, although in an imperfect manner, it is also clear from what has been said (ST I.13.1,2) that they have diverse meanings. For the idea signified by the name is the conception in the intellect of the thing signified by the name. But our intellect, since it knows God from creatures, in order to understand God, forms conceptions proportional to the perfections flowing from God to creatures, which perfections pre-exist in God unitedly and simply, whereas in creatures they are received, divided and multiplied.

As, therefore, to the different perfections of creatures there corresponds one simple principle represented by different perfections of creatures in a various and manifold manner, so also to the various and multiplied conceptions of our intellect there corresponds one altogether simple principle, according to these conceptions, imperfectly understood. Therefore, although the names applied to God signify one thing, still, because they signify that [one thing] under many and different aspects, they are not synonymous.

Once the texts have been read together, and reread a number of times in that mutual proximity, one can usefully proceed to notice certain similarities and differences.

b. Finding Similarities

As one might expect from the fact of my choice, the texts are indeed somewhat alike. Aquinas, like Amalānanda, wants to preserve the unity of God and also the meaningfulness of the multiplicity of namings of God found in scripture. Those names can serve, as in Advaita, to foster or exclude certain ways of talking about the relationship of the creator and the created. As Aquinas adds, they can also signify, from the multiplicity of created experience, the perfections which exist in perfect simplicity only in God; each moment of awareness of the possible perfection of a part of created reality undergirds a possible different naming of God as the source and realization of that perfection. Amalānanda and Aquinas agree that there is a point to using multiple, inadequate "namings" for Brahman and God, respectively.

Both Aquinas and Amalānanda are theologians who respect the scriptural basis of their work. Both want to prevent the collapse of scriptural and theological language in the face of the perfectly simple unity of the transcendent, and to show how the rich variety of that (imperfect) language needs to be appreciated if we are to know the transcendent better. Though description must remain connected to the practical, gradual and shifting compositions of theology undertaken in each tradition, and though one needs to take into account the sources of theological writing about either God or Brahman in either tradition, it is still possible to recognize in such descriptive endeavors a real ability to speak of God and of Brahman—and in an objective fashion, even if the features of this speaking might still have to be described according to the distinctive temporal and spatial features of each tradition.

A careful reading that continues along these lines, however complexly, will confirm all the more strongly the initial impression that the comparison is plausible and the similarities real, and with such texts it would be possible to construct more complex comparative theological structures. One might describe, for example, how imperfect language provides us with salvific knowledge of the transcendent; or, from attention to individual words, one might work toward the examination of more complex similarities, such as those governing the relationships of Brahman or God to the human person who speaks of either.[7] For the sake of such descriptions, one might grant to one or the other text the leading position, but without making the other entirely dispensable. Finally, because generated from attention to both thinkers, the resultant theological position would be genuinely unprecedented, even in its sophisticated and self-consciously "postcomparative" formulation, since it would be composed out of and after the two traditions as they are reread together.

c. Finding Differences ✓

However interesting the similarities and the further possible projects might be, attention to these is not enough. To utilize discovered similarities while overlooking obvious differences accomplishes nothing. Whatever the similarities of the two texts, it is also obvious that they are not identical, that they were written in quite different contexts. They have outstandingly different features, and these differences, distances, and tensions must be preserved—in part because the resistance of texts to complete assimilation is a major part of what is important and interesting about comparison.

Some readers may decide more boldly that the two texts are not at all about "the same thing," whether by "the same thing" one means "God" or "Brahman," or simply "the same theological problem;" the possibility that any given comparison will be recognized as mistaken and therefore rejected need not be excluded in advance. But here I point out only several smaller differences.

First, one may ask if Aquinas' project of defending the application of different names to God is really the same as Amalānanda's project of justifying a procedure by which one transfers some but not all of the attributes of Brahman as the object of meditation from one act of meditation to another. The question is not whether Aquinas' text has spiritual overtones and is written in a context which values the spiritual assimilation of scripture through meditation; the *Summa Theologiae* is clearly sympathetic with such possibilities. Nor is it whether Amalānanda knows the difference between practical spirituality and theology; he clearly does. Rather, the question asks about the difference between Aquinas' effort to present systematically certain conclusions about what can be said about God, and Amalānanda's rooted-in-meditation, practical decision-making about what can be transferred or not from meditation to meditation. Do the markedly different contexts differentiate the two texts to such an extent that their similarities are only apparently real, or only marginal?[8] If one is not prepared to link the texts by merely presupposing that they are about "the same thing," how does one go about defending the connection that is put forth as the starting point for the comparative reading?

Although both authors deal with the problem of synonymity, Aquinas presupposes that all these "perfection-names" apply properly and first to God, while Amalānanda presupposes that no scriptural name can properly apply to Brahman; here we encounter a difference that may indicate larger differences in theories of creation, differences as to how contingent reality is related to the noncontingent. From starting points grounded in different metaphysics, our theologians would then be exploring, in ways increasingly different, the ways in which a multiplicity of names can be used to extend our knowledge beyond what any particular name would point to, and about transcendent realities differently positioned in each tradition. Some of us may decide that an important, initial difference of this sort—should it in fact be the case—would require us to differentiate more severely their apparently similar rejections of synonymity. If both theologians end up claiming that names are inadequate but useful, it may nevertheless be unsettling to say that this claim can be based either on the view that *all* such names apply to the transcendent, or on the view that *no* such names apply to it.

To resolve these difficulties, and to become able to recognize which differences matter and which do not in the formulation of a comparative context, we are eventually required to extend our knowledge of the contexts of the two texts, to put the selected texts in perspective, so as to be better able to know precisely how the similarities and differences operate in relation to the larger patterns of each system. We need to know more of the immediate textual contexts, but also of the larger projects of the *Uttara Mīmāṃsā Sūtras* and *Summa Theologiae,* of the historical and literary background of the two texts, etc. In its farthest reach, this process of proper contextualization implies a reexamination of the entirety of both theological traditions and of all that is relevant to them; it becomes an infinitely extended process, in which the texts in question become ever more specified as their context is more broadly articulated, as each discovery is complicated and further questions continually raised. Only at the ever receding horizon does one attain the ideally final, completed context in which one can finally decide if the systems are commensurable or not. Of course, every well-fashioned inquiry is challenged in this fashion, and prudent scholars always manage to impose limits on their research.

The point rather is that careful attention to the similarities and differences between two texts in order to discover their truth compels the comparativist into an increasingly demanding encounter with the Texts in which the truth of comparison is inscribed. As in Advaita itself, the comparative project discovers within its confines an enduring tension between its Text and its truth, the persistent concealment of its truth in the complexities of the compared Texts. As in Advaita, too, the resolution lies ultimately in the ability of the properly educated and accomplished comparativist, who is able to renounce comfortable presuppositions and convenient shortcuts to truth. It is that comparativist who can make the required series of sound judgments about what matters, about which further questions to ask and which to leave aside for the moment, about where the truth of comparison finally lies. But before taking up more extensively these questions of truth and reader, however, let us explore several other aspects of the practice of comparison.

d. Some Strategies for the Practice of Reading Amalānanda and Aquinas Together

The challenge posed to the reader by the juxtaposition of the texts cannot be reduced even to the more complex acts of recognizing and arranging similarities and differences; the practice is always richer and more potent than these component activities, and it is a mistake to reduce comparative work to them. In the following pages I highlight how one might attentively manage the extended practice of comparing juxtaposed texts, by presenting, in the briefest of sketches, five models for that practice. I sketch two possibilities drawn from the Advaita tradition and three from contemporary theological and literary studies: i. the Advaita practices of "coordination" (upasaṃhāra)[9] and ii. "superimposition" (adhyāsa);[10] iii. the notion of "a comparative theological conversation;" iv. Philip Wheelwright's understanding of metaphor; v. Jacques Derrida's practice of "collage."

i. Coordination (upasaṃhāra): Rules for Using Texts Together[11]

In Chapters 2 and 3 we examined coordination as a practical strategy adopted by the Advaitins to facilitate their judgment as to how texts from different upaniṣads could, or could not, be used together in meditation. The practice of coordination developed in continuity with other Mīmāṃsā strategies for the adjudication of differences among ritual texts, although the Advaitins had to refine a position of their own on how texts relate to Brahman as their (extra- and posttextual) referent. Coordination enabled the Advaitins to use texts together, taking advantage practically of their common terms, parallel structures and conclusions. They succeeded in meeting this practical need, while moving toward the position that because Brahman is one, some textual material is reusable outside its original context and beyond the usage warranted by the text and its context, and while at the same time continuing to preserve the distinctness of any two texts which were considered together. Texts were used together, not melded into one.

It is possible to think of the use together of Christian and Advaita theological texts as an instance of coordination, aimed at a more skilled rereading of them, one which takes into account comparable terms and themes and parallel modes of operation—constituted as such in all the complex and ambiguous ways suggested above—while yet not reducing the two texts to a single text, or subordinating both to a perspective which would undercut the textuality of both. Like coordination, this reflective juxtaposition would be a largely practical experiment. Nor would it require complement by a completed theoretical position or extratextual knowledge about the truth or status of the compared texts. The knowledge that is gained would remain posttextual, emerging from the practice of comparing familiar texts without the encumbering desire, or ability, to reduce them to a single body of information. Yet precisely because there is no overarching framework—not yet, at least—in which the compared texts could be accounted for, the studiously pragmatic strategy of coordination becomes all the more valuable.[12]

ii. Superimposition (adhyāsa): The Superimposition of One Text on Another

Superimposition (adhyāsa) is the act of imposing one reality—idea, person, thing, word—on another, for the purpose of an enhanced meditation on the latter.[13] In UMS III.3.9 and UMS IV.1.5 Śaṅkara characterizes superimposition as a form of meditation in which the meditator deliberately imposes one reality upon another for the sake of an enhanced meditation: when, for instance, one imposes a mental image of the sun on one's eyes in order to meditate on the latter, or a mental image of Viṣṇu on a small smooth stone. He identifies two necessary conditions for correct superimposition: a. one can fruitfully superimpose a higher reality on a lower (the sun on the eye, Viṣṇu on the stone,) because the proximate, lesser reality and the act of meditation on it are thereby enhanced; to impose the lower on the higher would be pointless. (UMS IV.1.5) b. In the course of meditation, neither reality is forgotten, and one remains aware of the act of superimposition. (UMS III.3.9)[14] A third attribute is implied: c. the superimposition is only temporary, for use in a particular meditation and for a set purpose; the meditator does not prolong it indefinitely nor is it claimed that the connection is a necessary one.

Thus explained, superimposition reflects what often occurs in comparison, intentionally or unconsciously. A member of one religious tradition superimposes a text from another tradition upon one from her or his own, remembering the difference, remembering when the superimposition is begun and when it is finished, and performing it not as an example of some deeper sameness, but for the sake of that enhancement which occurs through the partial identification and the subsequent defamiliarization that occurs due to superimposition. The familiar is seen anew, read differently because there is superimposed upon it something significantly different.

One may of course wish to explore further the implied evaluative moment in superimposition, in cognizance of Śaṅkara's observation that the superior is to be imposed on the inferior in a purposeful superimposition. The comparativist will have to decide whether to identify one tradition as superior to the other, estimating the practical advantages that would accrue from an explicit evaluation of that sort; she or he will have to ask whether the projected comparison does not in fact intend just such an enhancement of the more familiar text, even if this intention has not been stated explicitly. In the preceding pages I have referred more neutrally to a juxtaposition of texts, rather than to the superimposition of one upon another; but there is no reason to perform comparisons exclusively from a strictly neutral position.

iii. The Comparative Conversation

Drawing on the work of Hans-Georg Gadamer, David Tracy draws our attention to the advantages of conversation as a model for the way we appropriate texts, as we learn from an "other" who for a moment stands near us in an ongoing conversation, an other with whom we converse, and who is neither the same as us nor entirely different. Conversation

> occurs if, and only if, we will risk ourselves by allowing the questions of the text. We must follow those questions—however initially different, other, or even strange—until the

> unique result of this kind of interaction occurs: the exploration of possibility as possible, and thus as similarity-in-difference. In such moments of recognition, what is both disclosed and concealed as other and different becomes appropriated as possibility.[15]

Q
MO

The imaginative process of reading back-and-forth in the conversation of one's own tradition with another requires a genuine openness to unforeseen possibilities, the potential smaller and larger transformations of the self of the person who genuinely enters an encounter. As a literate conversationalist, the comparativist progresses through a reflective, gradual dialogue with the compared, conversational other, a conversation the conclusion of which one cannot theoretically predict.

The conversation model envisions a reading which must be reflectively performed, in which one is articulate but never completely so; what one has to say is in part determined by what one hears, reads, at any given point. One comes to the comparison with something to contribute, while yet remaining vulnerable to the implications of what one might hear. Only if the other is allowed to speak, can the conversation proceed. Our extended initiation into the world of the Advaita Text has taken into account the risks implied by an encounter with this complex, thoughtful and demanding "other," including the likelihood that the reader will become inextricably involved in a new Text and hence in its formulation of the world. Conversations, once begun, are sometimes not easily ended; sometimes the partners quarrel, occasionally they fall in love. As the Advaitins might put it, the conversation between the Texts instigates a desire to know which comprehensively transforms those who dare to read.

iv. The Comparative Tension: Metaphor, Epiphor and Diaphor

The event of resignification that occurs in comparison and rereading is helpfully illuminated also by attention to metaphor. One can entertain the idea that by the activities of comparative reading the compared texts are placed in tension, extended and transformed, as new meanings are articulated for each precisely in their juxtaposition.

Philip Wheelwright describes metaphor as the act of "tensive language" in which "man gropes to express his complex nature and his sense of the complex world . . . seeks or creates representational and expressive forms . . . which shall give some hint, always finally insufficient, of the turbulent moods within and the turbulent world of qualities and forces, promises and threats, outside him."[16] Wheelwright pays special attention to the intentional, creative act of juxtaposition: "what really matters in a metaphor is the psychic depth at which the things of the world, whether actual or fancied, are transmuted by the cool heat of the imagination. The transmutative process that is involved may be described as *semantic motion*; the idea of which is implicit in the very word 'metaphor,' since the motion (*phora*) that the word connotes is a semantic notion—the double imaginative act of outreaching and combining that essentially marks the metaphoric process."[17] This transmutation may occur through "epiphor" or "diaphor:" epiphor indicates "the outreach and extension of meaning through comparison," and diaphor "the creation of new meaning by juxtaposition and synthesis."[18]

The practices of epiphor and diaphor usefully extend our understanding of the practice of comparison, because the practice of them invites us to emphasize the way in which a comparison can be constructed so as to produce an initially uncomfortable tension—a semantic motion—at the moment when the texts are taken up in order to be read together, even the feeling that the comparison is unjustified, or too weak, or too hasty. One may be upset, disoriented, intrigued; but one is thereby enabled to reflect on the implications of that tension, appreciating it without making it more permanent than the momentary construct it may in fact be.

The powerful motion frequently achieved in poetry through the careful manipulation of words in relation to one another can be achieved also in the juxtaposition of texts from different traditions: placed unusually together, they come to mean differently, though only insofar as they also maintain their own meanings. The decision to read Amalānanda alongside Aquinas has an important effect on both texts insofar as they are read attentively together; yet one does not rewrite either text, nor reinterpret one so as to be entirely consonant with the other. Placing them side by side, either literally or as if in two columns, compels the reader either to extend both texts' meanings, and to recognize the new meanings produced only from both together.

v. Collage: Visualizing the Margins of Comparison

I draw a final model for comparison from the writings of Jacques Derrida, who excels in a way of reading that is rigorous yet unsettling. In helpfully describing Jacques Derrida's "grammatological" strategy of decomposing texts into selected "clippings" in order to release them from their controlling contexts, Gregory Ulmer has shown how some of Derrida's most exciting—and bewildering—writings proceed precisely by strategies of excision, recomposition and new juxtaposition, as these produce hitherto nonexistent meanings which could never be otherwise expressed.[19]

Ulmer appeals to the practice of "collage"—borrowed from the visual arts—to locate Derrida's way of producing new meanings through decomposition and the subsequent constructive modes of writing:

> The effectiveness of collage is that, like metaphor, the piece, displaced into a new context, retains associations with its former context. The two operations constituting the collage technique—selection and combination—are the operations characteristic of all speaking and writing. Moreover, as in language usage, the operations are carried out on preformed material. Derrida uses his decompositional, dissolving, collage technique to break up the clear and distinct outlines of the concept, with distorting effects similar to those achieved in cubism with regard to the conventions of representation in the visual arts... The use of collage permits Derrida to escape the traditional "intentionality" in favor of a writing that is productive outside the ideology of communication.[20]

The process of collage is most vividly pursued in *Glas*, a text composed entirely of quite different materials (drawn mostly from Hegel and Genet) juxtaposed in two columns which run the length of the book. The "collaged" texts meet, resist and intrude upon one another; they destabilize each other's meanings, and in turn unsettle the reader who is forced to learn to read differently if she or he is to master skillfully this disorienting material.[21]

Comparative theological reading shares features with this strategy of collage, as the constructive comparativist unsettles two (or more) traditions by excising important and familiar materials from their "legitimate" contexts in order to use them together newly, necessarily without prior warrant. The traditional interpretations woven around both texts, though recognized, are bracketed and rendered momentarily inarticulate. The reader, a member of either tradition who chooses to become a comparativist, is compelled to interact with the materials in a way that neither tradition would recognize as "its own way." She or he must work very hard with the newly aligned materials, each subjected momentarily to the disorienting power of temporary acts of decontextualization and recontextualization. The procedure is effective and productive, in part because there is no established, approved set of margins within which the reading can be contained; nor is there any entirely adequate summation, before or after the reading, of what the juxtaposition is supposed to mean.

This process of unsettling collage is in part what is accomplished in the juxtaposition of Amalānanda and Aquinas printed earlier in this chapter. The reader can, if she or he wishes, see/read each text differently because they are now located together, and thereafter interpret each differently in light of the new possibilities and constraints thereby introduced. Or one may resist the collage, and refuse to look at the texts on the same page.

These five models—coordination, superimposition, conversation, metaphor and collage—have been introduced in order to indicate ways in which we can imagine what we are doing when we read together texts from different theological traditions, and persist in this practice over time, and in a way more richly productive than the mere listing of similarities and differences. One may of course experiment with more than one of these models, since each focuses our inquiry in a different practical fashion: i. the strategies by which one makes the reading together of compared texts a manageable but not reductive reflection; ii. the temporal arrangements by which one text is allowed to enhance the other; iii. the engagement in multiple texts as the initiation of an ongoing and necessarily unpredictable conversation; iv. the construction of tensions by which the texts taken together are allowed to communicate more than either of them alone; v. the visualization of proximities by which the texts marginalize and destabilize one another.

Such value of these practices will be known only in their performance, as their potential benefits are available only after their enactment; and so we must leave open the question of the use of the models in any particular comparison, while inviting the reader to complete the process initiated here. In each case, the active contextualization of the texts of Aquinas and Amalānanda, or other such pairs, demands a commitment to reading and an increasing skill in reading, along with a deferral of those strategies of systematization which would obviate the arduous path back and forth through the juxtaposed texts. The demands of Text and texture imposed on us by the Advaita—demands doubled in the moment of retrieval of another Text such as the *Summa Theologiae*—require persistently textual responses, self-conscious strategies of reading and writing which achieve resolution only through and after the event of a properly enacted rereading.

2. *Are There Incomparable Texts? The Example of ST III.46.3*

With just one example we have embarked on a rereading of the entirety of the two Texts involved; the expected rereading is a comprehensive one, and no part of a Text, however central, can be appealed to as an excuse for not reading other parts of it; and no part can be ignored merely on the grounds that it is inconsistent with the general trajectory of the reading that is undertaken. We must therefore take into account the possibility that there are at least some parts of texts which resist comparison, which are so significantly unlike what is found in other texts that any possible comparison is likely to be unwarranted. Let us examine one such text, Aquinas' treatment of the Passion of Christ, which may appear incomparable, since it would seem that in Advaita there is nothing like the Passion, in fact or in principle.

After locating the Passion within the more comprehensive frame of Christ's departure from the world, Aquinas outlines ST III.46–49 as follows: "With regard to the Passion [ST III.46–49], there arises a threefold consideration: 1. The Passion itself (46); 2. the efficient cause of the Passion (47); 3. the fruits of the Passion (48–49)." ST III.46 explores the Passion by inquiring into its necessity, appropriateness, and efficacy:

> 1. Whether it was necessary for Christ to suffer for men's deliverance; 2. whether there was any other possible means of delivering men; 3. whether this was the more suitable means; 4. whether it was fitting for Christ to suffer on the cross; 5. the extent of His sufferings. 6. whether the pain which He endured was the greatest; 7. whether His entire soul suffered; 8. whether His Passion hindered the joy of fruition; 9. the time of the Passion; 10. the place; 11. whether it was fitting for Him to be crucified with robbers; 12. whether Christ's Passion is to be attributed to the Godhead.

In support of the view that the Passion was the most suitable way for the deliverance of the human race (ST III.46.3) Aquinas explains:

> St. Augustine says, "There was no other more suitable way of healing our misery than by the Passion of Christ." (*On the Trinity* XIII.10.) I answer that among means to an end that one is the more suitable whereby the various concurring means employed are themselves helpful to such end. But in this that man was delivered by Christ's Passion, many other things besides deliverance from sin concurred for man's salvation. In the first place, man knows thereby how much God loves him, and is thereby stirred to love him in return, and herein lies the perfection of human salvation; hence the Apostle says (Romans 5.8): "God commended his charity toward us; for when as yet we were sinners . . . Christ died for us." Secondly, because thereby he set us an example of obedience, humility, constancy, justice, and other virtues displayed in the Passion, which are requisite for

> man's salvation. Hence it is written (I Peter 2:21): "Christ also suffered for us, leaving you an example that you should follow in his steps." Thirdly, because Christ by his Passion not only delivered man from sin, but also merited justifying grace for him and the glory of bliss, as shall be shown later (ST III.48.1; ST III.49.1,5). Fourthly, because by this man is all the more bound to refrain from sin, according to I Corinthians 6.20: "You are bought with a great price: glorify and bear God in your body." Fifthly, because it redounded to man's greater dignity, that as man was overcome and deceived by the devil, so also it should be a man that should overthrow the devil; and as man deserved death, so a man by dying should vanquish death. Hence it is written (I Corinthians 15.57) "Thanks be to God who hath given us the victory through our Lord Jesus Christ." It was accordingly more fitting that we should be delivered by Christ's Passion than simply by God's good-will.

We find here a theological statement of some of the fundamental beliefs of the Christian tradition: Christ died for all; his death is the most suitable way for our salvation to have occurred; his death restores our dignity; it ought to evoke our gratitude.

As such, it is foreign to the Advaita tradition, devoid of obvious parallels or evident starting points for comparison. Even Mīmāmsā's theology of sacrifice is not of much help in providing analogues for the soteriological interpretation of the Passion. One may be tempted then to consider leaving it aside as unsuitable for comparison, or to use it to block further comparisons, because it is both central to the Christian faith and positively "incomparable." One can build a wall around it, as it were, and protect it from other texts.

A rereading of the *Summa Theologiae* after Advaita would be in vain were it merely to undercut a Christian belief as important as a central recognition of the Passion of Christ, or were everything in the *Summa* to be taken into account but one or two such passages. But these outcomes are unnecessary.

In itself, the passage raises no direct, immediate conflict with Advaita; if immediate points of similarity are missing, so too immediate points of contradiction. As examples of theological discourse—which they are, even if they may also be more than that—the claims of Advaita[22] and the Christian claims related to the Passion are both mediated in a complex fashion through the Texts in which they are inscribed. Before ST III.46.3 is either marginalized or allowed to preclude further comparison, some point of consonant or dissonant interconnection with Advaita must first be identified or constructed.

In other words, one must determine where one is in the process of reading the larger Texts together, so as to assess the significance of the (at least) momentarily disturbing incomparability one has discovered; and this determination can be achieved only through the very same process of careful reading that is at work in easier cases of intriguing similarity and interesting difference. In other words, comparative reading is not halted by this ostensibly incomparable passage; rather, it is intensified.

The comparativist who remains steadfastly faithful to the practicality of the comparative enterprise can notice and take into account the evident uniqueness of Aquinas' faith position regarding the Passion, and likewise the lack of any comparable belief or theological expression in the Advaita—and can do this without rushing to a judgment about the truth of the one, on the basis of the other. One might allow a text such as ST III.46.3 to stand noticeably and carefully uncompared, in order to specify and highlight that incomparability, while not overlooking other possibilities for rereading which continue to exist even in the face of this large incomparability.

More ambitiously, one might trace the processes by which the truth of the Passion had been theologically composed and recomposed throughout the tradition before Aquinas, and then in later systems, in order to become able to explore these (re)compositions, and the function of Aquinas' text in regard to them, in light of comparable Advaita recompositions of the truth of Brahman, thereby inaugurating a comparative soteriology. Or, one might go farther and ask which text's viewpoint corresponds most closely to the way the world really is: is it true that we are saved by the Passion of Christ, or is it knowledge of Brahman that liberates? There is no prima facie reason to dismiss this question, or to preclude any of the answers that might be made in response to it.

Whichever option one follows, there is still no persuasive reason to refuse to reread ST III.46.3 alongside a selected Advaita text, even if the juxtaposition highlights distance, inappropriateness and apparent incomparability. Since comparative reading does not depend on similarity, extreme dissimilarity is no reason to end such reading.

3. The Fruits of Recomposing the Theological Text: Retrieving the Bible and the Commentaries on the Summa Theologiae

A retrieval of the textuality of comparison and a reformulation of comparison as first of all an exercise in reading brings to the foreground two aspects of the *Summa Theologiae* which, though never entirely neglected, have been relegated to the background in the the main currents of Thomism in this century. First, we will consider the role of the Bible as a powerful textual resource which helps constitute the *Summa Theologiae* as a Text. Returning to the *Summa Theologiae* after Advaita Vedānta enables us to examine Aquinas' use of the Bible, asking in particular how his reading of this important source, and his strategic use of quotations from it, affect his explanation and rewriting of the theological doctrines and themes received from his predecessors. Second, we retrieve the commentarial tradition which developed in response to the *Summa Theologiae*; we open the door to a reconsideration of the great commentarial and textbook tradition on the *Summa Theologiae*, in order to understand better how this Text's possibilities have been traditionally read and used. Let us consider in turn these scriptural and commentarial retrievals.

a. Retrieving the Citation of the Bible

One can affirm without controversy that the Bible is not unimportant to the *Summa Theologiae* in its overall plan and in its details; few would doubt that that the *Summa Theologiae*, though not a commentary on the Bible and not exegetical in the sense that the UMS is, nevertheless gives evidence of a worldview deeply influenced by the Bible.[23] A bit more controversial, however, is the suggestion that we (re)arrange our reading of the *Summa Theologiae* with a more pronounced emphasis on the exegetical component, at least remedially focusing our attention, for a time, on the dynamics of the *Summa Theologiae* as a text written in light of certain, and not other, biblical texts, and regularly inscribing certain, and not other, Biblical texts within its inquiries. The way the Bible is used by Aquinas reflects the manner of his education in it and reading it, his reception and modification of what he learned from his teachers and predecessors. Given the prominent role of the Bible in almost all versions of Christian theology, knowledge of the particularities of Aquinas' Biblical literacy aids us in differentiating his theology from that of later theologians who, even if profoundly indebted to the *Summa Theologiae,* necessarily approach its inquiries differently because they use and understand the Bible differently. A sharper delineation of the particular modalities of his theological reception of the Bible is an important task before us. The project of spelling out his access to the Bible, his exegetical presuppositions, techniques and practices, and the theology built on those techniques, is a large one which, though taken up by a few modern scholars,[24] is incomplete; any significant advance in this area is certainly beyond the expertise of this author. Here, I merely observe that the broadened context established by comparative theology and by the specific experiment of a reading of Advaita makes Aquinas' use of the Bible more interesting and not less, for the example of Advaita urges us to notice attentively his ways of reading and the expectations his writing place on his readers. I offer a single example of where a more sharply focused attention to his usage might begin.

In the body of ST III.46.3, cited above, and in arguing that the death of Christ on the cross was the most suitable way for God to deliver the human race, Aquinas introduces four Biblical texts:

> St. Augustine says, "There was no other more suitable way of healing our misery than by the Passion of Christ." (*On the Trinity* XIII.10)

> I answer that among means to an end that one is the more suitable whereby the various concurring means employed are themselves helpful to such end. But in this that man was delivered by Christ's Passion, many other things besides deliverance from sin concurred for man's salvation. In the first place, man knows thereby how much God loves him, and is thereby stirred to love him in return, and herein lies the perfection of human salvation; hence the Apostle says (Romans 5.8): "*God commended his charity toward us; for when as yet we were sinners . . . Christ died for us.*" Secondly, because thereby he set us an example of obedience, humility, constancy, justice, and other virtues displayed in the Passion, which are requisite for man's salvation. Hence it is written (I Peter 2:21): "*Christ also suffered for us, leaving you an example that you should follow in his steps.*" Thirdly, because Christ by his Passion not only delivered man from sin, but also merited justifying grace for him and the glory of bliss, as shall be shown later. Fourthly, because by this man is all the more bound to refrain from sin, according to I Corinthians 6.20: "*You are bought with a great price: glorify and bear God in your body.*" Fifthly, because it redounded to man's greater dignity, that as man was overcome and deceived by the devil, so also it should be a man that should overthrow the devil; and as man deserved death, so a man by dying should vanquish death. Hence it is written (I Corinthians 15.57) "*Thanks be to God who hath given us the victory through our Lord Jesus Christ.*" It was accordingly more fitting that we should be delivered by Christ's Passion than simply by God's good-will.

Aquinas' argument is in part aimed at those who are skilled in the complex demands posed by a text which bears with it a rich body of supporting texts. One must be able to follow the logic of his argument, but also to appreciate each of the citations from other sources which are inscribed into that argument; the best readers are those who appreciate the actual citations as indications of the larger contexts from which they are drawn. One might of course simply read around the citations as mere appeals to authority, but better readers attend to them, notice the pattern of citations thus composed, and allow their reading thereby to be redirected back to Aquinas' predecessors' use of the same citations, and thereafter back to the Bible itself as it was received and read in Aquinas' lifetime.

In ST III.46.3 his defense of the appropriateness of the Passion is tightly woven together with the four cited scriptural texts. In reading the argument carefully, one proceeds from an initial familiarization with each of the individual quotations to an examination of each as it is resignified by its place in the argument. Cited together, the texts contribute to a new narrative that is neither the mere sum of the texts, nor merely the argument which includes them, as if "merely embellished" by them. One inquires into their cooperative effect on the communication of the intended argument, the way in which they help fix it, but also the way in which they nevertheless remain "unruled," possessed of their own original and richer meanings, and therefore resistant to any fixed subordination to the intended theological point.[25]

While noting what Aquinas thinks St. Paul or the author of I Peter meant, the reader is able also to read those texts in their original contexts, to examine their connections there, and then to reread Aquinas with attention to the differences in the way he uses them. More than proof-texts, the passages mark the broader worldview within which the statements on the Passion are able to persuade; by a reappropriation of the quotations in and out of their original contexts, we are made ready to notice in a variety of ways the arguments posed by Aquinas. One then begins to gain in regard to this Christian Text a scripturally sensitive appreciation similar to that which we gained, in Chapter 2, by noting the uses *Taittirīya Upaniṣad* 2 was put to by Bādarāyaṇa and Śaṅkara.

A retrieval of interest in Aquinas' use of the Bible can, of course, occur entirely without reference to Advaita. Nevertheless, this retrieval is one of the primary tasks the study of Advaita imposes on the comparative theologian who returns to Aquinas after the study of Advaita. As we have seen, the Advaitin is obliged to an intense engagement in a Text carefully composed according to a careful reading of the upaniṣads, and must become skilled in rules for reading that defend, build upon and remain faithful to that explicit scriptural grounding. The reader who has gradually become proficient in Advaita approaches the *Summa Theologiae* with an acquired habit of reading which adheres closely to the literary texture, the composed surface, of theological texts, and seeks to discover the significance of what is said and cited on that literary surface.

b. Retrieving the Reading of Commentaries: Cardinal Cajetan on ST I.13.4

As we achieve a sense of the *Summa Theologiae* as Text and become sensitive to its inscription of prior texts such as the Bible, our interest is raised regarding the nature and role of commentaries on the *Summa*, its extension and flourishing in acts of commentary. As readers of Advaita who are educated to take seriously texts, and texts within texts—to see commentaries as the living extensions of earlier texts and not as extrinsic additions to them—we become prepared also to reread the commentators of the Thomistic tradition with a fresh eye, to understand their readings of the *Summa Theologiae* as intelligent readings which draw from the range of possibilities encompassed by the *Summa Theologiae* as an incipient Text. Like the retrieval of Aquinas' use of the Bible, this retrieval of the Thomistic commentarial tradition is a formidable historical and theological task, daunting in its dimensions.[26] In illustration of the direction this retrieval will take, I can merely introduce the method of commentary practiced by Cardinal Cajetan (1469–1534), the theologian who composed the first complete commentary on the *Summa Theologiae*.[27] I draw my example from his comment on an article of the *Summa* examined above, ST I.13.4, which debates the apparent synonymity of words about God.

In ST I.13.4 Aquinas distinguishes and relates "idea" (*ratio*), "name" (*nomen*), "conception" (*conceptio*), and "thing" (*res*), in order to show how one can have an imperfect and complex knowledge of the simple God:

> But even according to what was said above (I.13.2), that these names signify the divine substance, although in an imperfect manner, it is also clear from what has been said

> (I.13.1, 2) that they have diverse meanings. *For the idea (ratio) signified by the name (nomen) is the conception (conceptio) in the intellect of the thing (res) signified by the name.*[28] But our intellect, since it knows God from creatures, in order to understand God forms conceptions proportional to the perfections flowing from God to creatures, which perfections pre-exist in God unitedly and simply, whereas in creatures they are received, divided and multiplied.

Cajetan summarizes as follows:[29]

> Our intellect "knows God from creatures;" [1.] therefore, our conceptions of God are "proportional to the perfections flowing from God to creatures;" [2.] therefore, these are varied and multiplied though corresponding to that which is entirely simple; [3.] therefore, ideas of this kind, connected with the names attributed to God, are diverse; [4.] therefore, names of this kind are not synonyms.

The emphasized sentence of Aquinas—"for the *idea* signified by the name is the *conception* in the intellect of the thing signified by the name"—is the basis for Cajetan's third step, "ideas of this kind, connected with the names attributed to God, are diverse."

Regarding this he introduces an objection which calls into question Aquinas' apparent equation of "conception" and "idea:"

> The following doubt arises: in *Metaphysics* IV, it is said that the idea which a name signifies is a definition; however, it is agreed that a definition is not a conception, which is identified with the object of definition. "Idea" names the "second intention," whereas "conception" names the "first intention."

If "idea" and "definition" correspond, and "conception" and the "object of definition," it seems inappropriate to identify "idea" with "conception." Cajetan's defense of Aquinas' usage requires a further set of distinctions:

> According to philosophers and theologians, the word "idea" in [Aquinas'] proposition can be taken in two ways, formally or denominatively. Thus, "white" formally pertains to "whiteness," but pertains denominatively to some thing

> that is white in color. If it is taken formally, it names a second intention, and signifies a certain relation. If it is taken denominatively, it signifies both a conception and definition, but in different ways. For a mental conception is termed "the idea corresponding to a name," because it is that by which the name refers to a signified which is outside the mind. But it is also termed "the definition," because it is by this that what is signified by the name is explicated.

Cajetan then makes use of the distinction to explain Aquinas' usage:

> In the present case [ST I.13.4], it follows that "idea" should be taken denominatively, as meaning "mental conception." [Idea] is [here] signified by name, because [name] is signified proximately, whereas a definition is the idea as it is ultimately signified by the name.

Aquinas' use of language is correct; indeed, under scrutiny it yields even richer insights into the material under consideration. His position is clarified and reinforced through a series of further fine distinctions. Though legitimately raised, the objection is shown to be lacking in force because of a further distinction appropriate to the context: "idea" can be understood in two ways, not just one, and so the objection is not sufficiently nuanced.

Cajetan does not claim to have improved on Aquinas' text, but ST I.13.4 is nevertheless enhanced by his exposition; the student who works through the objection and its clarification in a disciplined manner will understand more clearly the range of meanings available to Aquinas when he composed his arguments.[30]

Cajetan's distinctions and his subtle response to the objection would delight the heart of a sophisticated Advaita commentator such as Vācaspati or Amalānanda; one might in fact engage in an exercise in comparative commentarial nuance, by comparing Cajetan's explanation given here with an example we considered in Chapter 2, the fine distinctions Vācaspati makes in defending Śaṅkara's interpretation of the words "Brahman,"

"-maya," and "puccha."[31] Both are similar too, one must confess, in their ability to tax the energies and attentions of readers; they build upon their masters' thought only in the most careful and painstaking fashions.

A reader might study Advaita without ever engaging the thought of Vācaspati Miśra, and one might study the *Summa Theologiae* without exploring the problems and resolutions finely achieved by Cajetan. Yet attention to the larger connections which constitute Texts, and the practice of comparative reading that places a rereading of the *Summa Theologiae* after the Advaita Text together compel the attentive reader to take commentaries seriously, and to retrieve questions which may not have been immediately noted by the casual reader. One acquires, now in a comparative setting, a refined sense of discrimination, an appreciation of the subtle linguistic refinements which enhance a Text and amplify its significance.

A rediscovery of Cajetan in the comparative context is perhaps counter-intuitive, a reversal of the ordinary expectation about comparative work. Instead of a search for the original text or earliest, freshest insights, or for the genius of Aquinas untainted by scholastic analysis, or for the most general statement of theological positions, stripped of "local," scholastic detail, one learns actually to prefer the kinship of more difficult theologians such as Śaṅkara and Aquinas, Amalānanda and Cajetan, and these in the most precise and demanding of their writings. Comparative reading does not strip traditions down to elemental truths or experiences, but retrieves respect for the wholeness of their development; the particular complexities and refinements of traditions are revealed as cross-culturally most illuminative, most efficacious in teaching the theologian how to read comparatively.

Once the practice and intention and multiple effects of Aquinas' exegesis are brought to the fore as important objects of inquiry in a theological rereading of the *Summa Theologiae*, and once we have similarly begun to search out the history of commentary on the *Summa*, we thus begin to establish the *Summa* as a correlative adequately parallel to the Advaita Text opened up in the preceding chapters. Returning primacy to the actual reading of Texts, we begin to construct a richer, more complex field of comparison, now attuned to scriptural sources and their use, and to commentarial strategies and their refinement, as these are mapped out across the expanse of the newly juxtaposed Texts that are read together.

This consideration of a variety of the issues which arise in the construction of the proper context for comparison—the Context that is produced out of the intelligent and attentive juxtaposition of the Texts of two traditions—has extended the reflection on Text begun in Chapter 2; but it also reflects the incompleteness of Chapter 2, and our reassessment of theology after Advaita Vedānta remains at its beginning. We must consider now the question of the truth of comparison, whether comparative theological reading can be communicated and persuasive to one's "home" faith community. This question follows from Chapter 3, where we explored the inscription of truth in texts and its accomplishment after texts and not merely outside them, and is the topic of the next section.

III. The Truth of Comparative Theology

1. The Patient Deferral of Issues of Truth

Engagement in a comparative theological reading which draws upon two (or more) Texts leads eventually to a confrontation with the same question of truth that is taken up in the Advaita and Christian traditions themselves: how does one get beyond reading, in order to know and state persuasively one's views about the world that exists outside texts?

Though the questions become increasingly compelling the more one reads—what is the increasingly complex reading project *for*? what truth does one discover? — I nevertheless begin by defending a deferral of a response to them. Any hope of advance in our thinking from the practice of comparative reading to a realization consequent upon this practice relies in part on our determination to compose this further discourse only in a properly consequent fashion, as truly after comparison, and not merely as the restatement of an earlier position, after a brief detour into comparison.

Truth is inscribed in the Text; it is placed within, behind, after the Text, and there is no shortcut to it. As we saw in Chapter 3, even the Advaita truth of the identity of the self and Brahman requires a painstaking and circuitous articulation; as we saw earlier in this chapter, even the Christian truth of the universal significance of the Passion of Christ remains imbedded in one or another theological expression of it. A tradition's truths, in scriptural, theological and doctrinal forms, become accessible as expressed and as understood in words composed over a period of time; the consequent truth of comparison is no exception, and indeed is all the more a matter of patient elaboration. It takes time to know how the truths of one's tradition will affect comparison and how our articulations of truth will be affected by it; distances of language and culture need to be traversed before we can restate firmly our community's truths or state anew the truth of theology after Advaita Vedānta. Texts make religions and theologies readily proximate to one another, and yet only as a time-consuming prospect. So too, as I have shown at length in the preceding chapters, the learning of a tradition's theological language(s) and an understanding and fruitful appropriation of its texts are parts of a process which is completed only in a realization achieved by the skilled reader.

We therefore ought not move too quickly, too impatiently, in our quest to uncover the principles supposed to underlie the act of comparative reading, or the truths to be gleaned from comparison. The practical agenda of finding of a viable way to think about these Texts and their implied and explicit systematizations must proceed without prematurely formalized conclusions to the search. The affirmation of truth within a rich textual realm is only secondarily a theoretical claim; it is primarily a practice to be performed through the reading and rereading of the texts that are involved. Change occurs through a traversal of the path of reading, teaching and doctrine, and not in a timeless conceptualization. Hence, we must practice comparisons and learn from them, and be patient when our experiments at any given time are incomplete, inadequate, when we are more sure of the practice than of its import.

2. *Truth and the Conflict of Truths in Light of the Textuality of Doctrine*[32]

Nevertheless, if we read patiently and experiment patiently, extending and improving upon experiments such as those involving Aquinas, Amalānanda and Cajetan sketched earlier in this chapter, we can expect that the truth of the compared Text(s), and so also the retrieval of the viability of their doctrines, will gradually become accessible. If we can read, we can read comparatively and can be confronted by a truth of reading that is available only in a comparative context.

To gather the fruits of this practice as they can be expressed to a wider community, we need a differentiated notion of doctrine which can account for the complex fashion in which communities generate their teachings about their faith and practice out of their (previously) constituted scriptures, practices and traditions in general. We need to understand the ways in which those doctrines are composed in a form that then persists, and the ways in which other theological doctrines serve as the necessary but never entirely fixed or permanent vehicles of those doctrines.

Though important, a comparative rereading of a Text such as the *Summa Theologiae* after Advaita need not result in changes in Christian doctrine in any literal or constitutive sense. Comparative theological reading does not require the abandonment of any particular doctrines, nor a revisionist interpretation of the meaning of any particular doctrine; indeed, comparative theological reading depends on the perdurance of what is said, read, taught, written in a tradition; those who would expect from comparative theology sensational new teachings should inevitably be disappointed.

Nevertheless, even if the words of a tradition's doctrines remain exactly the same, they are painstakingly and exhaustingly reread in the light of the compared, other tradition and its Text; if that new reading does not end in new teachings, it must nevertheless conclude in some kind of assessment of what is achieved, or realized. If we are to avoid remaining comfortably immersed in endless textual resignification, rereading everything while yet insisting that there need not be evident changes in a tradition's teaching, we need then to project a way to the articulation of truths which can be scrutinized in distinction from the rarified and elitist realm of practice.

For example: in ST III.46 Aquinas recognizes the centrality of the Passion of Christ in the economy of human salvation. If we juxtapose Aquinas' explanation of the Passion with Advaita's teaching of the salvific power of knowledge of Brahman, we may find ourselves compelled to ask which of the following declarations is true:

1. The historical event of the Passion of Christ is the most fitting, and ultimately the only, source of the salvation for the world;

or,

2. Knowledge of Brahman is all that is required for salvation.

The two claims appear incompatible, and out of a desire to take truth seriously we may feel obliged, however reluctantly, to choose between them.

However, since both are rooted in the set of interpretive and communicative acts which constitute the faith lives of their communities, the choice cannot be an immediate, stark either/or. Tracing the genealogy of their contextualization through a retrieval of exegesis, and the genealogy of the reader's own contextualization through an assessment of his or her learning and prior commitments remains the primary task in the articulation and understanding of truth. Accounting for this contextualization is crucial in all cases, but most acutely in a case where we are trying to understand and relate the truths of more than one community.

If we carefully reread the compared claims, seemingly so opposite, the problems related to a comparative reading of them are diminished, though not eliminated. The initial and apparently inevitable choice—is it Christ's Passion and Death which saves, or knowledge of Brahman?—is restored to its practical status, once again woven in with the entire array of reading and writing strategies we have been considering throughout.

While a certain kind of honesty might seem to compel us to a choice, the affirmation of one claim and the denial of the other, the complex dialectical process of learning a new tradition and returning then, afterwards, to one's own in a series of acts of rereading, is not adequately comprehended by the reduction of theological truths to competing claims; though we may make them out to be claims, they subsist more complexly and richly within their broader traditional contexts, and now within the at least equally complex comparative context. Rather than seeing the field of comparison as a battleground where truth is under attack, or a courtroom where judgments can be swiftly passed, it is necessary to approach the issues of theological truth in a way attuned to the findings marked out in Chapter 3, and earlier in this chapter: though not reducible to their textual representations, theological truths occur only through their textual forms, and there is no other path of access to them.

Such truths therefore make their claim on us first of all as theological readers, whose comprehension will depend in large part on the kind of readers we turn out to be—how skilled, rigorous, attentive to context, careful in our derivation of truths from their scriptural roots. As theological truths which are argued, analyzed, compared and contrasted with other truth, they are rewritten in increasingly demanding forms, available only to the person who has worked them through in great detail and with great patience. The conflicts that most directly strike the person who has not been reading carefully are not necessarily those which concern the person who is engaged in reading. The apparent contest of juxtaposed claims is just the kind of sensationalization the comparativist learns to avoid, as he or she acquires a sense of the necessarily complex origins of even the simplest experiments in the comparing of truths, and the necessity of a patient commitment to read back and forth between those truths without premature claims regarding either one or both of them. Even in comparison, therefore, the apprehension of truth retains its elitist dimension.

To return to our example, the truth of Christ's Passion in juxtaposition with the truth of Brahman: the permanent location of theological truths in and then after their texts makes unlikely any direct contradiction between texts about the Passion and theological texts about knowledge of Brahman. As theological truths they are complex literary events, composed against certain written and oral backgrounds, subject to new readings in new contexts, and therefore available as true only in a series of distinct arrangements and upon consequent judgments. While it is possible to formalize such claims in such a way as to make explicit their truth, the full presentation of the truth retains a memory of its textual and communal roots.

Since in a comparative context there can be no such complete memory—no perfect reader—the explicit, asserted truths of the other community cannot be received in the same way as they have been communicated and learned in that other community itself, or in the same way that one's home community has appropriated its own remembered doctrines. Only through a long and patient process of reading and rereading does a particular reader approach the point where even one of the contested theological truths is apprehended as superseding its texts and as becoming simply "the truth;" even more rare is the accomplishment of a reader who can intelligently and skillfully apprehend the truth of two juxtaposed truths, so as to make a judgment between them conceivable.

A Christian comparativist may begin and end with a belief in the efficacy of the Passion of Christ, with a set of theological arguments in support of that belief, and perhaps with a preference for Aquinas' exposition of that efficacy. She or he will not be likely to proclaim, alongside or instead of the truth of Christ's Passion, that "knowledge of Brahman saves." But she or he will be in this position of maintaining the original Christian commitment only after undergoing an education in the nature of Advaita claims about Brahman, and in that process will lose, I suggest, the capacity to make claims such as "knowledge of Brahman does not save." Though this result may seem minimal in light of the desire for decisions of import, the progress made in this way toward a new and broader context for the Christian claim is significant, and irreversible.

Our consideration of the complexities which frame the apparent conflict of the two claims thus ends inconclusively, without answering the question as to which claim is true. The consideration may therefore be viewed with suspicion, as a merely convenient postponement of a difficult choice that needs to be made. But it may also be viewed as a hard-headed acknowledgment of the embodied, textured nature of the claims, and as a contribution to the necessary foundation for whatever progress one is going to make in evaluating theological truths in a comparative context.

3. *The Truth of the Theology of Religions*[33]

An important task within the larger project of reformulating theological truth after comparison is the recomposition of the questions posed in the theology of religions, questions such as these: "Is one religion more true than another?" "Is it true that Christ is the only savior? Is Christ the savior for Hindus too?" "What model of religions, as related to one another and to the truth, serves as the best basis for the comparative enterprise?"

I have deferred such frequently posed questions because the practice of reading comparatively needed to be justified practically before a reconsideration of theologies about religions. Whatever theological judgments we might draw regarding the validity of religious traditions, we can in fact read and compare, we do understand in part, misunderstand in part; we are in fact changed in the process, and we do in fact reread our traditions differently while yet remaining members of our original communities. All of this occurs regardless of our judgments about religions, and it precedes whatever might be achieved in the theology of religions. The priority of the engagement in comparison over our theories about it needs to be noted and preserved.

The various positions one might then articulate in a theology of religions—all religions are one; all religions are merely different; one religion alone is true, the rest untrue; the rest partially true—become interesting only after reading has taken place, when these positions can be refined in light of actual knowledge of one or more religions, and rearticulated as extensions of the practice of reading. Even if one wishes to place the theology of religions at the beginning of one's treatise about religions, this theology is nevertheless best composed only after comparison has already occurred.

A postcomparative theology of religions—in this case, a theology of religions after Advaita Vedānta—must replicate the dialectical activity of reading, whereby the "new" is read through and after one's original Text, and according to the rules by which we construct and read the world in terms of our community's privileged texts.[34] Like other acts of juxtaposition, this dialectical act of reading creates a new signification for the non-Christian texts, and may distort as well as enhance their original meanings; likewise, new meanings will be constructed for the Bible and the theological systems composed from it, new meanings that can occur only due to the event of juxtaposition with these non-Christian texts. Only in an attentive recognition of this creative juxtaposition can a useful theology of religions be composed.

The three standard theologies of religions may summarized as follows: the *exclusivist theology of religions* holds that salvation is in Christ alone, and that Christianity is the only authentic (human) mediation of salvation; the *pluralist theology of religions* holds that there are no grounds for privileging one religion as the best of religions, and that salvation is mediated equally through many religions; the *inclusivist theology of religions* holds that salvation occurs through Christ alone, but also that people of other religious traditions may nevertheless be saved in their own traditions, even if they do not explicitly recognize Christ.[35]

Whatever the merits such models may have, they are almost always essentially abstract designs, developed without reference to any particular religious tradition other than the Christian. To be taken seriously in a comparative context, each will have to be rewritten with a far great commitment to detail and examples. At this point, however, the inclusivist position—itself usually developed in abstraction—stands forth as the most useful of the three. With its distinctive tension between an adherence to the universal claim of one's own religion and an acknowledgment of the working of the truth of the Christian religion outside its boundaries, inclusivism best replicates the tensions and revisions which accrue to the reading process as I have described it throughout this book. Its insistence that salvation occurs through Christ alone, and is yet universally available, is a perplexing double claim which, if merely stated, may suggest incoherence or at least a reluctance to resolve the difficult issues involved. Yet in the context of the dialectic of reading and extended signification this perplexing complexity appears as part of its vitality. It neither abandons its starting point in faith and in a vision of the entirety of the world in Christ, nor does it imagine that world in so narrow a fashion as to excise the Christian faith from the universal context it is said to articulate; there is a world, it can and needs to be encountered, read. Just as the comparative theologian insists on reading back and forth from Text to context, in the act of creative amplification of what has already been "written" from the start, the inclusivist insists on salvation in Christ alone and the true universality of salvation, and the need to keep these truths together in creative tension. Moreover, both inclusivism and comparison mirror the tension we discovered in Advaita, between the simple and universally available truth of Brahman and the complexity of the Text in which that truth remains steadfastly inscribed.

A comparative theology allied with the inclusivist position would therefore begin with a reading of the Advaita Text, for this Text and its multiple literary riches and its theological possibilities are now all included in the set of Christian theological resources. This inclusivist appropriation would be committed to the practice of reading the Text, instead of replacing it with a theory about it, an abstraction such as "the sacred texts of the world" or "the Hindu experience of the eternal." This inclusive reading would happen even if the inclusivist does not confuse this Text with the Bible, which remains the privileged Text formative of the inclusivist's thinking.

The inclusivist position, thus revised, becomes the practice of including; this, in turn, is a major revision of the theology of religions as such, a shift from a theoretical enterprise to a set of strategies of practical and reflective engagement in a religious tradition other than one's own, particularly by way of reading. The required rewriting of inclusivism and its alternatives is yet another important task which confronts the comparative theologians of the next generation.

4. The Truth about God

Intention and method are important, as is the revision of the theology of religions. But such concerns are no more decisive in comparative theology than in other areas of theology; the comparative theologian is no more likely to make final decisions in these areas than are other theologians in their areas of specialization. Nevertheless, and again as in other areas of theology, the Christian comparativist needs at least to consider the possibility of a truth more basic than those of the practical and theoretical kinds already considered, one urgent enough that a consideration of it cannot be postponed until all lesser issues are resolved: the possibility that through comparison one does, or does not, learn more of God. The comparativist will have to consider not only the possibility that the other Text is reasonable, or comparable, but also the possibility that it actually speaks of God—in the way that Christian Texts do—and so increases our understanding of God—in the way that Christian Texts do.

The question of whether or not the comparativist learns more of God has a pragmatic importance. The comparative theologian is making a large demand, that all of the home tradition be reread after engagement in another tradition; the probability of a positive response to this demand by other theologians and by the larger believing community will be greatly increased if they are able to perceive that the theologian is bringing home something worthwhile—as would be the case, for example, if the Christian community finds that it learns something about God by a study of the *Uttara Mīmāṃsā Sūtras* or some particular Advaita commentary, at least in a way analogous to how that community learns something about God by studying the *Summa Theologiae* or Cardinal Cajetan's commentary.

Here too, a straightforward question will not get a straightforward answer. If comparison really does enrich our knowledge of God, this increase will occur only gradually, within the same structures of reading, comparison and communication that characterize comparison in general. We cannot tell at a glance what the other tradition will teach us of God. Even if we learn that it is naive to equate "God" and "Brahman," and equally naive to declare "God is not Brahman," the value of Advaita for a Christian audience's knowledge of God remains undetermined, a value to be measured in careful experiments. One might, for instance, recollect what one has learned of God from Aquinas' exposition ST I.1-119, and then rethink it in light of UMS I.1–4.

Each Advaita tenet is a complex theological doctrine generated from a series of developed strategies about the use of scripture, the dynamics of meditation practice, the nature of opposing viewpoints and the history of Advaita's apologetic response, etc.; each can be inscribed into Christian theological discourse only gradually, selectively, and with the candid admission that the doctrine as finally received will not be quite the same as it was for another tradition's theologian, e.g., Śaṅkara or Amalānanda. Since this inscription remains undone, the question as to what a reading of Amalānanda will tell Christians of God must be deferred, though recognized as the key question.

Deferral or not, the comparativist who recognizes that theology's truth about God is not identical with faith's truth may still have to face questions such as, "Do you now share the Advaita faith? have you personally found Advaita to be true? have you ever met anyone who is one with Brahman?" Such questions require personal responses which entail various decisions about how one lives one's life. The simple and straightforward question of faith turns our attention to the comparativist, that faithful reader who alone is able to make the necessary transition from much reading, thinking and writing—the complex dissemination of faith in the (comparative or precomparative) theological practice of a community—to the event of realization. Here, then, we find ourselves where we were at the end of Chapter 3, concerned with the resolution of the tension between reading and truth in the person who does the reading and seeks the truth; the tension between the act of comparison and its truth is, after all, only another version of the same tension.

IV. The Education of the Comparative Theologian

The identity of the person who performs the comparative reading is therefore the central issue, because in that person the practice of comparison and the truth of comparison converge. The identity of the comparativist depends in turn on his or her background and prior education, as well as the interconnected background and current skills and concerns of the comparativist's community, the possibilities opened by particular experiment in comparison that was undertaken, etc. Even before decisions are made about which texts one is to read and in what manner one is to read them, the reader is already a highly defined social being, who comes to the project bearing an agenda defined in important ways by prior education.

To advance beyond this general observation, we need to return to the issue of competence (adhikāra) discussed in Chapter 4: if the wisdom of comparison is a form of discernment, a discernment of the convergence of Text and Truth that is achievable only by a skilled reader, then who is in fact, and not just ideally, the competent reader? The comparativist must be educated and made competent, by being shown how to engage attentively in the compared Texts; and this provisionally achieved competence must be authenticated by the community and passed down as one of its modes of education, for the preparation of future competent comparativists. In the following reflections I first reemphasize the pedagogical nature of the Advaita and Christian texts under consideration, and then consider the comparativist as student and as teacher/writer.

1. Texts as Teachers[36]

The pedagogy of comparative reading emphasizes the reflective practice of being educated anew through a new combination of materials, drawn from more than one tradition which are then to be read together, in a process which (gradually) fashions a new literacy. The primary accomplishment of comparison is the person who makes the comparison—not as the bearer of certain religious experiences, but as the reader (and then writer) of texts, who is educated differently and made proficient in the skillful performance of comparative reading.

In Chapters 2 and 4 we saw that the Advaita Text is a profoundly pedagogical document. The same is true of the *Summa Theologiae*. In his preface Aquinas announces that it is a text for students:

> Because the Master of Catholic Truth ought not only teach the proficient, but also instruct beginners (according to the Apostle: as unto little ones in Christ, I gave you milk to drink, not meat [I Corinthians 3.1,2,]) we purpose in this book to treat of whatever belongs to the Christian Religion, in such as way as may tend to the instruction of beginners . . . we shall try, by God's help, to set forth whatever is included in this Sacred Science as briefly and clearly as the matter itself may allow.[37]

That the *Summa Theologiae* is written for the student is evident in several ways. First, we are dealing in it with the basics of theology, what needs to be known by the well-trained theologian, and not with overly specialized questions. Second, Aquinas structures the *Summa* according to the needs of the student, and so according to the structure of good learning: the order in which topics are raised and difficulties met is conformed to how the student can best assimilate it in a reflective learning process.[38]

The *Summa Theologiae* leads the student from an initial reflection on how we can be said to know anything about God, to an ordered consideration of God "in himself" and as creator, to a consideration of created reality, particularly of the human person who is enabled to know and relate to God, and finally to a consideration of Jesus Christ and the Christian order of salvation. Although this final consideration may of course have been the first concern for many students, it is not necessarily the first to be properly understood.

The consistency of Aquinas' pedagogical concern is revealed again in his comments on the master of theology in ST I.117.1, the teacher who needs to be able to organize a text like the *Summa Theologiae*, in order to make evident the whole of the faith in a form that works for the student. Students learn by their own research, wherein the interior innate principles of knowledge are applied "to particular things, the memory or experience of which he acquires through the senses; then by his own research advancing from the known to the unknown, he obtains knowledge of what he knew not before." Students learn also by external instruction, wherein "anyone who teaches leads the disciple from things known by the latter to the knowledge of things previously unknown to him . . ." The teacher offers helpful means of instruction: "for instance, he may put before [the student] certain less universal propositions, of which nevertheless the disciple is able to judge from previous knowledge . . ."; he also takes into account the relative weakness of the student's reasoning power, "inasmuch as he proposes to the disciple the order of principles to conclusions, by reason of his not having sufficient collating power to be able to draw the conclusions from the principles."

The *Summa Theologiae* replicates this teaching process, unfolding the knowledge of the learned teacher in an order that the student can understand with increasing proficiency. As in Advaita, the Text is teacher; to understand the *Summa* is to submit oneself to it, to allow oneself to be taught by it. Careful, ordered engagement allows the reader to advance in the array of appropriate knowledges—of the text, the tradition, the self, right behavior, God.[39] As a teaching founded in the Bible and beginning with a reflection on the capacity of language, the *Summa Theologiae* extends the letter of scripture in a language (direct, commentarial, pedagogical, translated, etc.) that has the power to teach.

Its pedagogical efficacy remains in force when it is reread after another pedagogical text such as the Advaita Text, and the pedagogical effectiveness of both is enhanced by their juxtaposition. We therefore find ourselves reading and comparing two Texts which are meant to educate their readers. Both are dedicated to the development and use of a correct(ed), sophisticated language about Brahman (for the Advaita) or God (for Aquinas'

Christian theology) and are accordingly committed to the elaboration of full theological systems out of careful exegesis. Both hold that the key referent, God or Brahman, cannot be adequately known through words, or directly described, though words can train the reader for posttextual insights. They therefore build into their texts strategies which limit the further conclusions one might draw on the supposition that language is reliable, while yet inviting their readers to continue to be readers, immersed in texts. Both offer a long series of "case studies"—to be argued vigorously—which help the student to become skilled in reading Texts correctly, with a gradually increased self-awareness and nuanced appreciation of their meanings.

Together, these Texts comprise an education which could not be afforded by either Text alone—a difficult, demanding, and yet potentially wonderfully effective education rich in potential insights. It is all the more important then that the comparativist take advantage of these pedagogical resources by committing a great deal of time to the Texts, individually and together, in order to be educated by them and thereby to become the good comparative student, the insightful reader who alone can realize and articulate the Truth of the comparisons undertaken.

2. *The Education of the Comparativist: Competence, Motivation and Limits*

As we saw in Chapter IV, competence (adhikāra) balances a recognition of innate ability with a set of specific internal and external preparations that one needs to undergo in order to be made into the kind of person who can read properly and learn the truth. The first prerequisite is the desire to know (jijñāsā), as a pure desire and also as the motivation to engage in intensive reading.

Accordingly, we need to examine the desires of the theologian who bothers to undertake comparative work, the goals this theologian hopes to accomplish in reading and then in writing from that practice. Like the Advaita jijñāsā, the contours of this desire/project must be mapped out simply and complexly: as a simple and original, uncaused desire to know the truth, to know God, but also as a commitment to learn comparatively by the complex practice of reading comparatively.

Much could be said on the former, but one would have to trace the faith and desires of the theologian as these began in the period preceding the undertaking of comparisons. Since important aspects would be shared with theologians engaged in other disciplines within theology, and some aspects would simply be personal, perhaps inexplicable, we will not dwell here on these common and rare elements.

But why does someone take up comparative work as a task, an inquiry, promising to engage in multiple Texts over a long period of time? Perhaps the comparativist takes pleasure, intellectual and spiritual, in the composition of a larger Text, composed from her or his own tradition as newly contextualized by one or more other traditions. For this new, larger Text promises rich possibilities of text and context, layers of commentary on top of one another, a series of ongoing incidents of resignification—and all of this as provocative of new connections and renovative of old ones. This promise of virtually limitless new meanings is an important justification for engagement in the comparative enterprise, and for some it may suffice.

One might also appeal to the traditional universalizing and in some cases evangelizing thrusts of religions. For the Christian, this pertains to the missionary task of the churches, the literal and figurative inscription of the world into the community founded in the Word of God. The effort to account for the world in terms of the Word of God, and to perform that Word by the work of evangelization, need not be considered separately from the practices of recontextualization stressed in this volume. The traditional translation of the Word into many human words is mirrored in the rewriting of theology in the context of the new words of new Texts.

The general situation in which any theologian does theology today may also provide some warrants as to why one would take up comparative work. Though richer, the world of religion is now smaller; the encounter with other religions is not the special experience only of those who travel to far-off places; the problems facing the human race are increasingly global. If religion is to contribute to their solutions, it is unconvincing to suppose that only one religion will make this contribution, or that religions best make their contribution in isolation from one another. Identities preserved, people of diverse religious backgrounds still do best to cooperate in the responsible practice of their religions. If theology is to be intelligently composed in the contemporary situation, the advantages of a theological discourse enriched by a series of particular contextualizations in multiple Textual traditions cannot be overlooked.

However one explains the beginning of the desire to make comparisons, the practice of comparisons cannot be evaluated merely in terms of predicted results, as if they could be stated in advance of their production. The practice of comparative inquiry will always possess an unpredictable component. When the comparativist begins to appropriate a new tradition and on that basis to make skilled comparisons, she or he is quickly confronted with an array of new questions and new choices, and encounters and assimilates vast amounts of new material. The comparativist may begin by storing it according to the already established categories of thought and locating the "new" next to apparently similar portions of the "old"—while also overlooking, or treating as unimportant, or placing in a file labeled "not understood," various items one has no precise place for. But if she or he perseveres in the reading process and pays attention to what is happening, the awareness of what is new and newly significant becomes an increasingly urgent and effective agent for change; the process of increasing one's comparative knowledge is increasingly accompanied by the rearrangement of one's prior knowledge and by new expectations regarding learning and how learning is to be organized. The new vocabulary, concepts, images, myths, theologies, etc., at some point accumulate to a point at which they can no longer be easily confined in their appropriate places in the theologian's already-established theological discourse.

The theologian then begins to draw on a broader and more varied set of theological materials—expanding the theological library, if not the theological canon. Alongside the Bible and the great books of the Christian tradition there now stand selected volumes from one or more of the world's religions. They stand there on one's shelves, full of possible meanings and uses, though without any label which helpfully determines how one is to assess and catalogue them, or to locate them in terms of importance and pedagogical value. Effective symbols of the expanded possibilities of learning and of what counts as theology, these volumes also contribute to a subtle transformation of the standards by which theological literacy is determined.

One realizes at that point that one can no longer be well-read if literate only in the home tradition. Then, for the sake of the community and the coherence of theological education, the comparativist becomes a good librarian, expert in the acquisition of texts, and in strategies of recataloguing—in the mind's library, but perhaps literally so too—so that texts are properly arranged, not merely according to religion or by theme, but according to the emerging schemata of comparative theology. As new books are introduced, the recognized classics of one's home tradition must inevitably be granted less space, and priorities set up about which books are sent to storage, so to speak, to make room for the new books. So too, the new learning is not easily assimilated to the old, and requires its own support systems of grammars, dictionaries, atlases, journals, etc. In turn, the expected student who comes for an education is faced with this larger array of materials, and her or his reading is slowed down considerably, as a mastery of new writings is only gradually acquired and familiar texts slowly reread in a new light, for new purposes. In the short run, the student may seem merely to know less about more, and there may be some honest doubt as to the value of this arduously achieved superficiality. In the long run, however, the theological possibilities opened by this new learning are immeasurable.

The most important implications of this expanding practice of comparison are those which are most practical, most directly issues of education. For eventually one has to devise new ways of educating theologians, and so new versions of the entire theological curriculum, the list of what needs to be researched and to be taught. The undaunted comparativist begins then to identify a series of special questions which may be formalized and undertaken as ongoing projects, in a series of revised theological disciplines ranging from "comparative soteriology" and "comparative ethics" to "comparative exegesis" and "comparative apologetics," to "comparative mysticism" and "comparative popular devotions," etc. Each of these requires historical and social investigations as well regarding each side of each comparison. Not all of these need to be—or could be—undertaken by the same person. When differentiated, the comparative disciplines will also develop their own increasingly professional standards and criteria, and fortunately become less dependent on the intuitions or powers of persuasion of any particular theologian.

The comparative project and the revision of the curriculum cannot stop at any merely posited endpoint; if we understand what happens in the practice of comparative reading, we find everything to be different. The theologically sensitive juxtaposition of one's scripture and theology with what one recognizes to be another theological version of the world, narrated according to different texts, traditions and practices, makes one aware of the margins of one's theological universe. This awareness may dawn even before one has any inkling of the proper way to talk about these margins and what is beyond them. Whatever one wants to do after the juxtaposition of texts and acts of comparative reading, the theological and religious awareness of the "other" will remain in place, along with an unformalizable measuring of the margins of one's own universe of thought. Because unformalizable, this measure never becomes a proper topic within the system. It remains unwritten, but noticed; unobtrusive, it changes everything.[40]

3. *The Comparativist as Educator*

The remaining question has to do with how the comparative theologian is to communicate the smaller and larger results of the successive acts of reading and rereading. The comparative theologian's personal learning has been accomplished through a process of reading and rereading over an extended period of time, through the reception and construction of the words, sentences, paragraphs and texts of the other tradition; he or she is reeducated, taught to speak and write differently.

If the series of such exercises in reading inscribes not simply conclusions or theories in the theologian, but also new memories and new habits of reading, then it is pointless to offer the expected audience a mere set of conclusions which bypass the requirement that one learn by experiment and practice. Detached from details, abstracted from the experimental context, mere conclusions will inevitably be received by the audience in terms of its general, already established categories; thus invited to enter the process at its end, without having been first prepared to receive what the comparativist intends to communicate, the community is unlikely to understand what is the purpose of all the effort.

If the preparation of the audience is intrinsic to the goal, the comparative theologian will have to determine how to go about "defamiliarizing" the discussion, frustrating the community's tendency to apply its already familiar categories, so as to engage the community in the actual practice of theological comparison. Examples—loci of thought and speech (*articuli, adhikaraṇāni*)—must be composed and introduced, and readers cajoled into taking them seriously and working them through.[41] The theologian has to enable the community to read comparatively, by writing into her or his text one or more such opportunities, cases which can be understood satisfactorily only by a working through of local details according to the possibilities of the local vocabulary.

The juxtaposition of UMS III.3.11–13 and ST I.13.4 earlier in this chapter is a smaller example of this construction of a local opportunity; readers are invited to journey onto unfamiliar terrain, without any single mode of procedure agreed upon in advance. Although Chapters 2, 3 and 4 of this book serve primarily to introduce the Advaita Text in such a way as to explain and illuminate the particular mode of comparative theology that I have developed largely in response to that material, those chapters themselves comprise a detailed example, which may provide some readers with an extended opportunity to begin to think and read theology differently.

In the experimental and largely uncharted milieu of comparative work, the comparativist has no alternative but to become the kind of person in whom the connection of the new (Con)Text of theology with the community's truth is realized. The enduring public expression of that realization, however, requires a community which maintains its basic commitments while allowing new formulations of its traditions, its educational structures, and its claims about itself and others, in a world in which the possibilities of comparison have been irreversibly inscribed. The true event by which the truth of comparison is accomplished, therefore, is like the event of Advaita realization: it is a moment of simple insight, personal and communal, which is nevertheless prepared and practiced in an entire range of specific activities of reading and writing, initiated by individuals but carried on and perfected over generations.

V. *Finishing the Experiment*

These concluding reflections on the possibilities of comparative theology must be put forward modestly, without a sense of finality and without the added claim that no other way of thinking through the problems of comparison is possible. Numerous reasons come to mind for this required modesty, but the following is the most pertinent. The example that has entirely occupied this volume is but one example: the Advaita, that Advaita in its primary identity as the Uttara Mīmāṃsā, and a rereading and rewriting of a certain form of Catholic Christian theology after that Advaita. Advaita hearkens back to Mīmāṃsā, itself a thoroughly ritual discourse attuned to the temporal, practical, textually structured nature of ritual events. An experiment in comparative theology which is committed to the Advaita as Uttara Mīmāṃsā is a limited one, which constructs the patterns and dynamics of comparative theology according to the same commitments to practice, text, time and event.

Were the preceding reflections rooted in other materials, this book and its final chapter's statements about the practice of comparison would surely have had other emphases. For example, attention to Advaita has brought consistently to the fore the tension between the complexity of language and the simple realization which occurs due to and after those words. Had we focused instead on that transformed version of Mīmāṃsā and Vedānta which develops in the south Indian Śrīvaiṣṇava encounter with the songs of the Tamil-language Ālvārs, the most prominent tension would rather have been that between the dynamics of hearing and those of seeing, between the temporal formalities of language and the spatial complexities of vision. A different version of comparative theology would then have been articulated in light of that different experiment.

In any case, the singleminded devotion of this book to a single experiment precludes large generalizations, and no effort will be expended on them here. We must end tentatively: at this early stage in the articulation of comparative theology it is important to accept patiently the richness of the variety of comparative models which can be generated out of specific exercises, and to resist the urge to draw attractive conclusions for which there is neither a basis nor a need. As an Advaitin might claim, at every stage in comparative theology the reach of words is always inadequate; learned readers must compose their own conclusions.

Notes

Foreword

1. David Tracy and I edited this collection of essays that was published by SUNY Press in 1990.

2. For *Myth and Philosophy* see *ibid. Mencius and Aquinas,* written by Lee H. Yearley, was published as Volume II (SUNY, 1991). *Discourse and Practice,* which is another collection of essays that I edited with David Tracy, was published as Volume III (SUNY, 1992).

3. For Clooney's fullest statement on the earlier Mīmāṃsā tradition see *Thinking Ritually: Recovering the Pūrva Mīmāṃsā of Jaimini* (Vienna: Indological Institute of the University of Vienna, 1990).

Chapter 1. Comparative Theology and the Practice of Advaita Vedānta

1. My usage throughout is as follows: "Vedānta" refers to the thinking of the upaniṣads, and to this thought as it is received and systematized by thinkers in the various schools gathered under the name "Vedānta." "Advaita" indicates the "non-dualist" school of Vedānta, of which Śaṅkara is the most famous teacher. In a second usage, which will be clear in context, "Vedānta" refers to the Advaita insofar as it achieves the contours of a philosophical or systematic theological system, in which case it will be contrasted with Advaita as "Uttara Mīmāṃsā," that extended and revised version of Mīmāṃsā ritual thinking in which exegesis and commentary remain the primary vehicles of thought. For reasons that become clear in this chapter, I prefer to use "theol-

ogy" as a categorization of Advaita rather than "philosophy," even though Advaita does not describe itself as focused on "God" or "the gods."

2. On the general range of issues related to comparative theology in relation to the study of Advaita and religion in India see also, Clooney 1990c and 1990d.

3. Pierre Bourdieu (1977, 1984, 1990) has very helpfully analyzed the modes of relationship among theory and practice, in order to describe a practical understanding that is not detachable from practice. He proposes a "theory of practice" which builds on but is not reducible either to practice or to theories (merely) about practice; in his formulation of it he distinguishes three modes of theoretical knowledge. First, there is the phenomenological model of theory, in which theory "sets out to make explicit the truth of primary experience in the social world, i.e., all that is inscribed in the relationship of familiarity with the familiar environment, the unquestioning apprehension which, by definition, does not reflect on itself and excludes the question of the conditions of its own possibility." (1977, p. 3) Second, there is the objectivist model, in which theory "constructs the objective relations (e.g., economic or linguistic) which structure practice and representations of practice . . . It is only on condition that it poses the question which the *doxic* experience of the social world excludes by definition—the question of the (particular) conditions making that experience possible—that objectivist knowledge can establish both the structures of the social world and the objective truth of primary experience as experience denied *explicit* knowledge of those structures." (1977, p. 3) Third, there is the practical, in which theory "has no other aim than to make possible a science of the *dialectical* relations between the objective structures to which the objectivist mode of knowledge gives access and the structured dispositions within which those structures are actualized and which tend to reproduce them." (1977, p. 3) Bourdieu argues that this third mode of theory is not a reversion to "lived experience" and "subjectivity," but a path beyond the objectivist-subjectivist dichotomy, precisely through an exploration of the tension between the practical and the theoretical.

4. Comparative theology thus adheres most closely to Bourdieu's third model of theory (described in the previous note), in which the dynamics of practice, in their temporality, spatiality and according to the strategies of their transaction, are the primary object of attention.

5. Bourdieu correctly notes the distortion that occurs in a presentation of theoretical knowledge which abolishes this temporal component. Using the example of the dynamics of gift-giving as a social practice (1977, pp. 4–7), he shows that the variables of interval and deferral of return are crucial to the

value of practice, and that an abstract analysis of the giving and reciprocation of gifts loses sight of this temporal facet. Bourdieu strikingly insists that "to restore to practice its practical truth, we must therefore reintroduce time into the theoretical representation of a practice which, being temporally structured, is intrinsically defined by its *tempo*." (1977, p. 8)

6. Bourdieu 1977, p. 9.

7. A primary goal of comparative theological reading is therefore the development, protection and reinforcement of what Bourdieu has named the "habitus," the constructed, acquired, and interiorally appropriated practical self-presentation by which members of a society—as a community, and as individuals—differentiate, distribute and position the components of social reality in relation to one another. The practical challenges which comprise life's daily course are understood and provisionally resolved by this kind of implicit, learned, but afterwards taken-for-granted set of skills and strategies. See Bourdieu 1977, pp. 78–84.

8. Yearley 1990, especially 175 ff.

9. Yearley focuses on the concept of virtue in the traditions represented by Aquinas and Mencius.

10. Yearley 1990, p. 7.

11. Yearley 1990, p. 12.

12. Yearley 1990, p. 177.

13. Yearley 1990, pp. 188 ff. He concedes the relative rarity of clearcut, decisive similarities involving Mencius and Aquinas vis à vis their worldviews or their notions of virtue and of specific virtues.

14. Yearley 1990, p. 188.

15. Yearley 1990, p. 188.

16. Yearley 1990, p. 197.

17. Henceforth UMS.

18. Sūtras, as laconic and serviceable as mnemonic devices, never constitute a self-sufficient text which can be picked up and read; sūtra-texts were presumably always accompanied by a teacher's amplification of each sūtra's meaning in its proper context; see Renou 1963.

19. See Chapter 2, p. 70–71, for a more ample outline of the UMS.

20. These paragraphs preview the fuller interpretation which makes up the major part of chapters 2, 3, and 4.

21. Śaṅkara refers to an older author, known simply as "the commentator" (*vṛttikāra*). On the pre-Śaṅkara Vedānta, see Nakamura 1983.

22. Dasgupta (1922, vol. II) remains a valuable source of information for an overview of the Advaita tradition. Hacker (1950) is an invaluable study of Śaṅkara's immediate disciples, Sureśvara, Padmapāda, Toṭaka and Hastāmala. Neither work, however, focuses on the Advaita in its commentarial aspects.

23. On the debate over the meaning of this inaugural word, see Chapter 4, p. 130.

24. I.e., the deity Śiva.

25. Here and throughout, all translations of Vācaspati's comments on UMS I.1.1–4 are drawn from the 1933 translation by S.S.Suryanarayana Sastri and C. Kunhan Raja. Translations of later portions of Vācaspati, and of later commentators, are my own. Throughout, references are usually given simply to the appropriate Sanskrit śloka or sūtra; only in the case of particularly long commentarial passages will I give page numbers (to the Sanskrit or the translation), for the reader's convenience.

26. Steps first described in the *Bṛhadāraṇyaka Upaniṣad*, II.4.5; I return to this text in Chapter 3.

27. Cited by Appaya Dīkṣita with slight variation.

28. In elaborating Amalānanda's third verse, which compares smashing ignorance to smashing the head of the elephant in rut, and to the abrupt manifestation from the pillar of Viṣṇu as a man-lion, to destroy the devotee Prahlāda's foe, Appaya Dīkṣita emphasizes again the connection between knowledge and texts: "thus, Brahman, reached by the rising of manifestation, is the fruit of those acts of hearing (*śravaṇa*), reflection (*manana*), and meditation (*nididhyāsana*)."

29. Parpola (1981) offers helpful reflections on the original unity of the two Mīmāṃsās and on the origin of the terms *Pūrva Mīmāṃsā* and *Uttara Mīmāṃsā*. But as I have indicated elsewhere (Clooney 1990b, pp. 25–32), a decision on whether the names do or do not indicate an originally single system must proceed from a thorough understanding of both, and cannot by determined by largely extrinsic standards.

30. See Clooney 1990b for a description of the nonphilosophical Mīmāṃsā which is the true predecessor to Advaita.

31. These points too will be treated extensively in the succeeding chapters.

32. Deussen 1973, pp. 88–115.

33. Nakamura 1983, p. 116, and see 108–116 for his presentation of the Vedānta as a scripturally-based system of thought.

34. Modi (1956) correctly argues the centrality of III.3 in the UMS system.

35. See for instance his comments on UMS III.3.1.

36. Deussen (1973) so thoroughly takes up this task that he seeks to complete Śaṅkara's division of the exoteric and the esoteric by showing how Śaṅkara's doctrine of creation is exoteric only. See Deussen, p. 101.

37. Richard DeSmet (1953, pp. 8–24) has amply documented this modern tradition of scepticism about theology.

38. Anantanand Rambachan (1986, 1987) has skillfully shown that the Indian neo-Vedāntins of the 19th and 20th centuries have taken up the same project of making Advaita "respectable," and so have downplayed its ritual and exegetical components over against the claims of a higher truth, pure experience, etc.

39. Deutsch 1969, p. 6.

40. The place of reason in Advaita will be examined more closely in Chapter 3; Halbfass (1991) offers an excellent introduction to Śaṅkara's view of reason and revelation.

41. This is why the best synthetic works about the UMS, such as Prakāśātman's *Śārīrakanyāyasaṃgraha*, are those which present us a series of rules for reading and not summaries of the content of the text. So too other introductory manuals, such as the *Naiṣkarmyasiddhi, Vivekacūḍāmaṇi*, and *Vedāntaparibhāṣā*, in which an underlying commitment to textual knowledge persists.

42. Hereafter I use "Text" to indicate the larger Advaita Text to which this study is committed; "Text" includes the range of texts and contexts which the Advaitins read and write together, from the upaniṣads to the most recent of commentaries.

43. Each of these shifts has been explored by Roland Barthes (1979). See also Clooney (1990d) for a development of the correlation of my approach and that of Barthes. This description, and the conception of reading operative throughout this book, are greatly indebted, in various ways, to the following: Iser (1978), whose analysis of the reader-text relationship and the "mechanics" of

the interchange is extremely apt to this study; Oakes (1988); Riffaterre (1990); Said (1975 and 1983); Ulmer (1985) has been of great help in defining my use of Derrida's thought, and Scholes (1989) has helped refine my critical evaluation of Derrida's reading practices. Only more recently did I come across Altieri (1990), in which "Canons and Differences" has been a helpful complement to my earlier reading. Harold Coward (1990) offers a useful broad context in which one may consider Indian thought in light of Derrida, though Derrida primarily as a holder of philosophical positions.

44. Mīmāṃsā's firm exclusion of the author is stated and defended only within the articulation of a broader assertion of the textual location of dharma. See Clooney 1990b, Chapters 4 and 5.

45. See Clooney 1988, and Bilimoria 1988, pp. 164–234.

46. In accepting the Mīmāṃsā view that Vedic texts should not be understood as authored works, Advaita entertains a denial of filiation and of the concomitant shortcuts and privileges that come with the appeal to the author. However, here too the Advaita is maintains a "realist" notion of reading, in which texts are not thought to be open to endless meanings, it discovers meaning through the identification and use of a set of intratextual rules of meaning. By these rules a text means without being replaced by that to which it refers; the rules allow the text to mean, without this meaning being given in advance or after the text. Barthes (1979) notes that the Text "overtakes" the authored work and "undermines" its authority, and so "deconstructs" controlled, linear reading: ". . . the work is caught up in a process of filiation. [That is,] three things are postulated here: a *determination* of the work by the outside world (by race, then by history), a *consecution* of works among themselves, and an *allocation* of the work to its author . . . The Text, on the other hand, is read without the father's signature." (1979, p. 78) The Text's meaning is not entirely determined by an external-world, nor by the relation of individually identified works with one another, nor by attention to a single author's mind. Though studies of the authorial intentions of Śaṅkara cannot be dismissed as erroneous, they are also a distraction on the basis of which the problems and possibilities of the Text as a whole, in any of its stages (such as the *Bhāṣya* of Śaṅkara) or in the complexity of those stages taken together (over several generations of commentary), are neglected in an eagerness to pry from the Text what its authors meant when they wrote what they wrote. This book therefore has studiously excluded every kind of lateral study which would introduce the data of Śaṅkara's other commentaries and his noncommentarial *Upadeśasāhasrī*. Though this may appear an error in judgment to some, it is a move I share with the UMS commentarial tradition itself,

which never refers to Śaṅkara's upaniṣadic commentaries to explain his UMS *Bhāṣya*. I have also not engaged in a search for the "Śaṅkara of history," for what we might know about his life and times, etc. If we do become interested in the search for the historical Śaṅkara, and even if we take up the project as a legitimate corrective to our ignorance in various areas, we must at least admit that however we conceive our project we are using the Text differently than did its commentators; and we must still read the Text on its own terms.

47. Barthes suggests that "the Text must not be thought of as a defined object . . . [rather, it] is a methodological field . . . the Text reveals itself, articulates itself according to or against certain rules . . . *the Text is experienced only in an activity, a production.*" (1979, pp. 74-75). It is not there merely to be consumed. By contrast, the "work" is "concrete, occupying a portion of book-space . . . While the work is held in the hand, the Text is held in language: it exists only as discourse." (1979, pp. 75-76)

48. My comments on the transformation of the reader complement and situate textually the fine philosophical study of Śaṅkara in this regard undertaken by Taber (1983).

Chapter 2. The Texture of the Advaita Vedānta Text

1. Throughout, I refer to Advaitins as "readers," though early on "hearers" is of course the accurate term. Though there are striking differences to be expected in the responses of hearers and readers, the latter is the primary focus of this study.

2. Iser's emphasis (1978, p. 86) on the role of textual "strategies" is a useful starting point. A text is comprised in part of materials "selected from social systems and literary traditions." These make up its *repertoire*, and the reader actively engages this material in order to construct the meaning of the text. The *strategies* function "to organize this actualization . . . [they] organize both the material of the text and the conditions under which that material is to be communicated." The meaning of the text cannot be abstracted from these strategies, whose organizational importance "becomes all too evident the moment they are dispensed with. This happens, for instance, when plays or novels are summarized, or poems paraphrased. The text is practically disembodied, being reduced to content at the expense of effect. The strategies of the text are replaced by a personal organization, and more often than not we are left with a peculiar 'story' that is purely denotative, in no way connotative, and therefore totally without impact." At the heart of the problem is the

unexamined supposition that meaning can be detached from the language in which it is expressed, and from the ways in which that meaning is composed and elaborated, without much being lost in the process. The detachment of this meaning from its textual expression must be recognized as a significant act of reinterpretation which requires careful reassessment. Texts must be appreciated first as texts, even if our goal is to skillfully build systematizations on them. Though Iser's treatment of fiction requires some modification if it is to be applicable to theological texts, his notice of what is lost in summarization compels us to reconsider the relationship between the reading we do, the way we gain our understandings, and the manner in which we "write these up" in acts of communication for larger and different audiences. Whatever their differences, theological texts too have their own repertoire of strategies, to which we must remain sensitive in our treatment of them.

3. On the importance of the *Chāndogya* for the Vedānta, see Deussen 1973, Modi 1956, and especially Bhatkhande 1982.

4. All translations from the upaniṣads here and below are drawn from the excellent Bedekar/Palsule (1987) English rendering and correction of Deussen's German translation; occasionally, I have made small modifications for the sake of clarity in English and in order to follow the Sanskrit word order more closely.

5. Below we shall return to this text, to examine how the Advaitins argue the meaning of the upaniṣads within the structures of the Text.

6. The "verses," signalled by quotation marks, comprise the *mantra* portion of the text; the rest is the *brāhmaṇa* portion.

7. Brian Smith's study (1989) of earlier and parallel Vedic materials and much of what counts as knowledge is organizational and homological: to know is to know where things are properly located in relation to one another, and therefore what they are akin to, like. The organizational reconstruction of the known occurs regarding, and by, a model of the Vedic ritual and the traditional Vedic knowledge. This can occur, as implied, by a strictly spatial model, according to which knowledge is rearranged on a spatial grid; but it can also occur according to temporal/genealogical ordering, as what is here and now known is traced back to its source. We move from what happens to be first known to the underlying source of that knowledge, upon which it depends.

8. On the possibility of a more straightforward reading of the PMS, which are more accessible than the UMS, see Clooney 1990b, pp. 34ff.; the obscurity

of the UMS is one reason why this present volume does not devote more space to a retrieval of Bādarāyaṇa's system. Modi (1956,) however, lays the foundation for a complete retrieval of Bādarāyaṇa.

9. Rāmānuja and other Vedānta commentators join or divide some sūtras differently, with a resultant variation in the total number of sūtras.

10. Renou (1961, p. 207) suggests that sūtras are perhaps deliberately obscure, so as to ensure that they will be transmitted properly, only under the guidance of approved teachers.

11. Defining the boundaries of an adhikaraṇa—how many sūtras constitute the unit—is the first task of a commentator, and prerequisite to further analysis. Schools of Vedānta may disagree on the exact definition of adhikaraṇas; Rāmānuja frequently divides adhikaraṇas differently than does Śaṅkara. Modi's occasionally severe criticism of Śaṅkara's divisions of adhikaraṇas is instructive. For a discussion of the connections among adhikaraṇas, see below, pp. 59–63.

12. Except where noted, all translations of Bādarāyaṇa's sūtras and of Śaṅkara's *Bhāṣya* are those of Swami Gambhirananda (1983), with occasional slight modifications. Only when Śaṅkara's commentary on a sūtra is exceptionally long will I give a page reference for the cited portion. All references to the Sanskrit of the *Bhāṣya* and the subsequent commentaries are from the 1981 edition.

13. Bourdieu is helpful in appreciating the importance of significance of this forensic style. He notes that temporally situated practical thinking proceeds not only or primarily according to the demands of logical coherence, but by the "messier" more expansive procedures of debate and argument: "Those who are surprised by the paradoxes that ordinary logic and language engender when they apply their divisions to continuous magnitudes forget the paradoxes inherent in treating language as a purely logical instrument and also forget the social situation in which such a relationship to language is possible. The contradictions or paradoxes to which ordinary language classifications lead do not derive, as all forms of positivism suppose, from some essential inadequacy of ordinary language, but from the fact that these socio-logical acts are not directed towards the pursuit of logical coherence and that, unlike philological, logical or linguistic uses of language . . . they obey the logic of the parti pris, which, as in a court-room, juxtaposes not logical arguments, subject to the sole criterion of coherence, but charges and defences . . . . Quite apart from all that is implied in the oppositions, which logicians and even linguists manage to forget, between the art of convincing and the art of persuading, it is

clear that scholastic usage of language is to the orator's, advocate's or politician's usage what the classificatory schemes devised by the logician or statistician concerned with coherence and empirical adequacy are to the categorizations and categoremes of daily life." (1984, p. 476) To be faithful to the Text we read, we need to return to Advaita the temporality of the reading process, and so infuse our discussions of Advaita with an awareness of this temporality.

14. Here and throughout this book I render sūtras amply, and without the encumbrance of bracketed words or footnotes.

15. E.g., *Taittirīya* 2.7.1, 2.8, 2.9, 3.6, 3.9.

16. "Then, when one receives this essence, he becomes full of bliss."

17. For instance: in the course of his first exposition of the adhikaraṇa, in commenting on sūtra 17, Śaṅkara argues that because we know from the whole of the upaniṣads that Brahman and the human self really are one, it is only for the purpose of argument that Bādarāyaṇa observes here that the self functions as if it were not Brahman: "In the case of ordinary people, it is seen that, though the Self ever retains its true nature of being the Self, there is a false identification with the body, etc., which are non-Self.... [This sūtra is spoken] taking for granted such a difference between the supreme self and the self identified with the intellect." [*Bhāṣya* on UMS I.1.17] Accordingly, and as the whole first interpretation of the adhikaraṇa suggests, the upaniṣad can be read as presuming duality. But later it needs to be reread with a directly present sense of the nonduality of self and Brahman. Śaṅkara's reading of the sūtra introduces a temporal dimension—the time needed for learning—by insisting that it be read twice, "for present purposes" and after one knows "really."

18. Another of his striking reinterpretations of an adhikaraṇa (UMS IV.3.7–14) is treated in Chapter 3, pp. 99–102.

19. See the beginning of Śaṅkara's second version of the adhikaraṇa, after the conclusion of the first explanation of UMS I.1.19; tr. 71–2.

20. Tr. 73.

21. Tr. 75.

22. Their commitment is reverent and intelligent, not merely repetitious. On occasion they differ from Śaṅkara: thus, Vācaspati, Amalānanda and Appaya Dīkṣita debate at length Śaṅkara' interpretation of "mantra" and "brāhmaṇa" according to sūtra 15, and offer alternate interpretations of the sūtra.

23. In the following paragraphs I summarize Vācaspati's comments (Skt. 186–7), from the second version of the siddhānta.

24. Different again, of course, is the case of "things" outside the Text—trees, rocks, men and women, gods; though these exist and are not textually constituted, as renunciation is made out to be by Advaita, they too are irrelevant until their textual location is identified.

25. Often translated as "states" or "stages" of life. I retain the Sanskrit *āśrama*, to avoid the dispute as to whether the āśramas are "really" four consecutive stages in a single course or rather four (potentially unconnected) states.

26. This Mīmāṃsā reasoning is drawn from the ritual situation where one or another action clearly occurs in a rite, though no justificatory text can be found; since action takes precedence over its texts, the fact of the fact demands the positing of a (currently unavailable) text.

27. The decision that there is a fourth āśrama entails a further consideration as to whether it has distinguishing marks; in turn, this entails a discussion of whether asceticism (*tapas*) is that adequate mark. The conclusion is that since asceticism is characteristic of the third āśrama it cannot be *the* distinctive mark of the fourth.

28. Skt. 884, 890; emphasis mine. We shall return to this aspect of the discourse about renunciation in Chapter 4: by verbally legitimated renunciation one traverses the gap between the complexity of textual knowledge and the simplicity of an Advaita apprehension of Brahman. It is possible to be permanently free of words—after one has been schooled in the Text. In his commenting, Amalānanda introduces a textually structured discussion as to whether renunciation entails the discarding the topknot of hair and the brahmanical thread and the carrying of either the triple staff or the single staff. This discussion proceeds on the basis of a new array of scriptural texts, and Appaya Dīkṣita amplifies it at great length. Ostensibly extratextual issues constitute the topic of the adhikaraṇa, but only in a textual (re)formulation. No social data is directly introduced, not even the behavior of those worthy of respect. Questions—asked inside and outside Vedānta—about the ordering of the orthodox spiritual life are rephrased in a thoroughly textual fashion. Each right reading advances that knowledge which culminates in a perfect, precise discrimination among texts and consequent perfect discrimination of correct living. See Olivelle (1986) for a full discussion of the Vedānta debate over renunciation, based on materials other than the UMS Text.

29. From a different starting point and for a different end, Pollock aptly summarizes the position enunciated here: "Even the act of ascetic renunciation, which is in its very essence the withdrawal from the rule-boundedness of social existence, depends on the mastery and correct execution of shastric rules." (1985, p. 509)

30. I take UMS I.4 as a supplement to the main project of the adhyāya.

31. I draw here on the explanations offered by Vācaspati Misra and Amalānanda; but for UMS I.1.22, I have relied on Advaitānanda's simpler exposition of the adhikaraṇa.

32. Deussen (1973, pp. 121–2) noted the evident sequence of texts drawn from the *Chāndogya*. The following texts are considered in order, in the following UMS adhikaraṇas (topical sections): *Chāndogya* 1.6.6 [UMS I.1.20–21]; 1.9.1 [I.1.22]; 1.11.5 [I.1.23]; 3.13.7 [I.1.24–27]; 3.14.1 [I.2.1–8]; 4.15.1 [I.2.13–17]; 5.11–24 [I.2.24–32]; 7.23 [I.3.8–9]; 8.1.1 [I.3.14–18]; 8.12.3 [I.3.19–21 (passim) and I.3.40]; 8.14 [I.3.41].

33. This is Advaitānanda's interpretation.

34. A standard rule of Mīmāṃsā exegesis is that the beginning (*upakrama*) and end (*upasaṃhāra*) of a text are keys to the meaning of the whole text, particularly when they agree.

35. The most well-known example of the applicability of the whole in each of its parts is the *Aṣṭādhyāyī* of the grammarian Pāṇini.

36. Skt. 179.

37. See also Appaya Dīkṣita's use of UMS III.3.38 in commenting on UMS I.1.22, and of UMS I.4.17 in his comment on UMS I.1.31.

38. We can note also that the Advaitins regularly read UMS adhikaraṇas in light of, and in subtle relation to, siddhāntas accomplished in the PMS. To give but a few examples from UMS I.1.12–19: PMS II.3.16, and the general Mīmāṃsā reflection on "place" (*sthāna*) is appealed to by Appaya Dīkṣita in the course of analyzing whether the location of "made of bliss" as the fifth and last in a series of sheaths tells us something definitive about its identity, whether it is like, or different from, the preceding sheaths. Vācaspati appeals to Kumārila Bhāṭṭa's *Tantravārtika* on PMS II.2.22—wherein the possible differences among three related towards (*jyoti* ("light"), *viśva-jyoti* ("the pervasive light") and *sarva-jyoti* ("the light of all")—are weighed and analyzed) to explain why it is that ānanda ("bliss") and ānanda-maya ("made of bliss") can be said to refer to the same reality, Brahman. In the second version of UMS I.1.12–19, Vācaspati, Amalānanda and Appaya Dīkṣita also appeal to PMS IX.3.15, in order to explain why the sūtras can legitimately be interpreted differently than they had been before; in the course of that explanation, Appaya Dīkṣita also refers to PMS III.1.22, and PMS I.4.23. On Śaṅkara's use of Mīmāṃsā siddhāntas as nyāyas, see Devasthali (1951), Moghe (1984) and Sastri (1989).

39. See Clooney 1991 and forthcoming c.

40. Modi 1956, vol. II, pp. 187-214.

41. That is to say, one must think like a Mīmāṃsaka. Coordination is the extension to the upaniṣads of a Mīmāṃsā practice whereby rules were spelled out as to how ritual performers could "borrow" details of ritual performance from the texts of other schools. For more on coordination, see Chapter 3 and Clooney, forthcoming c.

42. The UMS III in general is a reflection on the presuppositions of meditation, including the order of the world (UMS III.1), the nature of human self and Brahman (UMS III.2), and the orthodox identity of the meditating person. (UMS III.4.)

43. Here I follow Appaya Dīkṣita's comments on UMS III.3.1. Modi, interested in retrieving Bādarāyaṇa's system and in a consequent critique of Śaṅkara's version of the sūtras, offers a different explanation of the pāda's structure.

44. Vācaspati distinguishes between qualities which always attest to Brahman's nature ("being," "truth," "bliss," etc.) and those which do pertain only as posited in specific contexts ("being that toward which all blessings go," or "whose desires are true"). The former belong everywhere, the latter only where introduced. Appaya Dīkṣita adds the point, significant for the Advaitins, that even the basic qualities are more of the nature of boundaries than essential characteristics.

45. Tr. 21.

46. A more elaborate description is of course needed. Modi broke new ground by building an interpretation of the UMS beginning from UMS III.3, which in his view "holds the key of the Sūtrakāra's scheme of arranging the Śrutis for discussion in the first three Pādas of the first Adhyāya of the Brahmasūtra." (1956 vol. II, p. 187); see the whole of volume II, ch. 9, especially 196ff. Although Modi is sharply critical of the Advaita reading of UMS III.3, his sense of where one's attention to the Text ought to begin is useful even in interpreting the Advaita. See also Nakamura (1983, pp. 429-34) who adheres to the view that the core text was originally dedicated to an organization of meditations and claims generated by the *Chāndogya Upaniṣad.*

47. The Advaitins, from Śaṅkara on, argue that UMS IV.1.1–12 completes UMS III; Govindānanda says that whereas in UMS III.4 treats explicit statements regarding renunciation, UMS IV.1.1–12 considers what can be extrapolated from statements about the results of renunciation.

48. It is useful if one wishes to segment the Text, so that it parts might be conveniently moved around and treated in an order more amenable to another modes of interpretation. Deussen's important and influential *System of the Vedānta* is perhaps the first such reordering which utilized the identified divisions into pāda and adhyāya.

49. I discuss this important sūtra in Chapter 4.

50. This is so even if, as Potter (1982) and Sawai (1986) have correctly pointed out, Śaṅkara defends the possibility of a "sudden leap" into liberative knowledge, without any specific preparation. As we shall see in Chapter 4, the sudden leap marks that ideal (and ever receding) point at which one resolves the tension between Text and truth, knowledge as practice and knowledge as pure consciousness; in theory, the resolution may occur at any moment, though in practice great skill is required to make the leap.

51. Edward Said's reflections on "beginnings" are helpful background here, particularly his "meditation on beginnings," (1985, pp. 29-78.)

52. Such rules are known in the the Advaita and other sastras as *paribhāṣas*; they regulate the reading and use of the text of which they are a part. Chakrabarti (1980) is a helpful introduction.

53. Similarly, Śaṅkara's famous prologue on superimposition (*adhyāsa*)—the mistaken, disastrous identification of the self (ātman) with the phenomenal and changing world—can be read either as a distillation of the Text into the real underlying issue, the problem of epistemological error or as propaedeutic to the ensuing Text. By the former interpretation, it is the long-desired and welcome apprehension of the "real" underlying problem which had for generations been gotten at indirectly, clumsily, gradually, in the upaniṣads and interpretation of them in the UMS, the problem of a mistake, a confusion of identity, which has profound cosmological and spiritual results and which, once one has come to a proper understanding of it, can be investigated and resolved philosophically, with increasingly diminished need for the scriptural accoutrements with which the whole issue had previously been adorned. By the latter and more apt interpretation, it can be taken as a "final"—thought last, placed first—clarification of why it is that a proper understanding of scripture, the achievement of knowledge, can lead to that salvation desired by the Advaitins who meditate their way through the Text: because the problem confronting humans is a "mistake," an erring which has happened but which need not have happened, and so which can never be provided with a predictable metaphysical underpinning, the response to it is legitimately a practical one, a correction in the way one thinks. Attention to superimposition informs

us that the problem is wrong knowing, a problem to be cured by a right knowing—right knowing is achieved precisely through education according engagement in the Text.

Chapter 3. The Truth of Advaita Vedānta

1. In Chapters 1 and 2 I insisted that one must move beyond talking about the Text to an engaged, patient reading of it; whatever is said about it must be said only after and out of reading, not due to the privileges of any shortcuts. In particular, I argued that whatever one's position might be about the importance and function of the authors of texts, one frustrates the pedagogical expectations of the Advaita Text if one retreats into speculation about the intentions of Śaṅkara, the mind of Śaṅkara, as a device for "speed-reading." If one focuses on Śaṅkara and delves only sporadically into the later commentaries, one will constrict Advaita to its initial stages and deny oneself its full blossoming and fruition. One will know something about Śaṅkara, but not enough about Advaita. As I take up the topics of this chapter and the next, on the truth of Advaita and the reader of Advaita, I see no reason to qualify the positions thus taken. Nevertheless, the task of communicating—of choosing to write a book about Advaita—immediately imposes on the writer the requirement to say more than, "Read the Text." One gets caught in the tension between a simple truth (reading is the starting point for comparative work) and the complexities of the actual reading that must occur (the massive task of learning to read, of differentiating commentarial positions, judging what can be omitted and what cannot). In Chapters 3 and 4 I handle this tension haltingly, by skeptically taking some of those shortcuts I have called into question: I speak of topics in the Text, for here it serves little practical purpose, were it even possible, to refer to the whole, all at once; I refer a great deal to Śaṅkara's views, for his words offer a manageable place to stand when confronted with the rich (over)abundance of the Text; even when I use the later commentators I never give them a chance to speak their own word fully, but excerpt them selectively. My justification, if any, lies in the hope that while I am quite far from a mastery of the Text, I am far enough "into it" that my shortcuts occur after reading, not instead of it; they are posterior to the "after Vedānta" transformation of the way I think and go about writing. Readers are advised read these chapters with a sense of irony, recognizing an instance of the difference between what one says ought to be done and what one actually does.

2. For another presentation of truth in Advaita, see Deutsch 1969, pp. 86–90.

3. The following observations rely on *Fictional Truth,* which seeks to offer "a systematic scrutiny of the textual mechanisms and the verbal structures that represent or imply the truth of a fictitious tale." (Riffaterre 1990, p. xii.) In his foreword, Stephen Nichols characterizes Riffaterre's project as the effort to offer "an historical corrective to the reigning critical orthodoxy as the principal—in some critics only—legitimate form of art's interaction with the social formation that produced it." (Riffaterre 1990, p. vii) Mutatis mutandis, the same applies to this retrieval of Advaita.

4. Riffaterre 1990, p. xiii.

5. Riffaterre 1990, pp. xiii–xiv.

6. Riffaterre 1990, p. 3.

7. Riffaterre 1990, p. 2.

8. Riffaterre 1990, p. 3.

9. Just as world renunciation and the abandonment of texts is legitimated Textually; see Chapter 2, p. 55–58.

10. This is P.M. Modi's assessment of UMS II.2: "This Pāda (UMS III.2.) seems to deal with the different states, *jāgarita, svapna* and *suṣupta,* of the individual soul and of the Supreme Being. The first Sūtra (*saṃdhye sṛṣṭirāha hi*) refers to the Śruti, "*saṃdhyaṃ tṛtīyaṃ svapnasthānam.*" (*Bṛhadāraṇyaka Upaniṣadad* 4.3.9) Therefore, *sthāna* in this Sūtra means the *states* of *jāgarita* [being awake], *svapna* [sleep] and *suṣupta* [dreamless sleep] . . . If we interpret the world *sthāna* in this sense [as indicating "states"] we have not to suspect this discussion of the Supreme Self (UMS II.2.11–41) to be an interpolation because we can then say that Pāda II of Adhyāya III deals with the states of the individual soul *and those* of the Supreme Soul." (Modi 1956 vol. I, p. 3)

11. The precise nature of Brahman's possession of two forms is not entirely made clear by Modi: "The Śruti [text] referred to under Sūtra 13 says that Brahman is simultaneously both *arūpavat* and *rūpavat* . . . In Sūtra 14 the Sūtrakara says that this is possible because Brahman is *chiefly arūpavat* and *secondarily rūpavat.* In other words, if Brahman were *both rūpavat* and *arūpavat* in the literal sense, there would be a self-contradiction and then the Śruti in question would not be rationally explained. But such is not the case. Brahman is *only arūpavat,* because it is *chiefly arūpavat* . . . So on the strength of the Śruti [text] one can say without being inconsistent that Brahman is *simultaneously* both *arūpavat* and *rūpavat,* as the Sūtrakara [Bādarāyaṇa] does in Sūtra 11." (Modi 1956 vol. I, p. 11) It is not clear what it means to say that Brahman is *only* without form, because it is *chiefly* without form, or that Brahman is simul-

taneously with and without; it is a surer path to take read these as textual claims. So too, his solution implies that scripture ought not be taken literally: it doesn't, or can't, mean both kinds of statements about Brahman. What he does not do, however, is explain how we are to decide when scripture is to be taken literally.

12. Tr. 623.

13. The preceding discussion may be usefully located against the background of Riffaterre's discussion of "subtext:" "[A subtext is] a text within a text. From the viewpoint of the text in which it appears, a subtext is a unit of significance. From the viewpoint of the readers whom it helps to perceive and decode the significance of long narratives, the subtext is a unit of reading that is a hermeneutical model . . . It is not a subplot and must not be confused with a theme, for it has no existence outside the text in which it appears. A subtext is usually strung along the main narrative line in separate successive variants that may overlap with other subtexts. The story it tells and the objects it describes refer symbolically and metalinguistically to the novel as a whole or to some other aspect of its significance." (Riffaterre 1990, p. 131) A subtext points to the truth of a text because it "always constitutes a second reading of what the text surrounding it is about, a poetic or humorous metalanguage of the narrative. The subtext thus actualizes the relationship of referentiality." (Riffaterre 1990, p. 28) The texts which speak of Brahman without qualities serve this function of metanarrative, not as if they constitute a discourse within the discourse, but because their denial of the evident primary discourse—Brahman can be spoken of and meditated on in many ways—compel the reader to enter into a different and more complex, temporally sensitive relationship to the rest of the text, questioning it differently and vigorously rereading it against itself.

14. "You are that," repeated nine times in *Chāndogya* 6, has a privileged place in the Advaita tradition. Śaṅkara refers to it frequently as a distillation of the meaning of the upaniṣads, and in later Advaita, inside and outside the UMS Text, it becomes a key organizing tool in many Advaita expositions. For example, the third chapter of the *Naiṣkarmyasiddhi* of Sureśvara, a disciple of Śaṅkara, is an exposition of the meaning of *tat tvam asi,* including its necessary scriptural contextualization, the meanings of *tat* and *tvam,* and the proper linguistic tools by which the statement can be parsed properly. Similarly, Dharmarāja Adhvarīndra's *Advaita Paribhāṣā* a popular and concise presentation of Advaita epistemology, metaphysics and soteriology, structures its 7th chapter, on the content of Advaita, around an exposition of *tat tvam asi.* The decisive transformation of the disciple's consciousness in the *Vivekacūḍāmaṇi* is achieved through reflection upon an analysis of these same words.

15. Thus, in commenting on UMS I.1.6, Śaṅkara explains *Chāndogya* 6.8.8, of which "You are that" is the conclusion, as follows: "By [first] saying, 'That is the self,' the text presents that reality, that subtle self, as the self under consideration; then, in the text 'You are that, O Śvetaketu,' there occurs the instruction about it as the self of the conscious being Śvetaketu." See also his use of *tat tvam asi* in UMS II.1.14 and UMS III.2.27.

16. The great sayings continue to be used by the later commentators as a tool for the organization of the Text. For example, at UMS III.3.1 Amalānanda comments that UMS III.2 was devoted to an analysis of the *tvam*, the human self (in UMS III.2.1-10) and the *tat*, Brahman (in UMS III.2.11 ff.); consequent upon this analysis, UMS III.3 now takes up the means of meditation, the texts themselves. Or, the second version of the topic at issue in UMS III.3.16–17 inquires into the relation between *Chāndogya* 6 and *Bṛhadāraṇyaka* 4.3–4. Amalānanda and Appaya Dīkṣita explain the siddhānta—that although the texts seem to have different topics they can be meditated on together—by showing how the two passages are both about *tat tvam asi*, the *Chāndogya* beginning with *tat* and concluding with *tvam*, and the *Bṛhadāraṇyaka* moving in the reverse direction. Hence, the two texts are useable together because of their common emphasis on the single "great saying."

17. As we shall see in Chapter Four, in UMS IV.1.2–3 the pūrvapakṣin questions the efficacy of "you are that" and the other great sayings. If such a statement has liberative meaning, it will communicate it upon first reading, or not at all. The siddhāntin defends the value of reading and rereading, insisting that only gradually does the meaning of the statement become clear and effective in the experience of the reader. The great sayings are not magically effective, but are rather regulative distillations of the larger texts of which they remain part (in earlier Advaita, at least).

The preceding analysis too is indebted to Riffaterre, who provides a way to understand the function of great sayings. Though the great sayings too might be interpreted as subtexts (see above), I wish to consider them simply in terms of a second of Riffaterre's strategies, that of "ungrammaticality," discussed in Riffaterre 1978 and 1990. When the reader first reads a text, she or he looks for meaning, tries to understand; but while succeeding in discovering the (apparent) references of words, the reader is also able to perceive "incompatibilities between words: for instance, to identify tropes and figures, that is, to recognizes that a word or phrase does not make literal sense, that it makes sense only if he (and he is the only one around to do it) performs a semantic transfer, only if he reads that word or phrase as a metaphor, for example, or as a metonymy . . . This reader input occurs only because the text is ungrammatical." (1978, p. 5) These ungrammaticalities "signal that the subtext's meaning does not derive from the chain of events of the surrounding narrative, but from references to an intertext that remains the same for each successive version of the subtext . . . These ungrammaticalities are the most effective and conspicuous, not just because they disturb verisimilitude, but because in a time-oriented context they focus on an unchanging intertextuality, deriving their significance from their reference to an intertext that has no past, no future, no temporality, an image therefore of unchangeable truth . . ." (1990, p. xviii) This other frame of reference is the "intertext," the elusive, never-present text to which the text is connected through those ungrammaticalities which make sense only by reference to the absent intertext. The intertext is not another text, nor a marginal "text within the Text;" it remains as it were the perennial "unconscious" of the text; a path to it may be traced by clues such as ungrammaticalities in the text.

18. Riffaterre 1978, p. 12.

19. Riffaterre 1978, p. 13.

20. How this happens can be illustrated also and by attention to a Mīmāṃsā discussion presupposed by Advaita. PMS I.1.24–5 is devoted to both an establishment of the proper subject matter of Mīmāṃsā—dharma—and to a preliminary explanation of how dharma is to be known; one adhikaraṇa addresses the problem of how dharma can be the object of language. The objection is that even if individual Vedic words are authoritative, Vedic sentences—groupings of words—have no definite, unchanging reference, and so lack authority: "Even if the relationship of word and meaning is original, words cannot be expressive of dharma; for that purpose is not known by means of words." (PMS I.1.24) The siddhānta takes the position that the cohesion of the words into authoritative units is original to the Veda itself, and these larger and smaller units of words cohere with corresponding, always-being-enacted rituals: "On the contrary, they are authoritative, since there is a handing down together of words, already formed prior to use, for the sake of action. This handing down together is the means to the knowledge of that purpose, dharma." (PMS I.1.25) On these sūtras, see Clooney 1990 b, pp. 90, 115.

A long argument begins here, later formalized as the debate between the Bhāṭṭa and Prābhākara schools on the opposing positions of *anvītābhidhānavāda* (the Prābhākara view that the meaning of a sentence is more than the meaning of its words) and *abhihitānvayavāda* (the Bhāṭṭa view that the meaning of sentences is constructed out of the meanings of the individual words). At the core of the debate is the issue of how the Veda, in its individual sections related to individual sacrifices, imparts meaning. The pūrvapakṣa is that meaning is accumulated out of component meanings, such that the meanings of sentences are composed of the meanings of the words which comprise that sentence.

When the reader knows all the words—and presumably that to which each refers—she or he understands the sentence. The siddhānta is that the meaning of a sentence is found in its purpose, that wholeness to which all the parts contribute but which is communicated neither by any one of them nor by all of them merely added together. Vedic sentences signify through their "performance" in the construction of ritual actions to which they can be said to refer, but which, more properly, are engendered out of attention to these particular sentences. Significance therefore subsists in this creative interaction of a verbal whole and a whole of practice. It is a truth that occurs only in the totality of the practice of intelligent reading; here, it seems, the positions of Prābhākara and Riffaterre stand close together.

21. Both coordination (upasaṃhāra) and harmonization (samanvaya) have been introduced in Chapter 2.

22. *Chāndogya Upaniṣad* 6.2.1.

23. *Taittirīya Upaniṣad* 2.5; for an interpretation of this text, see Chapter 2.

24. *Chāndogya Upaniṣad* 4.15.2, "He is called 'the unifier of all that is pleasant' for he unites all that is pleasant; those who know this unite all that is pleasant."

25. Amalānanda's entire comment occurs under UMS III.3.11, Skt. 766–7.

26. Amalānanda's comments under UMS I.1.2 (Skt. 93–4) complement the preceding ones.

27. Tr. 47.

28. Sattva is the first of the three characteristics (*guṇa*) of which all reality is constituted; it is often characterized positively as light, pure, open, etc.; the debate here is whether parallel qualities of consciousness can also be attributed to it.

29. Tr. 48.

30. There follows a critique of Sāṃkhya's theory of three constituent elements (*guṇa*).

31. See UMS I.1.5; tr. 49.

32. UMS I.1.5; tr. 50.

33. See tr. 50.

34. UMS I.1.5; tr. 51.

35. See UMS I.1.5; tr. 51.

36. Tr. 51–54.

37. E.g., *Śvetāśvatara Upaniṣad* 6.9.

38. As we saw regarding UMS I.1.12–19.

39. The *lakṣaṇa* of something is not its essence, but rather its distinguishing characteristic, that which marks it off from other things—its definition, in the more active sense of marking off its boundaries.

40. Then, in the next section, I look forward to UMS II in order to show how the ambivalent reasonable-scriptural characterization of Brahman is accompanied by a deliberately fragmenting, designedly insufficiently reasonable characterization of competing viewpoints.

41. Tr. 14.

42. Tr. 14–15.

43. Tr. 15.

44. Tr. 17.

45. Amalānanda's dense comments (Skt. 93–4) may help to clarify the issues involved. He asks whether Brahman, supposed to be known from the words of scripture, can actually be characterized by any word or group of words. When the siddhāntin observes that "bliss" in *Taittirīya* 2 also entails "truth," etc.—because these terms are always connected—the pūrvapakṣin objects that even when taken together these words still fail to communicate. If the words are distinct in their meanings, they do not add up to a definition of Brahman, which is distinctionless; if they are not distinct, then the meaning of a statement (composed of them) can never be determined, since words communicate only together, specifying and delimiting one another. Either way, they are not communicative. Unless the words are distinct in meaning, their use together as a sentence is merely repetitive, and means nothing. The siddhāntin responds that when the meaning of a word is already known, that meaning can be put forth and specified by other meanings; but since the word "Brahman" is not a word of that sort, what we understand of it is achieved only by the collocation of words in the sentence altogether. Together the words communicate what is not the referent of any single one of them, and without it being a complex referent of all of them.

46. Deussen 1979, p. 108.

47. The text is given in translation in Deussen 1979, pp. 109–115.

48. *Chāndogya Upaniṣad* 4.15.5.

49. Tr. 892.

50. Tr. 884.

51. Tr. 886.

52. In keeping with earlier discussions in UMS III.3, he concludes that if the result of meditation is liberation—if knowledge saves—it is untenable to posit distinctions in Brahman or between Brahman and the self.

53. Tr. 890–1.

54. Tr. 891–2.

55. In III.2.11–21; see the treatment of this adhikaraṇa earlier in this chapter.

56. See "Human Reason and Vedic Revelation in Advaita Vedānta" (Halbfass 1991, pp. 131–204) for an overview of the issues involved in the following sections.

57. Skt. 449. Vācaspati further specifies reason's limitation, saying that reason is most unreliable when it comes to trying to understand the cause of the world.

58. Tr. 313–14.

59. Tr. 321.

60. Tr. 322.

61. Śaṅkara puts forward a more systematic claim when he responds to the charge that were Brahman the material cause, it would bear all the impurities evident in the world. He proposes an Advaita theory of causality, *satkāryavāda*, the view that effects preexist in their causes (UMS II.1.7; see also UMS II.1.14.)

62. The remainder of UMS II.1 defends the coherence of Advaita by addressing a series of questions and objections: 13: whether Advaita unreasonably denies the distinction of experiencer and experienced; 14, 15–20: whether it is possible to state that Brahman and the world are nondifferent; 21–23: why the nondual (human) self does not always acts to its own best interest; 24–29: how Brahman functions as material cause; 30–31: whether Brahman is omnipotent; 32–33: whether Brahman has any motive to make the world; 34–36 whether Brahman is to be blamed for suffering.

63. UMS II.2.1; tr. 368.

64. The following comments are simply my own suggestion as to how the whole may be read, since this pāda is a case where the commentators do not

offer convincing arguments in favor of one or another reading of progress of the whole. There are some identifications of saṃgati; for instance, Śaṅkara says that the link between the consideration of the Vaiśeṣika position (12–17) and the Sarvāstivāda Buddhist position (18–27) is that whereas the former is "half-nihilist," the latter is "completely nihilist;" or, more picturesquely, Ānandagiri comments (Skt. 479) that the analysis of the Buddhist positions (18–32) is followed by that of the Jainas (33-36) because the former are "those whose garments hang loose" (*muktakaccha*) while the latter are "those whose clothes have been discarded altogether" (*mukāmbara;*) he then notes (Skt. 487) that after the Jainas (33–36) the Śaivas (37–41) are treated, because whereas the former are those "whose hair has been plucked out" (*luñcitakeśa*) the latter are those "who wear their hair twisted in braids." (*jaṭadhāri*)

65. By contrast, Advaita is portrayed not as rejecting matter, but as subsuming it into consciousness.

66. 32 summarizes the positions related to Buddhism.

67. Ānandagiri identifies four sects: Śaiva, Pāśupata, Kāruṇikasiddhāntin, and Kāpālika. (Skt. 488)

68. Although a thorough analysis of this pāda remains to be done, some of the problems with the Advaita portrayal of the various positions have been duly noted. Ingalls (1954) drew our attention generally to the nature and limitations of the Advaita presentation of Buddhism, and more recently Darling (1987). Larson (1979) has sketched and defended the Sāṃkhya position against its Advaita description. Even if one concedes that Buddhists or Sāṃkhyans would on their own portray and defend their positions more convincingly, the main point is to read each Advaita portrayal in context, and to read UMS II.2 within the whole of the Text. The positions are distorted by Advaita not merely because of deficient or distorted presentations of their details, but primarily because they are written into an alien script—a script which is all the more difficult to understand because it also has an interest in constraining and weakening the role of reason, and in showing the impossibility of the emergence of *any* clear, reasonable viewpoint on the whole matter.

69. The pedagogical rationale for the pāda is stated clearly in an argument which occurs at its very beginning. Śaṅkara recognizes the following objection: "It is proper to establish one's own point of view for the sake of determining what the right knowledge is, as a means to the attainment of liberation by people seeking release; but what need is there of demolishing others' points of view, which amounts to being inimical to others?" (Tr. 367) Śaṅkara replies, "There are some people of dull intellect who, on noticing that the great scriptures of the Sāṃkhyas and others are accepted by the honored ones and that

they proceed under the plea of bestowing the right knowledge, may conclude that these too are to be accepted as a means to right knowledge. Besides, they may have faith in these, since there is a possibility of weight of reasoning and since they are spoken by omniscient people. Hence this effort is made to expose their hollowness." (Tr. 367–8) Vācaspati appeals to the objectivity of truth: "Just as it can be understood from the Advaita texts that Brahman is the source of the world, so too it can be understood from the inferences of the Sāṃkhyans, etc., that something nonconscious—the material principle, etc.—is the source of the world. But it is not possible to combine the view that the conscious is the source, with the view that the nonconscious is the source, since the views are contradictory. Regarding an established entity, one cannot entertain contradictory opinions." (Skt. 487–8)

70. This constitution of the world by its inscription in the Text is not novel to Advaita, which follows the lead of the Brahmanical world in general, and Mīmāṃsā in particular. The Mīmāṃsakas defined the world (*loka*) only in distinction from the ritual-scripture world (*veda*): the "world" is the "Vedic world" minus its coherent intelligibility. On the Mīmāṃsā view of the "world," see Clooney 1990b, pp. 131–7. This scriptural construction of reality is not a denial of a world outside the Text, just as the Advaita view of Brahman as the sole cause does not replicate a Buddhist denial of a world outside of consciousness. Mīmāṃsā (followed by Advaita) reserves to the Veda the power to regulate the world's significance; the world's intelligibility is not inherent, but is constructed by a proper arrangement of it according to the canons of intelligibility gleaned by the Mīmāṃsakas from the Vedic ritual-scriptural whole. Just as the Mīmāṃsakas arrange the elements of the world—wood, fire, rice, humans, words, gods, etc.—according to their position in relation to the sacrifice, the Advaitins bestow meaning on heterodox positions by locating them in relation to the proper Advaita understanding of consciousness and its relationship to material reality, and using their truths properly, within the complete (Advaita) comprehension of the world.

71. These first two sūtras draw on the *Sāṃkhya Kārikā* 15.

72. Tr. 372.

73. In UMS II.1.24 by the siddhāntin and here by the pūrvapakṣin.

74. Tr. 380.

75. Tr. 383.

76. Lindbeck 1984.

77. Lindbeck 1984, p. 31.

78. Lindbeck 1984, p. 16.

79. Lindbeck 1984, p. 33.

80. See especially chapter 6.

81. Lindbeck 1984, pp. 63–69.

82. Lindbeck 1984, p. 63.

83. Lindbeck 1984, p. 64.

84. Lindbeck 1984, p. 64.

85. Lindbeck 1984, p. 65.

86. Lindbeck 1984, p. 66.

87. Lindbeck 1984, p. 68.

88. The grammar and intratextual organization of the Text itself constitutes a significance irreducible to any of the meanings included within it, and available only to the careful and patient reader.

89. Lindbeck also observes that the further refinements of religious language through the articulation of "technical theology and official doctrine," are more and not less distant from the possibility of ontological reference. For in these statements, "one rarely if ever succeeds in explaining, defending, analyzing, and regulating the liturgical, kerygmatic, and ethical modes of speech and action within which such affirmations from time to time occur. Just as grammar by itself affirms nothing either true or false regarding the world in which language is used, but only about language, so theology and doctrine, to the extent that they are second-order activities, assert nothing either true or false about God and his relation to creatures, but only speak about such assertions. These assertions, in turn, cannot be made except when speaking religiously, i.e., when seeking to align oneself and others performatively with what one takes to be the most important in the universe by worshiping, promising, obeying, exhorting, preaching." (Lindbeck 1984, p. 69) These remarks on the linguistic constitution of the believers' world and the transition from intrasystemic truth to a performative, "liturgical" connectedness to the inscribed world aid us to understand how Advaita as a theological system adequately accounts for its truth, while yet not adopting experiential or propositional models of truth. The bottom line, in Advaita and Lindbeck, is an involved and literate commitment to the Text and all that is thereby implied.

Chapter 4. Advaita Vedānta and Its Readers

1. For an epistemologically sensitive presentation of some of the issues addressed here, see Bilimoria 1988, pp. 292–302.

2. Vedāntins in general agree that knowledge itself cannot be enjoined, though the upaniṣadic texts clearly encourage some complex activity. The Advaitins and the Viśiṣṭādvaitins dispute various technical points regarding the *Bṛhadāraṇyaka* text, pertaining to the apparent injunctiveness of each apparently injunctive part—must be seen, must be heard, must be understood, must be meditated on—and thence of the statement as a whole.

3. Though "seeing" appears to be the beginning of the process, in Vedānta it is identified as the end of the process too. The logic of the text may be that earlier moments of vision initiate new cycles of hearing, understanding, meditation, vision.

4. Let us also recall from Chapter 1 how Appaya Dīkṣita, in commenting on Amalānanda's introductory sloka 2 to the *Vedāntakalpataru*, sketched the connection between the steps of meditation, as described in the *Bṛhadāraṇyaka* text, and progress in Advaitic knowledge. The parallel and interconnected structures of knowledge and meditation are replicated in that specifically Advaita knowledge which is generated by reading one's way through the Text. For another use of the *Bṛhadāraṇyaka* text, see Amalānanda's comments on UMS III.4.47 and 50, where he correlates *śravaṇa, manana* and *nididhyāsana* with the categories of learning (*pāṇḍitya*), childlikeness (*bālya*) and silence (*mauna*).

5. The portion considered here is found in the translation, pp. 34–36.

6. Tr. 35; Skt. 129.

7. Tr. 35; Skt. 129. Vācaspati says that such apparent injunctions of knowledge refer back to the basic command that one should memorize one's texts in the proper fashion (i.e., perform *svādhyāya*) and so become literate in a preliminary fashion. (Skt. 130) This preliminary memorization, which can be commanded, is the material prerequisite for engagement in the intelligent inquiry which is the activity of Advaita; it is therefore preliminary to knowledge of Brahman, which cannot be commanded. This reference back to prior learning affords the commands to hear and understand a definite role in the extended learning process of Advaita.

8. Amalānanda explains in more detail why the knowledge of Brahman cannot be enjoined, even as an act of reading texts: "Hearing is the apprehension of the purport of the text 'you are that,' in regard to Brahman [as] the self;

[it is an apprehension gained] by a pondering which begins with [actually] hearing the word 'that.' [Knowledge cannot be enjoined] because it is not possible for one to realize the 'that' as something to be done, when there is not yet any apprehension of the idea [of 'that'] differentiated by some further specification [e.g., by attention to the 'you'] of its referent; when the 'that' is apprehended, then the hearing has already come to be, and so is not something that can be done, or cannot be done, or be otherwise done. So too, understanding [is not subject to injunction,] because it is not something that can be done as long as it lacks apprehension [of its object] through rational scrutiny focused on some specific aspect of the object [of inquiry]. So too meditation: repeated reflection according to [prior] apprehending and understanding must be repeated two or three times for apprehension. So the intended object of injunction is not an object of injunction, when known. And it should be clear that seeing is not something that can be done." (Skt. 130) At UMS III.4.26, Amalānanda summarizes succinctly the process of realization that begins in verbal knowledge: "Refinement (*bhāvanā*) is the result of verbal knowledge; this in turn results in complete manifestation (*sākṣātkāra*), which in turn results in the achievement of salvation (*apavarga*). Ritual action is not required for any of these. Indeed, the notion of being a brahmin, etc., which is the reason for competence for ritual action, is cancelled by this verbal knowledge; for in the time after [verbal knowledge], there is no more ritual action." (Skt. 899)

9. Śaṅkara takes up the question twice, in two versions of the adhikaraṇa: first in general (in UMS IV.1.1–2) in regard to meditation on scriptural texts, and then more specifically (in UMS IV.1.2) in refutation of the view that since Brahman is extratextual and not subject to the differentiations of time and space, it can not be known by the repeated reading of texts.

10. Tr. 814.

11. Tr. 815.

12. Tr. 816.

13. Tr. 817. Śaṅkara concludes by warning that repetition must not be allowed to become a goal in itself: " . . . to one to whom this realization does not come promptly, this very repetition is meant for bringing about the realization. Even there, however, the teacher should not distract him from the understanding of the sentence, 'you are that,' in order to direct him to mere repetition." (UMS IV.1.2; tr. 818)

14. Skt. 932.

15. Skt. 933–34.

16. Skt. 935.

17. See also Vācaspati on UMS I.1.4 (tr: 170 and 232–33), and on UMS IV.1.2; and the Govindānanda at UMS III.4.47.

18. Vācaspati, tr. 79.

19. Skt. 58. Appaya Dīkṣita further explains the process by which training enhances one's ability to hear the notes more distinctly, with a conscious knowledge of the particularity of each. (Skt. 58–59)

20. I use here the translation of Patañjali's terms by J.H. Woods (1913).

21. *Yoga Sūtras* III.3. Vācaspati cites the sūtra with the added word *dhyānam,* as implied by Patañjali. Amalānanda adds, "hearing and understanding are fixed-attention because they consist of bringing the mind to dwell on Brahman, by means of [upaniṣadic] sentences and reasoning. Because "seeing," as manifestation in the form of a mental state, enters upon Brahman, it is as if emptied of form, and so is concentration." (Skt. 615)

22. Skt. 615.

23. Vācaspati, tr. 78.

24. Vācaspati, tr. 72–73.

25. At III.4.26, Vācaspati correlates the four stages of realization (*prapatti*) of Brahman in the *Bṛhadāraṇyaka* text examined above—*śravaṇa, manana, nididhyāsana, darśana.* "The first is a realization gained simply from hearing the upaniṣadic texts, and this they call *śravaṇa.* The second is from the same upaniṣadic texts, accompanied by *mīmāṃsā,* and this they call *manana.* The third consists of continuing reflection, and this they call *nididhyāsana.* The fourth has the form of manifestation, and this is no different from *kaivalya* ['isolation']." (Skt. 898)

26. A third, visual example also attests to the convergence of meditation and the acquisition of textual knowledge. At UMS I.3.19 Śaṅkara makes this comparison: "Just as before the perception of distinction, the transparent whiteness, constituting the real nature of a crystal, remains indistinguishable, as it were, from red, blue, and other conditioning factors; but after the perception of distinction through the valid means of knowledge, the crystal in its latter state is said to attain its true nature of whiteness and transparence, though it were exactly so even earlier—similarly, in the case of the individual soul, which remains indistinguishably mixed up with such limiting adjuncts as the body, etc., there springs up a discriminatory knowledge from the upaniṣads constituting his rising from the body; and the result of the discriminatory

knowledge is the attainment of the real nature, its realization of its nature as the absolute Self. Thus unembodiedness or embodiedness for the Self follows respectively from the fact of discrimination or non-discrimination . . ." (tr. 193) Vācaspati elaborates with yet another image: "By the repeated practice of hearing, understanding and meditating they are liberated by that knowledge which is discrimination. This knowledge which is discrimination has as its result the manifestation of the pure self, its appearing in its own true nature; this manifestation, in the form of a mental process, destroys the evolved world; then, like the *kataka* fruit, it too is dissolved, because [as mental process] it too is part of the evolved world." (Skt. 304)

27. Because *jijñāsā* indicates both the desire to know and the inquiry instigated by that desire, I have generally left it (and the correlate *jijñāsin*) untranslated, to leave open both possible meanings.

28. He considers, and rejects, the following four possibilities. First, the inaugural "atha" cannot indicate the beginning of the desire to know Brahman. The desire cannot be identified with the beginning of a text, and necessarily precedes the student's (motivated, purposeful) reading of it. Vācaspati observes that the desire to know always precedes any inquiry which is intended to satisfy that desire; the desire instigates the process, and must be operative before the undertaking of a process. Second, "atha" does not signal the beginning of a new enterprise, as if "something were effected on the mere hearing of that word 'atha,' as on hearing the sound of the drum or the conch." Although knowledge does progress, and new knowledge is acquired, knowing is not an activity that can be inaugurated so expediently. Third, "atha" cannot indicate that the desire to know Brahman arises only after a knowledge of ritual has been achieved; for it is obvious that the desire to know can arise without ritual knowledge. Fourth, the knowledge of ritual is not even a necessary though subordinate accessory of knowledge of Brahman, necessarily its accompaniment though not a cause for it. Ritual and Brahman are distinct topics and there is no necessary connection between the two. Śaṅkara dismisses all four interpretations and opts instead for a fifth, "proximity" (*ānantarya*). In Mīmāṃsā, proximity (PMS III.1.24) is a weak, noncausal connection, mere sequence. It indicates nearness in time or space, without any further subordination of one of the related elements to the other. In claiming that brahmajijñāsā is "after" only in this limited sense, Advaita argues not that knowledge is without precedents or proximate environs, but only that being a proper Advaitin is not connected causally to those precedents. This minimalization of connection is important in several ways. First, it defends the Uttara Mīmāṃsā as an enterprise posterior to and distinct from the Pūrva Mīmāṃsā, and so justifies it as a separate undertaking. Second, it emphasizes

the way in which the desire to know, and then knowledge itself, are not material projects which can be quantifiably measured and predicted, nor predictably caused; the sum total of the proximate factors which (seem to) contribute to desire and then to knowledge never make knowledge inevitable. Third, it indicates that Brahman is not like the complex of words, actions, things, people, etc. which constitute a sacrifice and which form the material object of the Mīmāṃsā inquiry; knowledge of those things cannot be shown to be requirements for knowledge of Brahman. Fourth, the whole discussion pertains to the originating desire which inaugurates the pursuit of knowledge, and then to the resultant knowledge. It does not pertain to the procedures of knowing, the way by which knowing as actually practiced is dependent, contextualized and linked with precedents.

29. Tr. 9.

30. *Taittirīya Āraṇyaka* 2.15.1. On the complex semantics of *svādhyāya* and *adhyayana* see note 44 below.

31. In Śabara's *Bhāṣya* a great deal of energy is devoted to examining whether the inauguration of Mīmāṃsā as further study violates the command that after study one should take up the life of a householder.

32. In general, the Advaitins are not entirely clear, particularly in polemical contexts, in their estimation of Mīmāṃsā—whether it is simply a how-to knowledge of ritual, or a more speculative understanding of ritual.

33. Tr. 66–7.

34. Vācaspati brings out this point strikingly when, after admitting that "it does not stand to reason that the [upaniṣadic] sentence requires ritual as an auxiliary," (tr. 71) he nevertheless goes on to attribute to the appropriately trained Advaitin precisely the set of skills one ordinarily gains from doing Mīmāṃsā: "in him who knows the connection of words and their senses; who comprehends the true nature of the principles regulating the use of sounds; who keeps in mind the relationships of subsidiary and principal, earlier and later, among things, and the requirements of expectancy, proximity and compatibility—in him there is seen the unhindered production of the knowledge of the meaning of the sentence, even though he has not performed any rites." (tr. 71).

35. Further on in his comment on UMS I.1.1, Vācaspati shows that brahmajijñāsā advances beyond dharmajijñāsā in terms of content: "By those who desire the nature of Brahman, the mass of bliss, the means thereto, i.e., knowledge, should be desired. That [knowledge] results from the Vedānta

BL

texts not of themselves, but as aided by the inquiry into Brahman." (tr. 108–9) That is, "through desire one is directed to the inquiry into Brahman (*brahma-mīmāṃsāyām*), and not [merely] to the Vedānta texts (*vedānteṣu*) or to the intention to declare their meaning; for this [attention to the meaning of texts] is already attained by the aphorism, *athāto dharmajijñāsā* [for this announces the Mīmāṃsā enterprise in general, because it] aphoristically expresses the injunction to proper study (*svādhyāya*), this signifying the fruitful understanding of the meaning. The apprehension of religious duty, since it implies the sense of the Veda, secondarily implies Brahman too, in the same way as what is not religious duty." (tr. 109)

36. See Clooney 1989d and 1990b, pp. 189–94.

37. Wives participate along with their husbands; see PMS VI.1.6–24, and Clooney 1990b, pp. 187–9.

38. See PMS VI.1.39–42. The case of deities is not raised by Jaimini in the sūtras of PMS VI.1, but only by Śabara and thereafter.

39. See PMS VI.1.25–52; see Clooney 1990b, pp.189–94.

40. See Clooney 1990b, Chapter 5 on the resistance of Jaimini to an anthropological perspective.

41. The question of the competence of women for study of the upaniṣads is not discussed in detail by the Advaitins, though the comparable ritual question was discussed at length by the Mīmāṃsakas (see Clooney 1990b, pp. 187–89.) The Mīmāṃsā conclusion is apparently taken for granted. However, in the course of surveying alternatives available to śūdras, Appaya Dīkṣita notes the suggestion that they get the information they need from books, just as women learn from their husbands. (Skt. 358)

42. Tr. 205.

43. Skt. 318.

44. "Svādhyāya" indicates both the portion of the Veda properly assigned to one and learned with one's guru, and the sanctioned memorization of that portion of the Veda; insofar as it can be distinguished, "adhyayana" indicates the activity of that study: the performance of svādhyāya as the act of studying the texts which are the svādhyāya. For a full consideration of the complex issues related to svādhyāya and adhyayana as the objects and activities of study, see Malamoud (1977, pp. 44–70) and Verpoorten (1987, pp. 23–30). The Mīmāṃsā and Advaita in large part constitute the intelligent appropriation of meaning which follows upon the properly performed study (adhyayana) of the one's proper portion of the Veda (svādhyāya).

45. Skt. 349.

46. Skt. 352.

47. Skt. 352.

48. Skt. 352.

49. PMS IV.4.19 [which in turn draws on PMS IV.3.13–16] is cited as a case when although no fruit is mentioned, heaven, the state of happiness, can be introduced as a presupposed but unmentioned goal; similarly, in the Advaita context, one can suppose a result attainable only through proper study, though such a result is not mentioned.

50. Skt. 353.

51. Skt. 353.

52. For an ampler consideration of this background, see Clooney 1990b, pp. 139–149.

53. Once, however, Śabara says that when courses of action based on these two goals turn out to be in conflict, the course of action determined by the sacrificial goal is takes precedence. See PMS XII.4.37.

54. The reference to the horse, either a commonplace analogy as to how something can be of instrumental value or a reference to the beginning of the *Bṛhadāraṇyaka Upaniṣad*, is obscure but interesting. See Modi vol. I, 262.

55. Tr. 783.

56. Though they are distinguished, according to a standard Mīmāṃsā calculation, in terms of the proximity of the aid they offer: the virtues being "near" or "interior" helps because they change the performer, while the rites being "distant" or "exterior" helps because their contribution to the rise of knowledge is not so directly evident. Vācaspati elaborates on this distinction of the "proximate" and "external" helps to knowledge, employing even more clearly the ritual metaphors of interiority and exteriority. It is helpful here to note the Mīmāṃsā calculus of how actions help other actions. In UMS III.4.26–7 and UMS IV.1.16, we find a balance which neglects neither rites nor knowledge. The apparatus of the compromise is itself borrowed from Mīmāṃsā. In both sections we see reference to "help from afar" (*ārādupakaraṇa*.) The distinction between help "from afar" and "from nearby" (*saṃnipātya-upakaraṇa*) is a Mīmāṃsā construction, intended to help sort out how different subsidiary actions help toward the completion of a ritual, now reused in order to locate action as a subordinate but real and indispensable part of the process toward

the achievement of knowledge. Two Mīmāṃsā distinctions are crucial here. First, in PMS II.1.9–12, Jaimini distinguishes two kinds of subordinate actions, the primary (pradhāna) and the secondary (guṇa). The secondary contribute to a rite by the change they effect in one of the materials used in a rite—e.g., cleaning, cutting, cooking some rice, a cake, etc. The primary contribute directly to the rite, in the sense that they do not effect any change in a material; thus, for example, circling the sacrificial arena is important to a rite, but not to any particular part or material of it. Knowledge is primary in this sense. Second, though in PMS II.1.9–12 Śabara does not use terms "near" (*saṃnipātya*) and "far" (*ārād*), later texts such as the *Mīmāṃsā Nyāya Prakāśa* (e.g., 1929, paragraph 121) use them as correlative to the guṇa and pradhāna as used in PMS II.1.9–12. Secondary (guṇa) actions are "near", because they are instrumental in directly changing an element used in the sacrifice. Thus, one beats rice grains in order to husk them, and by this direct—"near"—transformation of a sacrificial material one contributes to the rite. By contrast, primary (pradhāna) subsidiary actions contribute from "afar;" they contribute from a distance, simply by their performance as pre- or post-rites, for example, and not through the transformation of anything used in the sacrifice. Their contribution through action is indirect, from a distance. This line of thinking is important since those rites which contribute from afar are the primary subordinate actions, more important than acts which contribute from nearby, because they are directly contributory, precisely as actions and not by way of the preparation of things. These primary subsidiary actions are done before or after the major action, and are clearly distinct from it; yet they are necessary for the completion of what is primary. Thus, to call ritual action a "distant" help toward knowledge is not merely to concede it a minimal, remote helping role, but to specify that as activity, it helps toward the activity of knowledge, and does so more importantly than would activity conceived of as a proximate transformation of the Advaitin. On all of this, see Clooney 1989b.

57. *Bṛhadāraṇyaka Upaniṣad* 4.4.23.

58. I.e., the hearing (śravaṇa) and understanding (manana), mentioned in *Bṛhadāraṇyaka Upaniṣad* 2.4.5, which initiate the process toward that salvific knowledge which must be achieved through the upaniṣads.

59. Skt. 899. The concluding citation is *Chāndogya Upaniṣad* 6.8.7.

60. UMS III.4.28–31 deals with the topic of whether any of the orthodox restrictions on food still apply to the renunciant.

61. Intention is explored in PMS IV.3–4, as part of the general calculation of the relationship between the puruṣa-artha and kratu-artha.

62. UMS IV.1.16 adds, "However, the *agnihotra* ritual, etc., are for the same goal, for we see texts which state this." This occasions a further insistence that works and knowledge cooperate. In agreement with the sūtra Śaṅkara argues "the obligatory daily duties like the agnihotra, enjoined in the Vedas, are meant for that very result. The idea is that their result is the same as that of knowledge." This is so, he adds, despite the fact that of themselves knowledge and rituals produce different kinds of results. In the period before realization, works aid the origination of knowledge "from afar." Vācaspati stresses the temporality of the process, whereby the ritual has a sure but limited place: "there is no ritual action at the time of the arising of knowledge, nor after it, but only before it . . ." (Skt. 960–1).

63. This recalls a similar Mīmāṃsā discussion of those who may seem disqualified by physical, familial or economic defect; see PMS VI.1.39–43. Here, Vācaspati explains that since works help toward the beginning of knowledge, and not its accomplishment, those who are already desirous of knowledge, such as widowers desiring knowledge, cannot be held back from the goal by their nonperformance of rituals. Vācaspati's reference to Vidhura and others may introduce the possibility that certain śūdras too can proceed toward the goal.

Chapter 5. Theology after Advaita Vedānta: The Text, The Truth, and The Theologian

1. I continue in this chapter the usage established previously: "Text," or "Advaita Text," refers to the complex body of texts and contexts woven together by the Advaitins through the reading and writing together of texts from the upaniṣads to the latest of the commentaries on the *Uttara Mīmāṃsā Sūtras*. More generally, "Text" may be taken to refer to any theological tradition's complex set of (sacred) texts and commentaries as a whole act of writing and subsequently of reading.

2. The third of which remained unfinished at the time of Aquinas' death.

3. Each question (*quaestio*) is comprised of a number of articles (*articuli*), each of which begins with objections, followed by a statement of the correct position, and concludes with responses to the objects. Though there are important differences, both "question" and "article" are partly in correspondence to adhikaraṇa.

4. The *Summa Theologiae* of Aquinas ends here, with a large supplementary section appended, in which the study of the sacraments is completed (Supple-

ment, 1–68) and the final human destiny considered (69–99).

5. I have used the translation of the Dominican Fathers. Translations of Cajetan are my own.

6. See Chapter 4, pp. 121–129.

7. For a good example of a more complex comparison using Vedānta material, see Lipner 1978.

8. Yearley's sober estimation of the rarity of truly significant differences and similarities must be kept in mind here. See Yearley 1990, pp. 170–72.

9. Coordination is the practice, and the set of rules for the practice, of selectively combining different upaniṣadic texts and the characteristics of Brahman they present for the sake of unified meditations; see the treatment of coordination in Chapters 2 and 3.

10. In traditional Vedānta adhyāsa was the practice of superimposing one word or image or practice on another, to enhance the latter as an object of meditation.

11. See also Clooney, forthcoming c.

12. One may expect that if coordination is accompanied by the systematizing thematic project of harmonization (samanvaya; see Chapter 2), comparison as an exegetical act should be similarly accompanied by a thematization of its results.

13. See UMS IV.1.5 for the notion of "enhancement" (*utkṛṣṭi*).

14. The most well-known version of superimposition is represented as an epistemological error, a case of mistaken identity in which the prior act of superimposition is forgotten. This instance of error is merely an instance of the broader practice, which flourishes as long as the activity is not transmuted into a mere identity. As such, superimposition bears the burden of a certain infamy, since it is identified by Śaṅkara in his preface to the *Uttara Mīmāṃsā Sūtras* as *the* central problem of human existence. Humans superimpose all the imperfections and limitations of their earthly existence on their true self (ātman), which is unlimited and perfect. Because they confuse apparent reality with true reality; seeing only the former, they are subject to the array of miseries which plague the human race. However, this use of superimposition is Śaṅkara's (probably original) extension of a more neutral usage, reflected by his treatment of superimposition at UMS III.3.9 and UMS IV.1.5. In light of those two texts, the problematic superimposition (adhyāsa) described in the introduction to UMS I.1.1 can be shown to be faulty on all three grounds: a. one is superimposing the lesser, empirical self on the higher, true Brahman; b.

the difference of the superimposed and that on which it is imposed is forgotten, as the person forgets the difference of self and Brahman; c. the faulty superimposition is postulated to be the way things really are, and hence is carried forward as a way of life.

15. Tracy 1987, pp. 20, 93.

16. Wheelwright 1962, p. 46.

17. Wheelwright 1962, pp. 71–2.

18. Wheelwright 1962, p. 72.

19. Ulmer 1985.

20. Ulmer 1985, pp. 59–60.

21. Hartmann 1981, chapter 3.

22. Claims such as those examined in Chapter 3: the ultimate nonduality of the knower and the known; the distinction between Brahman with qualities and without qualities; the view that Brahman is the material and efficient cause of the world; the break with the orthodox Brahmanical tradition on (some of) the prerequisites to knowledge.

23. Corbin (1974) sets forth clearly the Biblical model underlying Aquinas' outline of the *Summa Theologiae*, its foundation in the dynamics of what may today be termed "salvation history."

24. See Reyero 1971.

25. In developing a more nuanced understanding of how theologians cite scriptural texts, Boyarin's distinction between paradigmatic and syntygmatic midrash (1990, pp. 26–38) is helpful. His comment on a midrashist's collocation of texts (about the splitting of the Red Sea) can, *mutatis mutandis*, be helpfully applied to Aquinas: "The midrashist has gathered all of these verses together, so that they may make the maximum impression on the hearer/reader. When each verse is encountered in its own place, as it were, its impact is relatively weak, but when all are encountered together . . . the dramatic and pictorial effect is enhanced greatly . . . it is the melding of these different texts into a single quasi-narrative that makes this passage work as midrash and ultimately gives each of the quoted verses its maximum power." 1990, p. 31.

26. A helpful place to begin in this reconstruction of the Thomistic tradition is Roensch 1964.

27. Cardinal Cajetan, Tommaso de Vio, wrote his commentary on the *Summa Theologiae* between 1507 and 1520. The revival of Aquinas studies in recent decades, in part defined as an effort to recover the genius of Aquinas himself over against his tradition, has been critical of Cajetan and the scholastic tradition for their reading of Aquinas. See Lonergan's brief comment on Cajetan in "Philosophy and Theology," 1974, pp. 193–97, and Corbin's comments (1974, pp. 818–20) on the "logicisation" of Aquinas' arguments.

28. "Ratio enim quam significat nomen, est conceptio intellectus de re significata per nomen." All emphases are mine.

29. P. 145. Beginning with *intellectus noster cognoscit Deum* . . .

30. The same point may be made with reference to Cajetan's comment on ST III.46.3. Here too, the purpose is precision, but the exploration unfolds in a more meditative, even reverent tone. After clarifying how ST III.46.3 takes up a point not considered in ST III.46.2, Cajetan goes on to say [p. 439, beginning with *ubi nota quod alii* . . .]: "Notice that other modes of human liberation occur either through some creature, or through the will of God alone. If we are liberated by means of some some creature, clearly and evidently this medium would more remote from an efficacious accomplishment of the goal than is the Passion of Christ; for the Passion is presupposed to be a divine medium, most efficacious in every way. This point was omitted by our author, since it is self-evident. But it would certainly be more expeditious if our liberation were accomplished through the will of God alone, inasmuch as only that will of God would [have to] concur. But it would not be so sweet a means of liberating humanity, nor leading to so many good things, as is clear from the many good things set forth in [Aquinas'] text." Cajetan then notes the refinement of Aquinas' reasons why the Passion was the most fitting way of liberating humans: "As for the reasons given in the text for the greater fittingness in liberating the human race through the passion of Christ, note that they can all be subsumed under two headings: pertaining to the sweetness of their disposition, and to human dignity. He looks to the sweetness of disposition of our consequent salvation when he says that we are led to salvation by the demonstrated love of God, by the example of Christ, by his merit, and by his preciousness, etc. He looks to our human dignity when he says that [by Christ] man saves himself, redeems, fights for himself, merits, conquers, satisfies, triumphs, rules, judges, etc." The text is opened up with care and reverence, the sweetness and dignity of the Passion are elaborated, reverently and with understanding, while at the same moment further refinements are made; the *Summa* text flourishes in Cajetan's words, and the reader appreciates its beauty more fully.

31. See Chapter 3, pp. 52–55.

32. See Chapter 12, "Doctrines," in Lonergan 1972, for an example of the way in which the required differentiation of doctrine might proceed.

33. For an exposition of the transition from comparative theology to the theology of religions, see Clooney 1990a.

34. See my comments on Lindbeck's understanding of the relationship between scripture and world, at the end of Chapter 3.

35. On these, see D'Costa 1987, Clooney 1989a, and Knitter 1989.

36. My understanding of Aquinas throughout this section is indebted to David Burrell's reading of Aquinas, particularly in his *Aquinas: God and Action* (1979).

37. Cardinal Cajetan notes that "student" and "beginner" here should not be taken to indicate that the *Summa Theologiae* is a mere primer; rather, its elegant simplicity is at the same time profound, and requires intensive, careful study.

38. This was recently aptly recalled by MacIntyre (1988, pp. 175–178), who correctly notes how carefully Aquinas keeps together the following concerns of the good teacher: to begin with simpler truths, to distinguish between premises and consequences while yet not expecting that the former be fully understood before the latter are worked through, to understand the process of understanding as it personally occurs in a student's ordinary experience and, finally, to pay attention to the quality of the life of the student, who learns properly only when properly prepared and thus making the connection between the practice of the good life and proper reflection on lived experience. See also Persson 1970, pp. 242ff., on how pedagogy and the structure of the "real" contribute to Aquinas' ordering of the *Summa Theologiae.*

39. Persson elucidates the pedagogy of the *Summa Theologiae.* He stresses that for Aquinas all theology is scriptural theology or, better, a *sacra doctrina,* a teaching "in other words" of the divine revelation which is available to us only in the Bible. Although the Bible is entirely adequate, it is difficult, accessible to those who have zealously studied it and probed its meaning. (Persson 1970, p. 58) In order to present its truth to the larger community of those who are not so well-prepared, the Church has always had to find ways of teaching the scripture; this teaching is the traditio of the Church, the doctrina. (47) Aquinas himself prefers the term "doctrina" to "theologia," in order to stress "the sense of teaching and the outward activity which clearly for Thomas constitutes the theological task." (71) Good theology is always an extension of scripture (89), which remains its norm. (83) He notes that when Aquinas in-

sists on the importance of the meaning of scripture, he means the *literal* meaning, *per voces* (54–55): "Thomas explicitly states (ST I.1.10) that the true sense of the scripture, *quem auctor intendit,* is not the spiritual but the literal sense of the passage." (55) While this does not indicate a total rejection of the medieval notion of the four-fold meaning of scripture, it does remind us of how rigorously Aquinas intends to root theology in scripture; in principle, it remains always prior to theology's ancillary components, such as philosophy. See also Corbin 1974, pp. 869–72. Aquinas insists that theology is a science, that its principles are beyond it, and that it is superior to all other sciences (ST 1.1.2, 5.) Burrell (1979) has brought our attention to the specific, grammatical purposes of the initial questions on God in the *Summa Theologiae,* and how it is unwarranted to read into these a complete, prior-to-scripture "natural theology" of God. He calls into question the common view that Aquinas had a theory of analogy, and argues that Aquinas refused to systematize his strategies on the analogous use of language and that the failure of the efforts of his disciples (ancient and modern) to do so vindicate Aquinas' reluctance to achieve that kind of synthesis. Particularly in the opening sections of his *Aquinas: God and Action,* Burrell indicates how to locate properly within Aquinas' overall theological project the construction of a proper way of speaking about God. He notes that in the medieval world the notion of "philosophical grammar" was operative and crucial: "The medievals' way of doing grammar is philosophical, since it reflects the background conviction that the form of one's discourse reveals something of the structure of the world." (Burrell 1979, p. 4) Consonantly, Aquinas' introductory discourse on "God" seeks to structure our use of language without giving the impression that "God-as-referent" is thereby understood. The reflective use of language affords us not with a scientific demonstration of first principles, but a *manuductio,* "an appropriately intellectual therapy in the pursuit of religious questions, rather than . . . an explanatory framework." (Burrell 1979, p. 14) Throughout the first *quaestiones,* Aquinas is not describing the nature of God per se, nor the God to whom we relate in worship. Rather, "he is engaged in the metalinguistic project of mapping out the grammar appropriate *in divinis.* He is proposing the logic proper to discourse about God." (Burrell 1979, p. 17) "The upshot of this exercise in transcendent logic is to announce concertedly the distinct ways in which any expression offered to characterize God—like 'wise and all-knowing'—will misrepresent its subject. In that indirect and reflexive fashion, something is conveyed to us of the nature of God. Grammar, after all, does give the nature of a thing, but never straightforwardly as people expect of a doctrine of God." (Burrell 1979, p. 17) An understanding of the grammar of religious language is reducible to neither the simple practice of religion nor a positive Christian theology expressive of revelation (Burrell 1979, p. 13), but is a significant aid and important starting point for the theologian's composition of language about God.

40. These remarks deliberately echo Jacques Derrida's "Tympan," his preface to *The Margins of Philosophy* (1982). In it he describes the problem of presenting to philosophy what is other to it, when one way in which philosophy defines itself is precisely through its appropriation of its other(s). In "Tympan" he outlines the strategies that occupy the volume, the tracing of the margins of philosophical texts, in order to raise uncomfortably the question of that other which those texts cannot account for. Though the project of finding the margins of theology through comparison is not identical with Derrida's project, his remarks are helpful in delineating the magnitude and contours of the process involved.

41. On the general problem of "generalization" and the "example," see Bourdieu 1977, pp. 16–22.

Selected Bibliography

A. Texts and Translations of Sanskrit Source Materials

ĀPADEVA. 1929. *The Mīmāṅsā Nyāya Prakāśa,* trans. Franklin Edgerton. New Haven: Yale University Press.

PRAKĀŚĀTMAYATI. 1939. *Śārīrakanyāyasaṅgraha.* Madras: University of Madras.

ŚAṄKARA. 1980. *Brahmasūtra Śaṅkarabhāṣyam with the commentaries Bhāṣyaratnaprabhā, Bhāmatī and Nyāya-Nirṇaya.* Delhi: Motilal Banarsidass.

ŚAṄKARA. 1981. *Brahmasūtra Śaṅkara Bhāṣya with the commentaries Bhāmatī, Kalpataru and Parimala.* 2 volumes. Parimala Sanskrit Series No. 1. Ahmedabad: Parimal Publications.

ŚAṄKARA. 1983. *Brahma-Sūtra Bhāṣya,* trans. Swami Gambhirananda. Calcutta: Advaita Ashrama.

ŚAṄKARA. 1962. *The Vedānta Sūtras of Bādarāyaṇa with the Commentary of Śaṅkara,* trans. George Thibaut. 2 volumes. New York: Dover Publications.

EIGHTEEN PRINCIPAL UPANIṢADS. 1958. Vol. 1. Ed. V. P. Limaye and R.D. Vadekar. Poona: Vaidika Samsodhana Mandala.

SIXTY UPANIṢADS OF THE VEDA. 1987, trans. V.M. Bedekar and G.B. Palsule from the German translation of Paul Deussen [1897]. 2 volumes. Delhi: Motilal Banarsidass.

VĀCASPATI MIŚRA. 1933. The *Bhāmatī of Vācaspati* [Catussūtrī], trans. S. S. Suryanarayana Sastri and C. Kunhan Raja. Adyar, Madras: Theosophical Publishing House.

WOODS, J.H. 1913. *The Yoga System of Patañjali*. Cambridge: Harvard Oriental Series.

B. Texts and Translations of Thomas Aquinas

AQUINAS, THOMAS. 1981. *Summa Theologiae*, trans. by the Fathers of the English Dominican Province. 5 volumes. Westminster, Maryland: Christian Classics.

AQUINAS, THOMAS. 1885–1906. *Summa Theologiae cum commentariis Thomae de Vio Caietani*. Vols. 4–12 in *Thomae Aquinatis Opera Omnia*.

C. General

ALTIERI, CHARLES. 1990. *Canons and Consequences*. Evanston: Northwestern University Press.

BARTHES, ROLAND. 1979. "From Work to Text." In Josué V. Harari, ed., *Textual Strategies: Perspectives in Post-Structuralist Criticism*, pp. 73–81. Ithaca: Cornell University.

BHATKHANDE, S.M. 1982. *The Chāndogya Upaniṣad and the Brahmasūtras of Bādarāyaṇa*. Bombay

BILIMORIA, PURUSOTTAMA. 1988. *Śabdapramāṇa: Word and Knowledge*. Dordrecht: Kluwer Academic Publishers.

BOURDIEU, PIERRE. 1977 [1972]. *Outline of a Theory of Practice*, trans. R. Nice. Cambridge: Cambridge University Press.

———. 1984 [1977]. *Distinction: A Social Critique of the Judgment of Taste*, trans. R. Nice. Cambridge: Harvard University Press.

———. 1990 [1980]. *The Logic of Practice*, trans. R. Nice. Standford: Standford University Press.

BOYARIN, DANIEL. 1990. *Intertextuality and the Reading of Midrash.* Bloomington: Indiana University Press.

BURRELL, DAVID. 1979. *Aquinas: God and Action.* Notre Dame: University of Notre Dame Press.

CHAKRABARTI, SAMIRAN C. 1980. *The Paribhāṣās in the Śrautasūtras.* Calcutta: Sanskrit Pustak Bhandar.

CLOONEY, FRANCIS X. 1988. "Why the Veda has No Author: Some Contributions of the Early Mīmāṃsā to Religious and Ritual Studies" *Journal of the American Academy of Religion* 55, 659–684.

———. 1989a. "Christianity and World Religions: Religion, Reason and Pluralism," *Religious Studies Review* 15: 197–204.

———. 1989b. "Dharmamātra Karma: A Reevaluation of the *Pūrva Mīmāṃsā Sutras* 2.1.9–12 and the *Bhāṣya* Interpretation" *Journal of Oriental Research* [Madras]: 157–168.

———. 1989c. "Evil, Divine Omnipotence and Human Freedom: Vedānta's Theology of Karma," *Journal of Religion* 69: 530–548.

———. 1989d. "Finding One's Place in the Text: A Look at the Theological Treatment of Caste in Traditional India" *Journal of Religious Ethics* 17: 1–29.

———. 1990a. "Reading the World in Christ: From Pluralism to Inclusivism," in G. D'Costa, ed., *The Myth of Pluralism: Christian Uniqueness Reconsidered.* Maryknoll: Orbis.

———. 1990b. *Thinking Ritually: Rediscovering the Pūrva Mīmāṃsāof Jaimini.* Vienna: Indological Institute of the University of Vienna.

———. 1990c. "Vedānta, Commentary, and the Theological Component of Cross-Cultural Study," in F. Reynolds and D. Tracy, eds., *Myth and Philosophy.* Albany: State University of New York.

———. 1990d. "Vedānta, Theology and Modernity: A Case Study in Theology's New Conversation with the World's Religions," *Theological Studies* 51: 268–285.

———. 1991. "Binding the Text: Vedānta as Philosophy and Commentary." In Jeffrey R. Timm, ed., *Texts in Context: Traditional Hermeneutics in South Asia.* Albany: State University of New York.

———. Forthcoming a. "Hearing and Seeing in Early Vedānta: An Exegetical Debate and Its Implications for the Study of Religion," *Festschrift for Dr. S. S. Janaki.*

———. Forthcoming b. "From Anxiety to Bliss: Argument, Care and Responsibility in the Vedānta Reading of Taittirīya 2.1–6A." In Laurie Patton, ed., *Arguing the Vedas: Studies in Authority and Anxiety.* Albany: State University of New York.

———. Forthcoming c. "Upasaṃhāra and the Articulation of Uttara Mīmāṃsā in UMS 3.3.5," *Sri Mandan Misra Felicitation Volume,* Delhi.

CORBIN, MICHEL. 1974. *Le Chemin de la théologie chez Thomas d'Aquin.* Paris: Beauchesne.

COWARD, HAROLD. 1990. *Derrida and Indian Philosophy.* Albany: State University of New York.

DARLING, GREGORY J. 1987. *An Evaluation of the Vedāntic Critique of Buddhism.* Delhi: Motilal Banarsidass.

DASGUPTA, SURENDRANATH. 1922. *A History of Indian Philosophy.* 5 volumes. Cambridge: Cambridge University Press.

D'COSTA, GAVIN. 1987. *Theology and Religious Pluralism: The Challenge of Other Religions.* New York: Basil Blackwell.

DERRIDA, JACQUES. 1982. "Tympan," in *The Margins of Philosophy.* Chicago: University of Chicago.

DESMET, RICHARD. 1953. *The Theological Method of Śaṅkara.* Dissertation for the Pontifical Gregorian University.

———. 1954. "Langage et connaissance de l'Absolu chez Śaṅkara." *Revue Philosophique du Louvain* 52: 31–74.

DEUSSEN, PAUL. 1973 [1883]. *The System of the Vedānta II: According to Bādarāyaṇa's Brahma-sūtras and Śaṅkara's commentary,* trans. Charles Johnston. New York: Dover Publications.

DEUTSCH, ELIOT. 1969. *Advaita Vedānta: A Philosophical Reconstruction.* Honolulu: East-West Center Press.

DEVASTHALI, G.V. 1951. "Śaṅkarācārya's Indebtedness to Mīmāṃsā," *Journal of the Oriental Institute* (Baroda). I: 23–30.

HACKER, PAUL. 1950. *Untersuchungen über Texte des frühen Advaitavāda.* Wiesbaden: Franz Steiner Verlag GMBH.

HALBFASS, WILHELM. 1991. *Tradition and Reflection: Explorations in Indian Thought.* Albany: State University of New York.

HARTMAN, GEOFFREY H. 1981. *Saving the Text.* Baltimore: Johns Hopkins.

INGALLS, DANIEL H. 1954. "Śaṅkara's Arguments against the Buddhists," *Philosophy East and West* 4.3.

ISER, WOLFGANG. 1978. *The Act of Reading: A Theory of Aesthetic Response.* Baltimore: Johns Hopkins University Press.

KNITTER, PAUL. 1989. "Making Sense of the Many," *Religious Studies Review* 15: 204–7.

LARSON, GERALD J. 1979. *Classical Saṃkhya.* Delhi: Motilal Banarsidass.

LINDBECK, GEORGE. 1984. *The Nature of Doctrine: Religion and Theology in a Postliberal Age.* Philadelphia: The Westminster Press.

LIPNER, JULIUS. 1978. "The Christian and Vedāntic Theories of Originative Causality: A Study in Transcendence and Immanence," *Philosophy East and West* 28: 53–68.

LONERGAN, BERNARD. 1972. *Method in Theology.* New York: Herder and Herder.

———. 1974. *A Second Collection*. London: Darton, Longman and Todd.

MACINTYRE, ALASDAIR C. 1988. *Whose Justice, Which Rationality?* Note Dame: University of Notre Dame.

MALAMOUD, CHARLES. 1977. *Le Svādhyāya: Recitation Personelle due Veda*. Paris: Institut de Civilisation Indienne.

MODI, P.M. 1956. *A Critique of the Brahmasūtra (III.2.11–IV) with Reference to Śaṅkarācārya's Commentary.* 2 volumes. Baroda: private publication.

MOGHE, S. G. 1984. *Studies in the Pūrva Mīmāṃsā.* Delhi: Ajanta Publications.

NAKAMURA, HAJJIME. 1983. *A History of Early Vedānta Philosophy,* trans. by T. Leggett et al. Delhi: Motilal Banarsidass.

NOAKES, SUSAN. 1988. *Timely Reading: Between Exegesis and Interpretation*. Ithaca: Cornell University Press.

OLIVELLE, PATRICK. 1986. *Renunciation in Hinduism: A Medieval Debate.* 2 volumes. Vienna: Institut fur Indologie der Universitat Wien.

PARPOLA, ASKO. 1981. "On the formation of the Mīmāṃsā and the Problems Concerning Jaimini," *Wiener Zeitschrift für die Kunde Südasiens* 25: 145–177.

PERSSON, PER ERIK. 1970 [1957]. Sacra Doctrina: Reason and Revelation in Aquinas.

POTTER, KARL. 1982. "Śaṅkarācārya: The Myth and the Man," in M. Williams, ed., *Charisma and Sacred Biography.* Chico, California: Scholars Press.

POLLOCK, SHELDON. 1985. "The theory of practice and the practice of theory in Indian intellectual history," *Journal of the American Oriental Society* 105: 499–519.

RAMBACHAN, ANANTANAND. 1986. "Śaṅkara's rationale for śruti as the definite source of brahma-jñāna: A refutation of some contemporary views," *Philosophy East and West* 36: 25–40.

———. 1987. "Where words fail: The limits of scriptural authority in the hermeneutics of a contemporary Advaitin," *Philosophy East and West* 37: 361–371.

RENOU, LOUIS. 1961. "Sur la forme de quelques textes sanskrites," *Journal Asiatique* 249: 163–211.

———. 1963. "Sur le genre du sūtra dans la littérature sanskrite," *Journal Asiatique* 251: 165–216.

REYERO, M. ARIAS. 1971. *Thomas von Aquin als Exeget*: Die Prinzipien seiner Schriftdeutung und seine Lehre von der Schriftsinnen. Einsiedeln: Johannes-Verlag.

RIFFATERRE, MICHAEL. 1978. *Semiotics of Poetry*. Bloomington: Indiana University Press.

———. 1990. *Fictional Truth*. Baltimore: Johns Hopkins University Press.

ROENSCH, FREDERICK J. 1964. *Early Thomistic School*. Dubuque: The Priory Press.

SAID, EDWARD. 1975. *Beginnings: Intention and Method*. New York: Basic Books.

———. 1983. *The World, the Text, and the Critic*. Cambridge: Harvard University Press.

SASTRI, K. BALASUBRAHMANYA. 1989. "Jaiminīya-nyāyānām anyatra Sañcāra-yogyatā," *Journal of Oriental Research* (Madras) XLVII–LV, 169–184.

SAWAI, YOSHITSUGU. 1986. "Śaṅkara's Theory of Saṃnyāsa," *Journal of Indian Philosophy* 14: 371–387.

SCHOLES, ROBERT E. 1989. *Protocols of Readings*. New Haven: Yale University Press.

SMITH, BRIAN K. 1989. *Reflections on Resemblance, Ritual and Religion*. New York: Oxford University Press.

TABER, JOHN. 1983. *Transformative Philosophy: A Study in Śaṅkara, Fichte, and Heidegger*. Honolulu: University of Hawaii Press.

TRACY, DAVID. 1987. *Plurality and Ambiguity: Hermeneutics, Religion, Hope*. New York: Harper and Row.

ULMER, GREGORY L. 1985. *Applied Grammatology: Post(e)-Pedagogy from Jacques Derrida to Joseph Beuys*. Baltimore: The Johns Hopkins University Press.

VERPOORTEN, JEAN-MARIE. 1987. "Le Droit à L'Adhyayana selon La Mīmāṃsā," *Indo-Iranian Journal* 30: 23–30.

WHEELWRIGHT, PHILIP. 1962. *Metaphor and Reality*. Indiana University Press, Bloomington.

YEARLEY, LEE. 1990. *Mencius and Aquinas: Theories of Virtue and Conceptions of Courage*. Albany: State University of New York.

Index of Key Passages from the *Uttara Mīmāṃsā Sūtras* and the *Summa Theologiae*

Summa Theologiae

Uttara Mīmāṃsā Sūtras

Index of Names

Cajetan, Cardinal [Tommaso de Vio], 183–187, 189, 196, 245 nn.27,30, 246 n.37
Chakrabarti, Samiran, 222 n.54
Clooney, Francis, 209 n.3, 210 n.2, 212 nn.29,30, 213 n.43, 214 n.45, 216 n.8, 220 n.39, 221 n.41, 227 n.20, 232 n.70, 239 nn.36,37,39,40,41, 240 n.52, 241 n.56, 243 n.11, 246 n.33,35
Corbin, Michel, 244 n.23, 247 n.39
Coward, Harold, 214 n.43

Darling, Gregory, 231 n.68
Dasgupta, Surendanath, 212 n.22
D'Costa, Gavin, 246 n.35
Derrida, Jacques, 168, 173, 248 n.40
DeSmet, Richard, 213 n.37
Deussen, Paul 26, 28, 99, 213 n.3, 213 nn.32,36, 220 n.32, 221 n.48, 222 n.51, 229 nn.46,47
Deutsch, Eliot, 28, 213 n.39, 223 n.2
Devasthali, G.V., 220 n.38
Dharmaraja Adhvarindra, 225 n.14

Gadamer, Hans-Georg, 170
Govindānanda, 17, 221 n.47, 236 n.17

Hacker, Paul, 212 n.22
Halbfass, Wilhelm, 213 n.40, 230 n.56
Hartman, Geoffrey, 244 n.21

Ingalls, Daniel, 231 n.68
Iser, Wolfgang, 215 n.1

Jaimini [author of the *Pūrva Mīmāṃsā Sūtras]*, 24, 100, 101, 142, 143

Knitter, Paul, 246 n.35
Kumārila Bhāṭṭa, 220 n.38, 225 n.20

Larson, Gerald, 231 n.68
Lindbeck, George, 115-118, 232 n.76, 233 nn.77-87,89, 246 n.34
Lipner, Julius, 243 n.7
Lonergan, Bernard, 245 n.27, 246 n.32

MacIntyre, Alistair, 246 n.38
Modi, P.M., 26, 213 n.34, 216 n.3, 217 n.8, 221 nn.40, 43,46; 224 nn.10,11, 240 n.54
Malamoud, Charles, 239 n.44
Moghe, S.G., 220 n.38

Nakamura, Hajjime, 26, 212 n.31, 213 n.33, 221 n.46
Nichols, Stephen, 224 n.3

Oakes, Susan, 214 n.43
Olivelle, Patrick, 219 n.28

Pāṇini [the Sanskrit grammarian], 220 n.35
Parpola, Asko, 212 n.29
Patañjali [author of the *Yoga Sūtras*], 236 n.21
Persson, Per Erik, 246 nn.38,39
Pollock, Sheldon, 219 n.29
Potter, Karl, 222 n.50
Prabhākara, 227 n.20, 228 n.20
Prakaśātman, 18, 213 n.41

Rāmānuja, 217 nn.9,11
Rambachan, Anantanand, 213 n.38
Renou, Louis, 211 n.18, 217 n.10
Reyero, M. Arias, 244 n.24
Riffaterre, Michael, 79–80, 87, 115, 214 n.43, 224 nn.3–8, 225 n.13, 226 n.17, 227 nn.18,19, 228 n.20
Roensch, Frederick, 244 n.26

Śabara, 24, 131, 238 n.31, 240 n.53, 241 n.56
Said, Edward, 214 n.43
Śaṅkara, 1, 64, 78, 90, 100, 101, 124, 127, 136, 149, 158, 209 n.1, 212 n.21, 217 n.11, 218 nn. 17, 19, 220 n.38,

Index of Subjects